WOMEN
WHO
DARED

From the Infamous to the Forgotten

Edited by
Ben Fletcher-Watson and Jo Shaw

EDINBURGH
University Press

Edinburgh University Press is one of the leading university presses in the UK. Publishing new research in the arts and humanities, EUP connects people and ideas to inspire creative thinking, open new perspectives and shape the world we live in. For more information, visit www.edinburghuniversitypress.com.

Edinburgh University Press Ltd
13 Infirmary Street, Edinburgh EH1 1LT

Typeset in Constantia
by Biblichor Ltd, Scotland
Printed and bound in the UK using 100% renewable electricity by
CPI Group (UK) Ltd

A CIP record for this book is available from the British Library

ISBN 978 1 3995 4943 1 (hardback)
ISBN 978 1 3995 4944 8 (paperback)
ISBN 978 1 3995 4946 2 (webready PDF)
ISBN 978 1 3995 4945 5 (epub)

EU Authorised Representative:Easy Access System Europe
Mustamäe tee 50, 10621 Tallinn, Estonia
gpsr.requests@easproject.com

Contents

Preface

The Dangerous Women Project was an initiative of the Institute for Advanced Studies in the Humanities (IASH) at the University of Edinburgh. It was founded in 2016 by Dr Peta Freestone and Professor Jo Shaw, with Peta as editor.

The Project asks: What does it mean to be a 'dangerous woman'?

The idea that women are dangerous individually or collectively permeates many historical periods, cultures, and areas of contemporary life (despite, and in some instances in response to, explicitly feminist movements).

We may take lightly the label attached by mainstream media outlets to women such as Shami Chakrabarti of Liberty, or Scotland's First Minister Nicola Sturgeon as being 'the most dangerous woman in the UK'. But behind this label lies a serious set of questions about the dynamics, conflicts, identities, and power relations with which women live today.

The Dangerous Women Project curated more than 365 responses to those questions from all over the world between International Women's Day 2016 and International Women's Day 2017, gathered together on our website at http://dangerouswomenproject.org

Each Dangerous Women Project essay explores, examines, or critiques the 'dangerous women' theme by inviting reflections from women of diverse backgrounds and identities, including poets, playwrights and other creative writers, academics, journalists, commentators, artists, performers, and opinion formers, and indeed anyone with an angle on the theme. All views expressed in the Dangerous Women Project's articles are therefore the views of the individual author, not of IASH or the University of Edinburgh.

Acknowledgements

We would like to recognise the work of numerous staff at the University of Edinburgh, first and foremost Peta Freestone, without whom there would simply be no Dangerous Women Project. Peta's incredible work made this book possible, and we will always be grateful to her.

Thanks also to the many interns who have worked tirelessly on the various stages of the Dangerous Women Project, including Abrisham Ahmadzadeh, Mouna Chatt, Isabelle Gius, Katie Graham, Amy Life, Amy McMonagle, Jana Phillips, Christina Neuwirth, Josephine Teng, Sarah Thew and Shy Zvouloun.

Our Advisory Group, consisting of Mary Bownes, Suzanne Ewing, Penny Fielding, Lesley McAra, Fiona Mackay, and Mona Siddiqui, have supported us every step of the way with wisdom and insight.

The staff at the Institute for Advanced Studies in the Humanities, especially Pauline Clark, have been invaluable. Lesley McAra and Sarah Prescott steered us superbly and generously helped the book become a reality.

We want to acknowledge our original supporters and funders from the beginnings of the project in 2016, including Scottish PEN, especially Jenni Daiches, the Binks Trust and the College of Arts, Humanities and Social Sciences at the University of Edinburgh.

Lastly, our heartfelt thanks must go to all our authors from around the world, and to all the Dangerous Women who have supported us on the way.

Introduction

Ben Fletcher-Watson and Jo Shaw

Ben Fletcher-Watson is Deputy Director of the Institute for Advanced Studies in the Humanities. He originally trained as a theatre director and dramaturg and worked in the cultural sector for a decade before his PhD. His research centres on contemporary Scottish theatre for children.

Jo Shaw has held the Salvesen Chair of European Institutions at the University of Edinburgh since 2005 and is now Head of Edinburgh Law School. She was Director of the Institute for Advanced Studies in the Humanities from 2014–2017 and, together with colleagues, launched the Dangerous Women Project in 2016. Her research has focused for the last two decades on ideas of citizenship, especially in a European and global context.

When we asked 'What does it mean to be a dangerous woman?' on International Women's Day 2016, we knew that a host of questions would sprout from our provocation: Who, or what, does she present a danger to? Who gets to say she is dangerous? Why call women dangerous? Does that woman in fact consider herself dangerous? And what do the answers to those questions tell us about societies past and present? About our social and political structures, about our everyday lives, and about our very identities?

These questions were inspired by a series of high-profile acts of sexism and misogyny that we had watched play out online.

In early 2014, Professor Mary Beard gave a lecture at the British Museum titled 'Oh Do Shut Up Dear!' She traced the public voice of women through history – or more to the point, the silencing of those voices.

In her talk, Beard discussed the Homeric idea that 'an integral part of growing up, as a man, is learning to take control of public utterance and to silence the female of the species'. Her lecture drew connections between that ancient attitude and the vitriol directed at women who speak out publicly today, particularly on social media.

As the year rolled on, more high-profile examples reinforcing Beard's points emerged in the digital space.

The year 2014 was the year of the Gamergate controversy, for example, where several women working in the video games industry (that year worth £3.9bn in consumer spend in the UK alone, and fast growing) were targeted by a collective harassment campaign threatening violence, rape, murder and the exposure of their personal information publicly online. Female commentators on video game production and marketing were also attacked for highlighting the under-representation, stereotyping and exploitation of women and minority groups in games.

That same year also saw a spike in young female celebrities threatened with the public release of private photographs showing them naked. From Jennifer Lawrence, known for her frank outspokenness about the policing of women's bodies and the gendered pay inequalities in Hollywood, to Emma Watson after she gave her UN Goodwill Ambassador's He For She speech, these women's privacy was held hostage or outright violated. Roxane Gay rightly reminded us that this public shaming and harassment of women existed before the internet. But digital spaces provide tinder for wildfires – just a single spark can burn to ashes reputations, livelihoods and self-confidence, and compromise safety and security on- and offline.

Amongst others, these events ensured that Mary Beard's lecture remained at the forefront of our minds.

Then in 2015, we were reminded of another way in which women's public voices are undermined – by portraying them as dangerous. In April 2015, the *Daily Mail* ran several headlines characterising Scottish First Minister Nicola Sturgeon as 'the most dangerous woman in Britain', prompting widespread debate in the media on the label and its accuracy. Before Sturgeon, Shami Chakrabarti, Director of Liberty, was marked with the 'dangerous' brand.

By 2016, we knew that the next public humanities project at the Institute for Advanced Studies in the Humanities had to be an exploration of the widest possible context of women and danger. So we asked people to tell us about historical figures famous or forgotten, give us a biography or memoir, shine a spotlight on a contemporary issue, spin us a fiction that might be uncomfortably close to the truth, or cut to the chase with research or analysis as sharp as a scalpel.

A vast, diverse community of contributors began to submit their responses, in a wave of energy that would sustain the Dangerous Women Project throughout the year of its inauguration, and for many years since. Women submitted reflections on their own identities, interviews, films, portraits, comics, short stories, roars of rage and flights of imagination that crossed political divides, geographic boundaries and demographics.

One of the first themes to emerge, within the first week, was history and biography. Unsolicited essays poured in featuring the stories of women from hundreds or even thousands of years in the past, daring to fight for change – and in numbers we hadn't expected. Some celebrated their own relatives pushing back and resisting within local communities; others used our theme of danger to reframe the debate around well-known figures; many chose to highlight a favourite forebear whose example had inspired them; a few blurred the boundaries between fact and fiction, using poetry or short stories to look at history obliquely, with fresh eyes.

This collection offers a snapshot of those thrilling contributions.

With a few exceptions, these are biographies of individual women, but always placed within the wider context of their society and culture. The book is not intended to be a comprehensive dictionary of notable biographies, just as the original Project can never be complete; rather, we hope to present readers with a mosaic of lives, all different and unique but linked by the glittering wire of danger.

Instead of a traditional chronological series, we have chosen to cluster contributions within five categories: those who fought for social change, such as women's suffrage; those who marked the world with their words, from authors to journalists; women wielding power and influence, often through religion; pioneers in fields formerly controlled by men, such as science or the arts; and those defined by politics – whether questing for peace or rallying for justice. Our clustering is fluid and deliberately provocative. By drawing together the lives of women thematically across time, the book seeks to highlight the common bond of danger as ever-present, a spur to action and a challenge to patriarchal suppression.

Women's history in the 1970s often addressed social histories, where the household and the workplace were scrutinised as sites of resistance. Later, the landscape opened up to embrace histories of race and Global South figures alongside analyses of class. Herstory, or history that emphasises the contributions of women – often by reclaiming 'lost' stories or retelling events from a female point of view – became an urgent movement.

Each of the chapters here is built on foundations laid by generations of historians, but those historians are not necessarily professional scholars. Family history and personal study purely for the love of it have been just as inspirational for our authors as the mainstream revisionism that drives contemporary gender history.

One omission that we must address is the lack of biographies of trans women. The Project received a number of submissions from LGBTQI authors, including prominent trans writers such as Jo Clifford and Elaine Gallagher. Queer artists in particular contributed a glorious body of work, from photography to performance poetry, that is still available on our website. Many of these pieces have also been published in our two previous collections, *The Art of Being Dangerous* (Leuven University Press, 2021) and *Dangerous Women* (Unbound, 2022).

However, of more than 370 essays preserved in the Dangerous Women archive, none addresses the lives of trans women from the past. The focus for our trans authors in 2016 and 2017 was personal reflection and autobiography, making their voices heard in the digital square. Perhaps if the Project were to reopen today, we would receive biographies too, such as the figures proposed in Sara Sheridan's foreword. Maybe the experiences of our ancestors would be reassessed in the light of modern conceptions of gender expression, leading to new ways of looking at the distant past.

What we do know is that 'what does it mean to be a dangerous woman?' continues to be a question with resonance. The more people we have talked to about the Project, the clearer that has become.

As artist susan c dessel told us at the end of the original Project:

> The Year of Dangerous Women filled my head and my heart with tales of women whose quiet courage, audacious behaviour, or willingness to put themselves in danger have made and are making a difference in societies around the globe.
>
> It energised me, it angered me, it strengthened my determination to continue to try to effect change however daunting the circumstances, and it thrilled me.
>
> It offered counsel on the importance of passing these stories on to others as we give voice to those still unheard. And it roared the folly of history that neglects herstory.

We hope that these tales will similarly energise, anger, strengthen and thrill you. It has been an honour to curate this third volume of essays, as a testament to the power of uncountable dangerous and daring women.

Foreword

Sara Sheridan

Sara Sheridan has a fascination for uncovering forgotten stories and diverse histories. In 2018, she remapped Scotland according to women's history to memorialise our forgotten foremothers in her imagined guidebook *Where are the Women?* This book was chosen for the First Minister's Summer Reading list at the David Hume Institute that year. Her novel *The Fair Botanists*, set in Edinburgh in 1822, was Waterstones' Scottish Book of the Year 2022. In 2024, her play *Robert Burns: His Psychotherapy and Cure* aired on BBC Radio 4, voiced by Elaine C. Smith. Her latest novel, *The Secrets of Blythswood Square*, was longlisted for the Saltire Prize 2024. The story is set in Victorian Glasgow and examines the early female gaze, bodily autonomy and the nature of shame, uncovering scandal in what was, at the time, Britain's second city of Empire. Sara mentors fledgling writers and outside her writing work has a number of other interests. In 2015, Sophie McKay Knight's portrait of Sara garnered media and critical attention at the National Gallery of Scotland. In 2016, Sara founded REEK perfume – its first scent, Damn Rebel Bitches, was dubbed the 'first feminist fragrance' in UK *Vogue*. A second fragrance in memory of the accused witches of Scotland launched in 2017 alongside REEK's blog, Bitches Unite. Artefacts from the project were collected by the National Museum of Scotland and the Glasgow Women's Library when completed. She continues to campaign for better memorialisation of minority contributions to our society and culture, including a recent campaign undertaken with historian Andy Arthur to re-dedicate a cairn in Holyrood Park to the memory of Ailie Hall, a victim of domestic violence killed by her husband in the 1720s.

If there is one thing that this collection demonstrates, it's that the history of women is about making change. Every woman in this book made change, from the long-dead and fascinating female Pharoah Hatshepsut, written about by Stephanie Aulsebrook, to the award-winning journalist Anna Politkovskaya, whose work is highlighted by Lucy Popescu. Each of the dangerous women on these pages went against the grain, either shifting perceptions or fighting for legal rights or both. Not all the women featured are traditional 'goodies' or on the right side of history in everything they did. Caroline Norton, written about by Francine Ryan, for example, while agitating for women's rights within marriage, specifically wrote to Queen Victoria to assure Her Majesty that she certainly did not support the cause of 'equality' – by which she probably meant women's educational rights and suffrage. Yet each of the featured women (Caroline included) is remarkable and, overall, every story here demonstrates that our past, both political and social, contains a great deal of nuance, which is often ignored by traditional historians in favour of easier stories that are more certain.

Everyone loves certainty, but here we are, in interesting times. It's easy to back dangerous women with the safety of hindsight; more difficult when they pop up in the present. It's one of history's more important lessons, in fact, to realise that the people (of all genders) who opposed women's higher education, suffrage or property rights within marriage believed themselves to be right. In the moment, nobody knows how an argument is going to play out. That certainly was the case at the genesis of all these changes. Ideas about equality, so certain today, felt outlandish and edgy. The horror at realising you're on the wrong side of history was captured in popular culture by comedians David Mitchell and Robert Webb in a 2006 sketch. The duo, dressed as Nazi officers, come to the realisation that what they have been fighting for is wrong. 'Are we the baddies?' Mitchell asks in disbelief. It is a comedy classic because it captures an essential truth: people don't want to be on the wrong side of history. They can hardly believe it when that's what transpires.

While I am certain I would have supported votes for women, I expect I would not have been a kick-ass suffragette like Lilian Lenton (written about here by Hilary McCollum), but more a measured suffragist like Millicent Garrett Fawcett (profiled by Gillian Murphy). Although I admire Lilian's tenacity and passion, I don't support violence. Still, today the extreme end of the suffragette movement is venerated, often by commentators who would decry violence in present-day arenas of contention like environmental activism. I wonder whether the actions of women like Lilian speeded up the process of obtaining the suffrage or slowed it down. Would non-violent means engaged in by suffragists – such as non-payment of taxes, for example – have been efficacious enough? I have to concede that it probably would have taken longer Millicent's way.

There are no more dangerous women today, in the eyes of some, than trans women. Accepting that sex and gender are not inextricably linked is the arena of equality activism now. Yet there are no trans women in this book. When the Dangerous Women Project was first commissioned in 2016, the rights of the trans community were not at the nub of debate. Reading the collection today, it feels as if the struggle for trans rights is missing. It has been a long seven years. Writing this now in 2025, I believe we are facing years longer, because that is another lesson from history. The rights we now consider basic – to be able to vote, to receive higher education, to own property, to sue for divorce, to have bodily autonomy in the matter of abortion – took decades or more to normalise enough to gain majority support. The first call for women MPs was in 1747; the first woman to win a Westminster seat (although not take it up) was Constance Markievicz in 1918.

Trans women hold their own narrative in wider women's history, proving that gender identity along with other forms of bodily autonomy are not new notions, although medical care and cultural acceptance have developed alongside language to make the trans community, in some respects, more visible in the present day. Assigning modern concepts of gender identity to people from history throws up as many issues as assigning sexuality posthumously – much of queer history has been written between the lines. However, two women whose gender identity certainly made them dangerous, and who I hope might appear in future histories like this series, are both black: coffee farmer Romaine-la-Prophétesse, leader of the Haitian slave uprising in 1791, and Frances Thompson, freed from enslavement and then the first transgender person to testify before a congressional committee after she was raped in the Memphis Riots of 1866. In the twentieth century and beyond, trans actress Christine Jorgensen, the first trans woman in the USA widely known to have had gender reassignment surgery, American trans activist Sylvia Rivera, Lili Elbe as the first European to undergo gender reassignment surgery in the late 1920s, and British performer April Ashley, whose MBE was awarded in 2021 for services to transgender equality, each has life stories that highlight firstly how dangerous society finds gender fluidity, and that trans identity while certainly a 'current' issue is hardly new.

Movement of the Overton window (the view on what is generally considered 'politically acceptable') takes a long time to shift. It's sobering to point out that despite the population being broadly 50/50 in terms of gender, we still do not have 50/50 representation in either the UK or Scottish Parliaments, and we are approaching 175 years since the idea of women MPs was first mooted (and laughed out of the Commons chamber). Legal rights are only a first step and they take decades, never mind fully shifting entrenched perceptions and, indeed, encouraging uptake of 'new' rights. In this, our history is very much present. We are where we come from and it is a long journey to truly get somewhere new. But the world, slowly but surely, has changed and is still changing, mostly in a more progressive direction, in Scotland among other European nations anyway. History is a tidal process, as demonstrated by Marianne Moen's essay on the Oseburg Burials – Viking women likely of high status, the memory of whom was demeaned by succeeding generations of male scholars unable to understand the achievements and talents of women because of the social, political and legal oppression of the women around them. Marianne's essay highlights the importance of diversity in the gatekeeping of our institutions.

I am also drawn to examine how rights are rolled back. The power of those Viking women was not in question during their own time. When things change, they do not always do so in a progressive direction. In the last few years, we've seen rights rolled back for women in the Middle East to the point where it is rebellion simply to dance, to want to educate yourself or even to publicly show your face. We have also witnessed concerted right-wing campaigns in our own country against abortion clinics, for example, seeking to reduce women's rights to autonomy over their own bodies. Women are as dangerous today as ever they were in history. Our lives continue to be a battleground.

As a writer and someone who is concerned with both equality and justice, my contribution has largely been through promoting the stories of our amazing foremothers. There is a solid function in both fiction and non-fiction for writers to point out inequalities and injustices and, importantly, represent the past as it was, not as it was later thought to be. In my book *Where Are The Women?*, which remapped Scotland according to women's history, I told the stories of around 1,200 women. While I was therefore not able to go into the kind of detail about each of my subjects that the excellent essays in this book dive into, I did manage to represent the huge number of stories that are missing from our day-to-day perception of where we come from. The scale of what we have lost from our cultural narrative is vast. Honestly, I could easily have written 1,200 more women into the book.

In researching these women, I came across glaring oversights in the records. Their voices were often completely missing – female creatives talking about their work, for example, did not 'blow their own trumpets', which would have seemed headstrong and arrogant according to the conventions of their time. What female creatives really wanted was a (probably white, definitely upper-class) man to publicly support their work. Likewise, in most archives, the lack of female documents and artefacts is acute. In 2016, historian and broadcaster Bettany Hughes estimated that female material makes up a mere 0.5 per cent of recorded history. It remains the case today that you are most likely to find historical material about women in paintings (where they pose as models) or in fashion collections, where their outfits are preserved. However, because dangerous women find themselves so much in the spotlight, we are likely to find more physical remains of them than the average, in court records, broadsheet publications and periodicals (or scandal sheets), and the like. As a novelist, I catch a tantalising glimpse of biographical material sometimes in-between the lines of journals and letters written by men. In terms of non-fiction, writing a woman's biography is usually a bigger and more difficult job than writing a man's life story because there is simply less left behind. That makes collections such as this one even more important. The Dangerous Women Project provides a valuable resource, pooling stories and making them accessible to readers.

The idea that women's history is solely of interest or import to women always shocks me. When I speak about history in schools, there is often a (cheeky) boy who comes up with the question of what it has to do with him. 'These are your grandmothers too', I say. 'You come from amazing. You need to know about it.' Most important for me though, I admit, are the girls. I go back again and again to being a child, walking along the main streets in Edinburgh where I was brought up with my brothers. The boys saw endless accolades to people with whom they could identify – statues on main streets as well as street names dedicated to male achievement. How empowering it would have been to see somebody like me on a plinth: to have female achievement recognised and fêted. To this day there are hardly any accolades to Scotland's brilliant, innovative, world-class women on the streets of our capital, or indeed our other cities. We are poor at remembering female successes. In fact, we are poor at remembering women at all. This year after an eighteen-month campaign, my friend Andy Arthur and I, with support from the University of Edinburgh's hub for gender and sexualities studies known as GENDER.ED, succeeded in bringing to Historic Environment Scotland's attention a tumbledown cairn on Duke's Walk in Holyrood Park in Edinburgh, near where a young woman was murdered in October 1720 by her husband. The monument was referred to on their maps by his name, not hers. To its credit, HES has amended the record and an interpretive board will soon be raised to Margaret Hall more than two centuries after her death. Positive change is, as I said, slow and needs to be pursued. Changing perceptions must be fought for again and again. Remembering to remember is important.

It is the case that all women are sidelined after they die, but this is more so the case for women who were marginalised in life. When Claire Mitchell KC set up the Witches of Scotland campaign shortly after reading *Where Are The Women?* she touched a nerve. The campaign has become hugely popular, spawning a chart-topping podcast with its demands for an apology, a pardon and a monument to the victims of this literal witch-hunt, one of the worst in Europe, whose victims were around 84 per cent female. It is an irony that advocating on behalf of these (mostly) women who were considered so dangerous in their time, Claire and her co-campaigner Zoe Venditozzi might be considered dangerous today. Likewise, librarian and writer Kirsten MacQuarrie's deep research into the life of twentieth-century poet Kathleen Raine might be cast as 'dangerous' because it calls into question the actions of Raine's platonic partner, Gavin Maxwell, who took the title of his most famous work *Ring of Bright Water* from one of Raine's poems. Fêted in life for her literary talent, Raine has been almost completely forgotten because of Maxwell's sidelining of her importance in favour of his own one-sided view of their relationship, not least in blaming Raine for a 'curse' that he claimed lay at the root of all his life's problems. She is commonly remembered (if she is remembered at all) as being a mad, lovesick witch, rather than a hugely talented and inspirational woman. MacQuarrie's novel *Remember The Rowan* successfully restates Kathleen's position after decades of Maxwell's voice being dominant.

Not all of today's emerging stories are about women who have been sidelined, however. Researchers, historians and writers are continually turning up dangerous women we haven't previously known about at all, like Marie Maitland who wrote lesbian love poetry in sixteenth-century Scotland (the first known of in Europe since Sappho) and whose contribution was uncovered by linguist Ashley Douglas. Hearing Ashley talk about Marie's work at the British Library in 2021 made me wonder how many of our other important, pioneering and relevant foremothers are simply missing in action. While Marie was high status because of her family situation, which meant that there are traces of her life in legal and historical records, women from lower stations are unlikely to be recorded and the work of remembering their contributions falls to historical novelists, like me, whose job it is to recreate the social fabric we come from by way of story. In my novel *The Fair Botanists*, I used slivers of information (sometimes a woman in the background of a contemporary watercolour or sketch, other times a name in a court record) to re-imagine what it must have been like in Edinburgh in the summer of 1822 for women in a variety of situations. Novelists like me get away without being considered dangerous. I'm not sure we're dangerous enough. In her day, Jane Austen was criticised for being subversive. In *Mansfield Park* she used the names of contemporary slavers alongside other cultural references that we have, over time, completely forgotten. It made some of her readers uncomfortable. Well done, Jane, and shame on us for remaking her legacy as something less dangerous than she intended it to be. When at a book festival recently, I said that I would love to be as contentious as Jane Austen; the audience laughed.

So if there is something that I hope you take away from this collection, it is perhaps the ability to step back from your own environment and view it with a longer lens. That, it seems to me, is the value of the Dangerous Women Project, which was founded not only to record and retell the stories of change and female achievement, but to encourage readers to question their own views and actions. The project's very name makes it easier to adopt the mantle of dangerous women by normalising it. Our culture sometimes asks us to give up our social and cultural power and to relinquish our voices. In this, the past provides us with both inspiration and hope, for what has gone before indeed proves that change is always possible. The world is in a constant state of flux. We must honour both our foremothers and our children by supporting positive change wherever we can. We must remember to look for and honour the women who do that around us, as well as those who have done so in history. I was, in my twenties, privileged to meet Ruth Adler, who set up Scotland's Amnesty International office in Edinburgh. She was somebody who fought for equality and justice for others, and seeing her do so, up close, certainly changed my life. For me, the most important thing that has happened since Ruth's death in 1994 is the development of a new and more diverse lexicon. As a writer, I appreciate the absolute value and the power of words. When you name something, you enable it. So best be Dangerous. That's what this woman says.

DISSIDENTS

AND

DISRUPTORS

More than 100 of the essays published during the Dangerous Women Project were biographies and autobiographical reflections. In whittling down the chapters for this book, we had to make some difficult choices: Should we focus on figures from history, or include living people as well? Should we prioritise women whose histories are familiar, where our authors often wished to reframe them as dangerous, or spotlight lesser-known women? Was there perhaps a place for autobiography? We decided to seek a middle ground, presenting some historical icons alongside the (wrongly) forgotten, overlooked or disregarded. With great reluctance, we have not included the many powerful self-reflections submitted to the Project, as a number of them already appear in our two earlier volumes. Few of the women in these pages are still alive, but their stories live on as inspiration, and, occasionally, as warning.

Our second decision was how to order the chapters. From a chronological thread to thematic clusters, we pieced together the manuscript in a number of ways, but eventually resolved to focus the chapters around five core themes. This section foregrounds women who made themselves dangerous in pursuit of change: socialists and terrorists, suffragettes and anti-suffragists, legal campaigners and those willing to be imprisoned for their beliefs. These definitions are of course fluid: Lilian Lenton used arson to fight for the vote and was repeatedly arrested, as Hilary McCollum describes in her chapter.

We could have populated this first section solely with figures from the suffrage struggle, given the huge number of submissions on that topic. Votes for Women remains a rallying call as we approach the centenary of the Representation of the People (Equal Franchise) Act that gave women in Britain the vote on the same terms as men.

However, the chapters here offer a broader view on women's rights, from Flora Tristan's famous cry, 'Workers, without women, you are nothing!' to the Red Zora's 'armed propaganda' in 1980s West Germany. Women's suffrage forms a significant part of the story of resistance, but the struggle against patriarchy has always been fought on a far wider field.

FLORA TRISTAN: 'WORKERS, WITHOUT WOMEN, YOU ARE NOTHING!'

Jelena Vasiljević

Jelena Vasiljević is a Senior Research Associate at the Institute for Philosophy and Social Theory, University of Belgrade. Her background is in political anthropology and citizenship studies. Her expertise and research interests include theories of citizenship, citizenship transformations in the post-Yugoslav states, memory politics, civic engagement, and social movements in South-East Europe. Presently, she is primarily interested in theories and practices of solidarity. She held research positions and fellowships at the University of Edinburgh and the University of Graz. She was an expert member of the Balkans in Europe Policy Advisory Group (BiEPAG) and currently sits on the European Alternatives Transnational Board.

Flora Tristan's name and work remain insufficiently recognised. Today, she is mostly mentioned as one of the overlooked, yet instrumental, representatives of French utopian socialism, together with Charles Fourier and Saint-Simone, as a grandmother of the famous painter Paul Gauguin, and as an immortalised heroine in Mario Vargas Llosa's novel *The Way to Paradise (El paraíso en la otra esquina)*.

If only her name was not attached to so many other male names before, we could recognise just how important and unique her life and work have been. History, in this respect, did not do her justice, as her pioneering work in feminism and socialism remains overshadowed by men, ironically silencing her famous cry: 'Workers, without women, you are nothing!'

Flore-Celestine-Thérèse-Henriette Tristan-Moscoso was born to a French mother and a Peruvian father who was a colonel of the Spanish Navy in Peru. Her whole life could be told as a series of struggles. Her personal struggles – for a divorce and for custody of her children, and for a family acceptance and inheritance – are reflective of a woman's degraded position in nineteenth-century society. As the personal is also political, her public activism echoed her life story, which was interwoven in her struggles for the improvement of the lives of workers, and especially of working women.

Upon her father's death, when Flora was four, the family fell into poverty, which marked Flora's youth and adolescence. Given some legal doubts regarding the marriage of her parents, she was not recognised as a legal heir of her father, whose brother was a viceroy of Peru. At seventeen, she married her employer, the engraver André-François Chazal. The marriage was violent, and four years later, after having two children and with a third on a way, Flora left her husband and began a desperate fight for a divorce. It was only after an incident in which Chazal shot and wounded her that she was granted legal grounds for separation.

Another struggle to secure her rights led Flora to undertake an unusual and dangerous journey – especially for a lone woman of her time. Determined to claim her paternal inheritance, she sailed to see her uncle in Arequipa, Peru. After spending a year there, she returned home with no inheritance, still considered an illegitimate heir of her father. Yet, she returned with a plethora of thoughts about oppression, subordination and the lonely struggles women are left to fight if they want to secure their rights. She wrote a travel memoir and personal diary of the everyday abuse she endured during her violent marriage, titled *Pérégrinations d'une paria* (*Pilgrimage of a Pariah*).

Flora was one of the first historical figures to write about the oppression of women in marriage, advocating for the right to divorce, and pointing to a societal rather than a personal problem: 'women's ignorance, hostility toward their husbands, or brutality toward their children [was] not their fault but that of society', she wrote.

Her ability to see the wider social and political causes of the terrible predicaments in which many individuals lived turned her to socialist ideas and the movements flourishing in pre-1848 France. Her influential essay, 'The Worker's Union' ('L'Union Ouvriere'), earned her a place in the Utopian Socialist movement. It was a pioneering work due to its blending of socialism and feminism. Flora claimed that the struggle to overcome the oppression of women had to be accompanied by the struggle to obtain better living and working conditions. She recognised the particularly vulnerable position of working women, realising that the fight for workers' rights and women's rights has to be a unified struggle. She insisted that the emancipation of the working class could not happen without the liberation of women, since women's subordinated position fractures the entire working class. In this respect, she was truly a pioneer of socialist feminism. Forty years before Friedrich Engels, Flora stated that the relation of the proletariat to the bourgeoisie is what the woman is to the family.

Her propositions were not merely theoretical. They were practical and focused on everyday needs. The proposed Union from her essay was envisaged as a body collecting dues of all members, to pay for the institutions dedicated to education and safety – primarily that of women and children. She proposed that unions should construct 'a series of "worker's palaces" to educate their children, to aid "the wounded of work", and to care for the aged'.

With the publication of 'The Workers' Union' she became a political activist, aligned with the utopian socialists of the time. However, unlike them, she did not believe in the enlightened middle class but chose to speak to the workers directly, telling them that they alone are the best representatives of their interests.

Practical as she was, she set off on another journey, with the intention to put her ideas to work. She embarked on a tour of France, visiting factories and delivering speeches to workers, aiming to set up committees to lay the foundation for the Union. She applied the same effort she invested in her arguments to her praxis. Disseminating her thoughts and concrete ideas about how to realise them is how she spent her last days, dying at the age of forty-one.

Flora Tristan was an illegitimate child and a social outcast, a woman who left her husband and fought her own battles, despite societal norms and expectations. She was often depicted as dangerous for her society, children and the general order of things, but she remained radical, fierce and ready to give her whole self to fight for what she taught was right and for the promise of a better future.

Commemorating her as a dangerous woman, though, does not do her full justice. It exoticises her and diverts our attention from the true worth of her deeds. We should remember her as the woman who was brave enough to fight for what she truly believed was right, having had nothing to rely on except her own thoughts about what is just and worth fighting for.

More reading

Tristan, F., 2007. *The Workers' Union*. University of Illinois Press.

Tristan, F., 2015. *Peregrinations D'Une Paria*. Createspace.

Tristan, F., Beik, D. and Beik, P., 1993. *Flora Tristan, Utopian Feminist: Her Travel Diaries and Personal Crusade*. Indiana University Press.

Vargas Llosa, M., 2003. *El paraiso en la otra esquina*. Alfaguara. (Trans. Wimmer, N., 2004. *The Way to Paradise*. Faber and Faber.)

CAROLINE NORTON: THE WOMAN WHO FOUGHT FOR – AND WON – RIGHTS FOR MARRIED WOMEN IN ENGLAND

Francine Ryan

Francine Ryan is a Senior Lecturer in Law and Director of the Open Justice
Centre at The Open University. Francine is the co-founder of the Open
Justice Centre, which empowers law students to deliver the social justice
mission of the university by inculcating a commitment to public service.
Her research interests explore access to justice and the intersection
between law and technology, focusing on how technology can be leveraged
to make the justice system accessible for all. Francine's work is inspired
by the incredible women who have pioneered and changed the law to
help others.

Victorian society labelled Caroline Norton a 'scandalous woman', but
was she also a 'dangerous woman'?

There is no doubt she was a remarkable woman. She had the audacity
to challenge the power of men and highlight the suffering of women.
What is fascinating about Caroline's story is that although she campaigned to change the law and ultimately secured a landmark victory
for women, she was not a feminist and she did not believe in equality for
women.

Caroline's story demonstrates the plight and vulnerability of Victorian married women trapped in unhappy and often violent marriages
because they had no legal status.

Caroline was born in 1808 into a genteel but impoverished family. In
1827, at the age of nineteen, she married Conservative Party MP, George
Norton. They had three sons. It was a turbulent marriage and Caroline
was subjected to physical and emotional abuse. George wanted to control his wife but she resisted. She openly mocked him and flirted with
other men. Caroline's family was associated with the rival Whig Party,

and she was greatly admired by Whig men and influential in political circles. It was rare for a woman to have such political influence, but Caroline was fortunate that she had friends in Parliament and was renowned as a political hostess. She held intimate gatherings of well-connected men, which allowed her to press her cause. Caroline could rely on her Whig heritage. Her grandfather was Richard Brinsley Sheridan, a famous playwright and politician, who had a reputation for campaigning for social justice.

Her husband, George Norton, was a failed lawyer and an unsuccessful politician. Despite his abhorrence of Caroline's connections to the Whig Party he demanded she use her influence to secure him a number of judicial positions. George openly encouraged Caroline's friendship with Lord Melbourne, yet felt humiliated by the gossip that ensued, which fuelled his misery and rage.

The marriage collapsed, and in June 1836 George Norton sued Lord Melbourne, the then Whig Prime Minister, claiming that he had an affair with Caroline. His motive was not only to destroy the government, it was also the first step towards obtaining a divorce. Women were deemed the property of their husbands, so despite the fact that Caroline's actions were the subject of the trial, she was not represented and could play no part in trying to defend her reputation. Although George failed to prove his case, and Caroline and Melbourne were exonerated, Caroline's reputation was ruined.

The Nortons were now separated, but Caroline remained the legal property of George. She was unable to divorce him and had no legal rights. George refused Caroline access to her children and her own property. Caroline learnt the perilous position of married women. The law offered women no legal protection, because women had no legal existence. Sir William Blackstone defined the position of married women:

> By marriage, the husband and wife are one person in law: that is, the very being or legal existence of the woman is suspended during the marriage, or at least is incorporated and consolidated into that of the husband . . .

Caroline was a fighter and she came to understand that the only way to remedy her situation was to start a campaign to change the law. She was already an accomplished and established writer with political allies. She produced a series of political pamphlets to educate the public about the plight of mothers and to influence MPs to support a change in the law.

In 1837, she published her first pamphlet entitled 'Observations on the Natural Claim of the Mother to the Custody of her Children as Affected by the Common Law Rights of the Father'. She campaigned for all children under the age of seven to remain in the custody of their mother and the decision of where older children should live to be decided by the court not the father. Caroline was able to enlist the support of the MP for Reading, Mr Talfourd, to introduce a bill into Parliament to give judges the power to allow either parent to have access to their children under the age of twelve.

She published a second pamphlet 'The Separation of Mother and Child By the Law of "Custody of Infants" Considered', in which she wrote:

> The fact of the wife being innocent and the husband guilty, or of the separation being an unwilling one on her part, does not alter his claim: the law has no power to order that a woman shall have even occasional access to her children, though she could prove that she was driven by violence from her husband's house and that he had deserted her for a mistress. The father's right is absolute and paramount, and can be no more be affected by the mother's claim, than if she had no existence.

She followed this with 'A plain letter to the Lord Chancellor on the Infant Custody Bill', written under a pseudonym. It was a struggle, but the bill eventually became law in August 1839; it provided that if a wife was legally separated or divorced from her husband and had not been found guilty of adultery, she was allowed custody of her children up to the age of seven and access thereafter. Caroline's campaign had brought the issue into the public domain and worn away opposition to the bill.

The significance of her achievement cannot be underestimated but the great sadness for Caroline was that despite her efforts it still did not restore her children to her. George moved the children to Scotland where the Act did not apply and it was not until one of her boys tragically died that she was able to see her remaining children.

Caroline recognised that the campaign was not finished. To protect married women, they needed to secure their property rights. To that end, she published 'English Laws for Women in the Nineteenth Century' in 1854 and in June 1855 wrote 'A Letter to Queen Victoria on Lord Chancellor Cranworth's Marriage and Divorce Bill'. In 1857, the Matrimonial Causes Act was finally passed. It contained sixty-eight clauses, four of which came from Caroline's pamphlets. These included a woman's right to form a contract, to receive maintenance as directed by the court, to inherit and bequeath property, and to keep possession of her own earnings.

Caroline was not seeking female equality; in her pamphlet to the Queen she wrote:

The natural position of woman is inferiority to man. Amen! . . . I never pretended to the wild and ridiculous doctrine of equality.

The fight for equality would come later by other women. Her battle was forced upon her by personal tragedy; where so many women felt they had no choice, Caroline would not accept that and for the first time a woman challenged the status quo. By Victorian standards that made her a dangerous woman – she defied the role of subservient wife, mother and woman. She would not accept the injustice of her situation and so became a catalyst for change. To Victorian society it was shocking that a woman would publish details of her own situation, but by highlighting the tragedy of her own story and the case histories included in the pamphlets, she contextualised the suffering of married women.

Caroline secured a significant victory for women. The passage of the Infant Custody Act gave legal rights for women for the first time and made them visible before the law. Women owe a huge debt of gratitude to Caroline Norton. Her determination kick-started the process of legislative change; without this, women could not start the fight for the vote. We need the bravery of women to share their stories to engender change, and Caroline Norton may inspire other women to follow bravely in her footsteps.

Caroline Norton is largely a forgotten figure but her story is timeless. It reflects the injustice women endured in Victorian society and continue to suffer today. So many elements of Caroline's story will resonate with women – women who have escaped violence, fought for custody of their children; their struggle was her struggle. Even today, women in many cultures are still fighting for the kind of freedom she championed.

More reading

Biju, S. and Preetha, M., 2024. Impact of industrialization on child labour: An analysis of Caroline Norton's 'A Voice from the Factories'. *Agathos: An International Review of the Humanities and Social Sciences*, 15(1), pp. 171–182.

Fraser, A., 2020. *The Case of the Married Woman: Caroline Norton: A 19th-Century Heroine who Wanted Justice for Women*. Weidenfeld & Nicolson.

Sheridan-Norton, C., 1833. *Poems: By the Honble Mrs. Norton*. Allen and Ticknor.

Sheridan-Norton, C., 1982. *Caroline Norton's Defense: English Laws for Women in the 19th Century*. Academy Chicago Publishers.

LETITIA YOUMANS:
THE WOMAN WHO STOOD UP

Janet Kellough

Janet Kellough is a Canadian author and storyteller whose books and stage works frequently draw from the folklore and history of early Ontario. *Wishful Seeing* (Dundurn Press, 2016), the fifth book in her historically based Thaddeus Lewis Mystery Series, was shortlisted for the 2017 Crime Writers of Canada Best Novel Award. In 2020, Kellough was awarded the Prince Edward County Heritage Award for Heritage Awareness and Advocacy. She has also published several contemporary novels and story compilations, and her feminist speculative thriller *The Bathwater Conspiracy* (EDGE, 2018) was nominated for a 2019 Alberta Book Award.

For a large part of the nineteenth century, drunkenness was the single greatest social scourge in Canada. And against all odds, the liquor trade's greatest enemy turned out to be a very dangerous woman, who unexpectedly found herself leading the campaign to control it.

Letitia Creighton Youmans was born near Cobourg, a small town on the north shore of Lake Ontario. In her 1893 autobiography *Campaign Echoes*, she writes that her father, a farmer with a relatively small holding, made great sacrifices to ensure that she was well-educated. The reasons for this are unclear, but the traditional female goal of marriage and children never seemed to be part of John Creighton's expectations for his eldest daughter. He somehow scraped together enough money to send Letitia to the Cobourg Ladies' Seminary and later to the Burlington Ladies' Academy, both of which offered women an academic curriculum. When she graduated in 1846, she accepted a position as an instructor at a Ladies' Academy in Picton, another small town along the shores of Lake Ontario. It seemed her life would be spent as a teacher.

However, in 1850 she met Arthur Youmans, a widower with eight children. He needed a wife and someone to raise his family. He asked Letitia if she would consider taking the job. It was not the most romantic of proposals, and in spite of the fact that 'the subject of matrimony had not engaged much of my thoughts', and that later she admonished young women to 'marry no man for the sake of a home', there must have been something she found appealing about Arthur, for she accepted and settled down to try to become a farmer's wife.

It was a position she was ill-suited for, a fact her neighbours lost little time in remarking upon. 'Some of them asserted that I could not even boil a potato without looking into a book to see how it was done', she wrote. 'To the latter part of this charge I will, to a certain extent, plead guilty.'

Aided by Catherine Stowe's *Domestic Economy and Recipe Book* she was soon turning out perfectly-formed loaves of bread, and that trickiest of things to make – beautiful bars of hard soap. She also found time to educate not only her adopted family, but the neighbourhood children as well.

But it was her role as a Sunday School teacher that led her to her real life's work. In 1874 Letitia attended a conference at Lake Chautauqua in New York State to discover the newest methods of instruction. There, she also came into contact with American temperance groups who were holding concurrent meetings. Mightily impressed and armed with information, support and organisational strategy, she returned from Chautauqua determined to form a Temperance Union in Picton.

The selling of liquor licences was a lucrative source of income for municipalities in the province of Ontario. There was a tavern at every crossroads and in the smallest of villages. Whiskey was freely available at grocery stores and children could purchase it to take home to their parents. Entire paycheques would disappear into a bottle, and the social cost was enormous. Families were left to struggle on pennies when the breadwinner spent all of his money on whiskey. Chronic public drunkenness was punishable by a jail, or even a penitentiary term, and when their alcoholic husbands were incarcerated, women and their children were left dependent on the scant charity of friends and relatives.

Letitia organised. Then, along with a small band of followers, she petitioned Picton Town Council to stop granting liquor licences to grocery stores in the town. Council members were aware of her efforts, and decided to meet secretly to issue the licences before the petition could be presented. It was a small town though, with a well-developed grapevine, and someone tipped off the temperance band. They rushed off to the secret meeting, where their petition – which should have been first put in the hands of a councillor – was laid on the table by the janitor.

The Mayor picked it up, and glancing over it said, 'There is a petition from the ladies. Who is to present it? Will any member of the council volunteer his services?'

He clearly expected no such volunteer, but unexpectedly the local newspaper editor, also a councillor, took the petition, read it, expressed his approval and laid it before his fellow council members.

The mayor countered by insisting that someone from the group of temperance supporters must advocate the petition, asking whether they had selected a gentleman to speak for them, or whether one of (the ladies) would address the council. It was a blatant attempt to embarrass them into going away, for in those days it was completely unheard of for a woman to speak in public. Letitia recalled the moment:

> Almost unconsciously I rose to my feet. A mountain weight of responsibility rested upon me and the pent-up agony of the past found vent in words which did not seem my own, but voiced the sentiments of another and a higher source . . . and should I have held my peace, the very stones would have cried out against me.

Everyone was astonished. Far from being embarrassed, Letitia spoke succinctly and with passion. The battle was not yet over, however, as another councillor suggested that they would withhold licensing if Letitia was willing to personally reimburse merchants for their loss of sales. She countered by asking if the families of drunkards would be compensated for their losses as well. And in a final salvo, the mayor insisted that the temperance supporters gather a petition consisting of 'the majority of ratepayers' by the next evening, when they would meet again. Letitia and her band did heroic work gathering names, but fell just short of a majority.

It didn't matter – she had found her voice. News of her confrontation spread and soon she was invited to organise Temperance Unions in towns and villages throughout the province. She travelled tirelessly, at times addressing audiences as often as five or six times a week. The movement gathered momentum, and soon municipal councils everywhere found themselves debating anti-liquor by-laws.

And throughout it all, she had the unwavering and proud support of her dear, unromantic husband Arthur. At one point, when Letitia was slapped with a defamation suit for anti-liquor remarks she had made at a meeting, Arthur vowed to defend his wife 'if it takes every last penny I have'. The suit was quietly dropped.

Letitia Youmans quickly rose to the highest ranks as an administrator and field organiser for the provincial Women's Christian Temperance Union and eventually became the first president of the national organisation. As her fame spread, she was invited to speak across North America, attended international conventions and was regarded as a powerful and influential figure in Canadian public life.

She emphasised what she termed 'home protection', rather than prohibition, recognising that the true curse of alcoholism was the social cost it exacted. She formulated three 'inalienable rights' – the right of every woman to have:

A comfortable home
A sober husband
Sober sons

She also saw women's suffrage as a necessary adjunct to social justice for women. In 1885, the Ontario government granted unmarried women the right to vote, but Letitia wrote:

> It is a problem I have not yet been able to solve, why a woman having a husband would be disqualified from voting any more than a man who had a wife ... If only widows and spinsters are allowed to vote, then surely bachelors and widowers should be the only men eligible to the same privilege.

Although it is fashionable in a modern age to dismiss the temperance movement in Canada as a parochial and church-sponsored moral crusade, in reality it was a response to a severe social problem, whose victims were mostly women and children. Letitia Youmans did not see alcoholism as a purely individual failing, but laid the blame for widespread drunkenness firmly on the shoulders of the liquor merchants, who made their product cheap and easy to get and who reaped enormous profits from their activities.

And in the end, her efforts were successful. Many municipalities in the province, and indeed in the whole country, eventually passed by-laws regulating the sale of liquor, and in many respects Letitia Youmans laid the groundwork for the social safety net that underpins modern Canada.

Letitia Youmans died in 1896 and was buried in Picton, where a historical plaque honours the memory of this giant of Canada's social reform movement.

More reading

Errington, E. J., 1995. *Wives and Mothers, School Mistresses and Scullery Maids: Working Women in Upper Canada 1790–1840.* McGill-Queen's University Press.

Hayes, B., 2024. *The Fourth American Institution: Understanding Circuit Chautauqua.* [Online] available at: https://ushistoryscene.com/article/chautauqua/ (accessed 11 October 2024).

Noel, J., 1995. *Canada Dry: Temperance Crusades Before Confederation.* University of Toronto Press Heritage Series.

Roberts, J., 2009. *In Mixed Company: Taverns and Public Life in Upper Canada.* UBC Press.

MILLICENT GARRETT FAWCETT: STEADFASTNESS AND COURAGE

Gillian Murphy

Gillian Murphy is the Curator of Equality, Rights and Citizenship at LSE Library. She is an archivist and curator who works with the Women's Library and the Hall-Carpenter Archives (a large LGBT+ collection). She curates exhibitions, researches archives, runs workshops with archives, manages events, and connects people with archives.

When I think about Millicent Garrett Fawcett, it is not the image of a dangerous woman that springs to mind. But, when I think about what Millicent achieved during her lifetime, I think of the tireless, fearless campaigner who pursued a radical, dangerous idea, that of women's enfranchisement, until it was achieved. This campaign lasted sixty-two years and helped to overcome prejudice and organised obstruction, which required courage, energy and gritty determination.

Millicent was a member of a large family. She was one of the younger daughters of Newson and Louisa Garrett, and sister of Agnes Garrett and Elizabeth Garrett Anderson. The family lived in Aldeburgh in Suffolk and keenly debated the political questions of the day. In July 1865, when Millicent and Agnes were visiting their elder sister, Louisa, in London, they were taken to hear one of John Stuart Mill's election addresses. Millicent was greatly impressed by Mill and later wrote, 'This meeting kindled tenfold my enthusiasm for women's suffrage.'

In the following year, the Reform Bill was under discussion, and it was clear that women who wanted the vote needed to speak up. A small committee was formed to put a petition together, including Elizabeth Garrett. Millicent was nineteen years old and too young to sign this petition, as women had to be over twenty-one to sign. However, she worked very hard to collect signatures from others. In less than a month, 1,499 women's signatures were collected and presented to Parliament by MP John Stuart Mill on 7 June 1866. Although this petition was unsuccessful, the Fawcett Society regard this moment as its foundation and the launch of an organised campaign for female enfranchisement.

On 20 May 1867, and now married to Henry Fawcett, Millicent sat in the Ladies' Gallery to hear the debate on John Stuart Mill's amendment to the 1867 Reform Bill. It was proposed that the word 'man' be changed for 'person' in the enfranchisement clause. Millicent wrote, 'the heavy brass trellis which then screened off these galleries, and their bad ventilation made them quite unnecessarily tiring and even exhausting, but the whole scene was new to me . . . It thrilled me to hear my sister and her successful efforts to open the medical profession to women referred to.' Again, Millicent was inspired by Mill's speech. Two months later, the first meeting of the London National Society for Women's Suffrage was held at Clementia Taylor's house on Campden Hill and Millicent went along as its youngest recruit.

At the early stages of this campaign, the suffragists believed that victory would be quick, but they were politically innocent. Nevertheless, these women were bold pioneers. They were doing something that was unusual for Victorian women to attempt to do. They also realised that public meetings would have to be held to advance their cause, which was seen as another extremely bold and dangerous activity for Victorian women to be involved in.

Millicent gave a short speech in her first public appearance in July 1869 at a public meeting in the Gallery of the Architectural Society in Conduit Street. She spoke again in 1870 in the Hanover Rooms and then delivered her first lecture on women's suffrage in her husband's constituency in Brighton a month later. In 1871, she embarked on a speaking tour in the west of England, organised by Lilias Ashworth. Millicent did not particularly enjoy public speaking but had become very competent by 1884 and she was inundated with invitations to speak publicly. In a letter dated 19 February 1884 to Jane Cobden, Millicent wrote, 'No one knows how speaking takes it out of me.' She was keen that new people should be found to speak for women's suffrage because 'I believe everyone can speak who has got anything to say. Of course they don't like it, but no more do I.'

The suffrage campaign attracted educated women, which brought it to the notice of educated men. On 20 November 1908, Millicent was invited to speak at the Oxford Union Society. This was the first time a woman had spoken there in its eighty-three-year history. The question for debate was 'That in the opinion of this House the time has come when the Government should be urged to remove the electoral disabilities of women.' She was received with great enthusiasm and courtesy. This was a popular event and members were given permission to sit on the floor and gangways because the hall was so full. In putting forward her case for women's suffrage, Millicent claimed that votes for women would probably result in higher wages for sweated workers, a benefit to the entire community. She said that women had proved themselves in local government, which was a veiled tribute to her sister, Elizabeth, who had been elected Mayor of Aldeburgh, in Suffolk, earlier that year. Despite Millicent's competent argument, the motion was defeated by thirty-one votes, which, in an all-male assembly, was a considerable achievement.

Millicent was not one to show her feelings readily and rarely wrote about them. One event broke that pattern and was in response to the defeat of the

Conciliation Bill in 1912. After walking up and down the Palace Yard, Westminster, with hundreds of other women, Millicent recounts, 'I remember what I felt when I heard the bad news . . . I felt that what I had been working for for forty years had been destroyed at a blow; but I also felt what beavers feel when their dam has been destroyed, namely, that they must begin all over again, and build it up once more from the beginning.'

It took Millicent some time to recover from this political disappointment. By January 1913, she had put a request in the *Common Cause*, newspaper of the National Union of the Women's Suffrage Societies, asking if she could rely on the 'steadfastness and courage' of the Union of which she was President, to carry on the extra work entailed by the lengthy campaign. The Union responded by surprising her with a parade representing 400 societies at an evening reception following the Annual General Council meeting on 27 February 1913. Millicent was presented with a beautiful brooch encrusted in green, red and white jewels, the colours of the suffragists. On the reverse is a gold-lettered message in blue enamel: 'Millicent Fawcett 1913 Steadfastness and Courage'. Millicent was overcome by this show of loyalty. In her reply, she said she would regard the jewel as a most precious treasure and would hand it down to her daughter, who would prize it equally.

It was five more years before the Representation of the People Act 1918 gave women over the age of thirty – and holding the requisite property qualification – the right to vote. It took another ten years before women achieved electoral parity with men in the Equal Franchise Act, which received Royal Assent on 2 July 1928. Millicent wanted to be present at this event because, almost sixty-one years before, she had heard John Stuart Mill introduce his suffrage amendment to the Reform Bill in 1867. She described herself as having had the great good fortune of seeing through the campaign for women's suffrage from its small beginnings to ultimate success. Her personal determination played no small part in that achievement.

Was Millicent Garrett Fawcett a dangerous woman? Certainly not, but she was perceived as such by the conservative, male, authoritarian political elite of her time because she dauntlessly pursued the idea of political gender equality to them. Her refusal to be thwarted and her sheer determination made her seem very dangerous indeed.

More reading

Crawford, E., 1999. *The Women's Suffrage Movement: A Reference Guide 1866–1928*. Routledge.

Fawcett, M. G., 1924. *What I Remember*. Fisher Unwin.

Terras, M. and Crawford, E., eds, 2022. *Millicent Garrett Fawcett: Selected Writings*. UCL Press.

LUMINA SOPHIE DITE SURPRISE: A SPARK IGNITING MULTITUDES

Vanessa Lee

Vanessa Lee is an academic and playwright whose research interests include postcolonial theatre and film, gender studies and European, Asian and Caribbean theatres. Her articles have appeared in the *Global Media Journal*; *Journal of Romance Studies*; *Transtext(e)s Transcultures* and *The Bulletin of Francophone Postcolonial Studies*. Her book *Four Caribbean Women Playwrights: Ina Césaire, Maryse Condé, Gerty Dambury and Suzanne Dracius* was published in 2021 by Palgrave. As a playwright and theatre practitioner she has written and translated plays, and directed and performed in several productions in the UK, France, Ireland and Sweden. Personal webpage: www.vanessalee.org

1870: Martinique. A twenty-one-year-old pregnant black woman leads a group of her peers in the first workers' protests since the abolition of slavery in 1848. These female insurrectionists, in charge of burning down plantations, were called *Pétroleuses,* a name shared with the women involved in the Paris Commune that took place months later. The Martinicans came first, but were the first to be forgotten. While official histories may have eclipsed these insurgents, they are part of the local mythology and imaginary of Rivière Pilote in Southern Martinique, the epicentre of the insurrection. The leader of the *Pétroleuses* was Lumina Sophie dite Surprise.

Her official name was Marie-Philomène Roptus. However, she is remembered and recorded in local and official histories as Lumina Sophie dite Surprise. The court transcripts of the trials that followed the quelling of the short-lived 1870 revolt feature the names of insurrection leaders and major offenders. The transcripts of the *Insurrection du Sud* read: 'Lumina Sophie dite Surprise, 19 ans, couturière, née au Vauclin, domiciliée à la Rivière-Pilote. [Lumina Sophie dite Surprise, 19 years, seamstress, born in the Vauclin, resident of Rivière-Pilote].' The official narrative had inadvertently allowed the myth of Lumina Sophie dite Surprise to seep in.

Lumina Sophie dite Surprise was born on 9 November 1848, the year slavery was abolished (for the second time) in the French Caribbean.

Hers was one of the first births of a free Martinican to a formerly enslaved woman recorded in Rivière-Pilote's birth register. She was registered under the name Marie-Philomène Roptus, daughter of Marie Sophie, known as Zulma, and granddaughter of Reine Sophie. 'Philomène' was shortened to 'Lumina'. 'Sophie' she bore as a matronymic bequeathed her from her mother and grandmother, and she was given the nickname 'Surprise', according to Gilbert Pago. She became a seamstress, and learned how to read and write. Her occupation and her literacy conferred her a certain status. Those she led and fought for during the revolt of 1870 were mostly fieldworkers and illiterate. So why sacrifice herself and her bright future?

In 1870, social and racial tensions persisted in Martinique after the formal abolition of slavery in 1848, despite the formerly enslaved population's shackles being replaced by workmen's contracts. Two events sparked the insurrection and brutal governmental repression that lasted from 22 September to 30 September 1870. The first was the Lubin case, where Léopold Lubin, a black man, had been tried for standing up against a white man, Augier de Maintenon, and sentenced to a term in prison. In contrast, a plantation owner, Louis Codé had previously been accused of sexually assaulting and leaving for dead a black woman, had only received a fine. It was this same Codé who initiated the second event that led to the Insurrection by running up a white flag – a nostalgic symbol of royalty and white supremacy. As Jacqueline Conti puts it, like many Martinicans, Lumina's fight was 'against racism, exploitation, and poverty'. More importantly, 'in 1870, like in 1794 and 1848 [dates of the first and second abolition of slavery], African descendants, with women at the forefront, were claiming equality of rights and social justice.'

It is believed that Lumina Sophie dite Surprise was pregnant by one of the revolt's leaders, Émile Sydney. She was arrested at the end of the Insurrection and dealt a life sentence of hard labour at Saint-Laurent du Maroni, in French Guyana. Her son, Théodore Lumina, born while she was in captivity in Martinique and separated from his mother at birth, died after seven months. In 1877, she was forced to marry a former prisoner in French Guyana, a farmer from Northern France fourteen years her elder, and she died two years later at the age of thirty-one. But her name lives on.

Today two schools in the French West Indies bear her name: 'Lycée Polyvalent Lumina Sophie' in Saint-Laurent du Maroni, French Guyana; and 'Lycée Professionnel Régional Lumina Sophie' in Schœlcher, Martinique. A high-rise building was inaugurated in 2012 and named after her, the 'Tour Lumina'. A roundabout was also dedicated to her and all other rebel 'slave' women, even though she was not enslaved. In addition to and more importantly than her name decorating the plaques of buildings and roundabouts, Lumina's life has also inspired artists, writers and musicians.

Lumina Sophie dite Surprise is the subject of songs by Martinican artists Lorraine Zacharie (*Lumina*) and MIZIK BO KAIL (*Lumina Sophie;* interpreted by Lea Galva). A sculpture by Élisa Albert and Alain Ozier was erected in Rivière-Pilote in 2013 and depicts her alongside two other insurgents: Louis Telga and Eugène Lacaille. A novel by Chantal Clem (*Moi, Lumina Sophie*, 2022) explores a fictive narrative of Lumina's life. Commemorative events in Martinique celebrated the 150th anniversary of the Insurrection through talks, workshops and performances such as a site-specific 'theatrical walk' retracing the steps of Lumina Sophie dite Surprise, her mother Zulma and her grandmother Reine.

In 2005, writer and award-winning poet Suzanne Dracius wrote an eponymous play entitled *Lumina Sophie dite Surprise*, about the last days of Lumina and her *Pétroleuses'* fight against government forces. The play sought to reinstate Lumina into local history, since according to Dracius, most Martinicans when prompted to name a young woman ready to sacrifice herself for a cause would answer Joan of Arc. Everyone knows Joan of Arc. Not everyone knows Lumina, the opposite in many ways to Joan: pregnant, not virginal; black, not white. The God who spoke to Joan Lumina called 'un vieux béké [an old slave-owner]', whom she would readily burn down along with the plantations.

Lumina Sophie dite Surprise might have been the opposite of Joan, but no less deserving of recognition as symbol of political, social and anti-racist struggle past and present.

More reading

Couti, J., 2020. Lumina Sophie, Nineteenth-Century Martinique. *As If She Were Free: A Collective Biography of Women and Emancipation in the Americas.* Cambridge University Press.

Insurrection du Sud (22 septembre 1870): conseil de guerre/Martinique. 2008. Gallica. https://gallica.bnf.fr/ark:/12148/bpt6k5470322h. Accessed 7 October 2024. My translation.

Pago, G., 2008. *Lumina Sophie dite 'Surprise' (1848–1879): insurgée et bagnarde.* Ibis Rouge.

FLORA SHAW: HOW IMPERIALISM ENDANGERED WOMEN'S VOTE

Pengpeng Wang

Pengpeng Wang is currently teaching English in China on the online platform YLYK, which champions English learning through intensive reading of classic English texts in the humanities. She completed her undergraduate degree in English Literature and History at Newcastle University, and then obtained a master's degree in English Literature at the University of Edinburgh. As a Chinese student, her experience in Britain led her to develop an interest in diasporic groups. In her second year at Newcastle, she worked on a university-funded research project on women, leisure and diaspora in the North-East during the First World War. There, Lady Lugard's prominent role in the relief work for Belgian refugees during wartime prompted her to find out more about this unusual woman.

It is easy to dismiss things when they are not obvious, and such is the case with Flora Shaw, later Lady Lugard. Previous biographers first dismissed the importance of her whole life, and later the early part of it before she took up journalism. Although the most recent biography demonstrates her prominent contribution to the imperial project, her anti-suffragist role is only mentioned in passing. This continued despite many studies on connections between imperialism and the suffragist movement. Shaw is often much less discussed than her anti-suffragist peers due to the comparative 'muteness' of her stance.

But was her role really that insignificant?

In fact, her eminence in other fields allowed her to endanger the suffrage movement in subtle ways. The reason why Flora Shaw did not feature as visibly in the suffrage debate was that votes for women was not her priority. Rather, her major devotion was to the British imperial enterprise. The traditional gender difference was a crucial prop of the Empire, laying the foundation for a hierarchical society. Rank and order guaranteed both the stability of the metropolis and that of the colonies, as well as helping to justify the analogous inequality between the centre and the province.

For the anti-suffragists, women's suffrage was incompatible with imperial ideology. It symbolised a gender transgression where women diverted themselves from their 'natural' station as domestic mothers to intervene in men's parliamentary politics. If effected, such a move would definitely 'emasculate' England. Women's suffrage was also seen as threatening women's social purity, a fundamental female quality in the Christian belief system – another mainstay buttressing the imperial project. Interestingly, the discourse of the 'domestic mother' was also deployed by some suffragists: women's indispensable role in the expansion and consolidation of the British Empire – as hostesses of the 'home' and helpmeets of men – would validate their share of citizenship.

However, this rhetoric of women's distinctive role was first employed by the anti-suffragist side. The ominous suggestion is, therefore, the ubiquity and wide acceptance of anti-suffragist ideology – so much so that it was not only justifiable but also became instrumental, even in the argument of their opponents.

Shaw's familial background and childhood experience in Ireland were crucial to her induction into the imperial project. She saw the cause as the only solution to poverty in Britain. Unsurprisingly, during the early stage of her writing career, in the last decades of the nineteenth century, she incorporated imperial values into her stories for children. Among the many dogmas, including fixed class distinctions and justifications for British rule over Ireland, the duty of the 'gentleman' and the idealistic 'Victorian gentlewoman' featured heavily. As prints were cheap and new developments were mushrooming in women's and children's education, such literature served the purpose of imprinting on the younger generation the gender roles implicit in imperial ideology.

By the time the suffragists won their battle in 1918, the little girls who once read Shaw's rather popular *Castle Blair* and *Hector* would have been middle-aged. It is therefore not hard to make the link between the influence of her stories on them from their youthful days and the apathy of many women, including even those of working-class backgrounds, to this new right to vote in the post-war era.

Shaw later moved into writing journalism, first for *The Pall Mall Gazette* and *The Manchester Guardian* and finally *The Times*, where she travelled around the globe as a colonial correspondent. She could then reach out to a wider audience, achieving a more significant political impact. Her words and deeds seemed contradictory: it looked as if she was actively opposing the gender standard she had been advocating. Nonetheless, a closer inspection reveals the inherent consistency between her action and her words.

In a speech to the Scottish Geographical Society, during her career as Special Correspondent of *The Times* in Australia, Shaw solicited that young and educated people of Britain be sent to farm the lands of Australia. Their laudable work in this 'store house of raw material' would substantiate her vision of the mutual benefits between Britain and her province. Deploring the small number of British women in Australia, she strongly encouraged them to go there, asserting, as can be expected, that '[d]airy, poultry-rearing, and fruit growing would fall naturally into their department'. To her, the issue of women travelling to colonies was not problematic, as long as they remained true to their 'God-given' position as the helpmeets of men and contented themselves with performing domestic duties.

What these women would achieve individually was not an expedition of the colony. Instead, it was a duplication of the domestic sphere, and their role in this 'new' land was still that of housewives. Collectively, they became the maternal hostess of the British Empire – the larger and greater 'home'. Shaw justified this concept of 'home' by asserting that Australians had in 'their veins . . . the British blood' and were thereby of the same 'race' as the British people. In the long run, this settlement of British women proved to be harmful to local feminisms: it necessitated an 'othering' of the native women to establish the white superiority and supremacy to suit the imperial ideology, questioning colonial women's deservedness to the rights advocated back in England.

Shaw reconciled her unusual experiences by claiming membership among these women harbingers of the British Empire. Her travels and interventions in the colonial policy were no more than tending to the domestic affairs of the imperial home. As for Shaw's political involvements, she always remained conscious of her gender role and adeptly cast herself as a figure of modesty after her late marriage. She lobbied for her husband's colonial enterprise as Lady Lugard, immaculately living up to the standard of the virtuous Victorian wife.

The printed media was not, however, her only channel to exert influence. During the First World War, Lady Lugard's relief work for Belgian refugees was so noteworthy that it gained her the title of Dame of the British Empire (DBE). The War Refugees Committee she set up was one of the most important charity organisations, and was conveniently imbued with her ideology. This was manifest in its constitution, where men held most of the leading positions while women were assigned to clothing and accommodation departments, and in its treatment of refugees, which was dependent upon class and gender.

Lugard virtually encompassed all the three major types of distinguished women anti-suffragists in Julia Bush's work: the maternal reformer, the woman writer, and the imperial lady. The title of DBE was more than an acknowledgement of her contribution. It erected her as an exemplar to be admired. Thus, her resplendent achievements made her anti-suffragist ideology likely to be accepted along with her admirable public profile. Considering that anti-suffragist women who brandished their attitude often incurred charges of hypocrisy, as their implication in politics was essentially against their own principles, the road Lady Lugard took was much more secure.

This dangerous imperialist-cum-anti-suffragist Flora Shaw/Lady Lugard imperilled women's suffrage not by flaunting her viewpoint. In fact, the anti-suffragist campaign might never have occurred to her as a worthy diversion. However, her unwavering dedication to bolster the British Empire was so successful that the anti-suffragism inherent to her ideology was approved of by many, along with her other codes of conduct. In other words, this female imperialist readily put the suffrage cause into danger in an almost sidelining manner. This, among many things, reminds us of the difficulties faced by the fighters for women's suffrage and the fragility of feminism – both in its early stages and today. Above all, it warns us against the insidious nature of imperial ideology, which jeopardises equalities of all kinds.

More reading

Callaway, H. and Helly, D. O., 1992. Crusader for Empire. In N. Chaudhuri and M. Strobel, eds, *Western Women and Imperialism: Complicity and Resistance.* Indiana University Press, pp. 79–97.

Carrington, B., 2008. 'Good, and lovely, and true': A consideration of the contribution & legacy of Flora Shaw's fiction for children. In L. Thiel et al., eds, *A Victorian Quartet: Four Forgotten Women Writers.* Pied Piper Publishing.

Grewal, I., 1996. *Home and Harem: Nation, Gender, Empire, and the Cultures of Travel.* Duke University Press.

Storr, K., 2010. *Excluded from the Record: Women, Refugees and Relief 1914–1929.* Peter Lang.

CHRYSTAL MACMILLAN: CHALLENGING AUTHORITY, CHAMPIONING EQUALITY

Helen Kay

Helen Kay spent several years researching and giving presentations on the work and life of Chrystal Macmillan. In 2014, the work was put on hold when Helen became the coordinator of an International History Working Group, preparing material for centenary exhibitions on the history of the Women's International League for Peace and Freedom. In 2024 she co-authored *Chrystal Macmillan, 1872–1937: Campaigner for Equality, Justice and Peace* (Edinburgh University Press) with Rose Pipes.

Why did five women graduates challenge the University of Edinburgh authorities in 1906?

Chrystal Macmillan, Elsie Inglis, Frances Melville, Margaret Nairn and Frances Simpson had the audacity to request voting papers for the parliamentary General Election under the university franchise. The university acknowledged that:

The women have been admitted to graduation in several of the faculties of the universities and their names have been placed on the Register of the General Council. They have attended and voted at the meetings of the General Council, and they have hitherto enjoyed and exercised all the privileges possessed by male graduates of the universities.

But to claim the right to vote for the university candidate in a parliamentary election was considered a step too far and the university authorities refused the women's request. The men were shocked by the audacity of the women when they pursued their application through the Court of Session in Edinburgh and on to the House of Lords in London. The university authorities spared no expense in hiring the best lawyers to represent the universities in court hearings, and when the women eventually lost their case, the university claimed legal costs of £111 14s 3d.

Even the Press were impressed by the women's arguments, naming Chrystal Macmillan the 'Scottish Portia', but the university authorities and the lawyers realised that this claim for a parliamentary vote, if granted, would create a dangerous precedent. The Law Lords supported the university's decision to refuse voting papers to the women on the grounds that the word 'person' in the relevant legislation did not include 'woman'.

Macmillan, who presented the women graduates' case in the House of Lords in 1908, was a pleasant but dangerous woman throughout her life, continually challenging the established order, trying to improve the situation for women. She campaigned all her life for women's right to full citizenship under the law, in Scotland, in Great Britain and internationally.

Macmillan's suffrage campaigning took her to all parts of Scotland, from Dumfries to Shetland, speaking at crowded public meetings.

Men have made a more comfortable world for boys and men than for girls and women; and the women now want the power to make the world more comfortable for the girls and women without doing any harm to the boys and men. It is not good for men that they should be in the position of tyrants.

By 1910, she was learning the power of monitoring proposed legislation as Scottish representative of the National Union of Women Workers (NUWW, later known as the National Council of Women).

She was always on the alert to 'spot' clauses which were prejudicial to women, or which differentiated their treatment from that of men.

In May 1913, Macmillan recommended that NUWW members wrote to local Members of Parliament urging that amendments to the Insurance Act should include a clause ensuring that 'one fourth of each Insurance committee of representatives of insured persons should be women' and that a clause be inserted in the Mental Deficiency Bill to ensure the inclusion of a Woman Commissioner.

Her reliance on the law to challenge established views gave her a sound understanding of legislation, so that when some women were granted the vote in 1918, Macmillan was called upon to write a pamphlet titled, 'And shall I have the Parliamentary vote?'

At the start of the First World War, Macmillan ran the relief office for the International Women's Suffrage Alliance (IWSA) in London. In response to a request from Holland for help in caring for 80,000 Belgian refugees suddenly displaced from Antwerp in October 1914, she raised the money and organised a load of food to be transported to Flushing, all within one day. She and a colleague, Mary Sheepshanks, travelled with the food to Holland, where the women toured extensively, listening to what the refugees and camp organisers needed, before returning to Britain to raise money for further supplies.

Many women in the international suffrage movement were unwilling to join in the patriotic fervour sweeping through Britain, France and Germany from the start of the First World War. In February 1915, twelve women from Belgium, Britain and Germany met with Dutch women to discuss how to maintain their international relationships. Macmillan became one of the organisers for an International Congress of Women which met in April 1915, when 1,200 women from twelve countries chose to face the dangers of travel through war-torn countries to meet in The Hague. With Macmillan as chair of the Resolutions Committee, twenty resolutions were passed expressing the women's horror at the bloodshed, providing an analysis of the causes of war, and advocating the use of mediation to resolve international disputes. The Congress elected five envoys to take the message to all the Heads of States in Europe and the USA, urging them to end the bloodshed and resolve the dispute through continuous mediation. Despite their efforts, no statesman would take the first step towards resolving the war through peaceful methods.

The women were not applauded by their fellow citizens for their efforts. In Germany, some women were imprisoned on their return home. In Britain, Millicent Garrett Fawcett thought their actions were close to treason, and Macmillan's family refused to talk about her involvement.

As Chair of the Political Committee of delegates to the Zurich Congress of Women in 1919, Macmillan presented the resolution criticising the Versailles Treaty. The women welcomed the establishment of the League of Nations but regretted that 'the Covenant of the League now submitted by the Allied and Associated Powers, in many respects does not accord with the 14 Points laid down as the basis for the present negotiations, contains certain provisions that will stultify its growth, and omits others which are essential to world peace.'

From 1916 onwards, Macmillan campaigned for a change in national and international law on the Nationality of Married Women. The international legal situation for women who married foreigners was messy. It was possible for women who married foreign husbands to have two nationalities imposed upon them: other women who married foreign husbands were left with no nationality, which, in practice, left them stateless, while others were deprived of all citizenship rights and benefits in the land of their birth.

The British position was stated firmly by Sir Cecil Hurst, Legal Adviser to the Foreign Office, who defined the legal situation in 1923:

'Our law in this country . . . is founded on the principle that husband and wife are one, and that one is the husband.' This meant that British women who married foreign men lost their British nationality, and, even if they remained resident in Britain, they were thereafter treated as aliens, having to register with the local police and being refused a British passport. Macmillan argued that 'there is no reason why the rights of a woman in connection with nationality should be curtailed because of marriage any more than are those of a man . . . The right to nationality in one's own person is the most fundamental political right.'

When the Government showed no sign of drafting new legislation, Macmillan could not accept this lack of action and, in 1921, drafted a document to illustrate what such a legislative change would look like. Two years later, she was the only woman called to give evidence to the British government's Commission of Enquiry into the Nationality of Married Women.

At international level, Chrystal Macmillan showed herself to be equally resolute. A committee member of several Women's International Organisations, she galvanised an International Demonstration of Women in 1930, and she organised a deputation to the League of Nations Codification Conference to promote the resolution 'That a woman, whether married or unmarried, should have the same right as a man to retain or to change her nationality'.

The lawyers and jurists, all men, were meeting in The Hague to discuss international issues of nationality. Macmillan wanted to make visible a major problem: the agenda for the Codification Conference made no reference to women, nor did it acknowledge that the situation of women under international law was different from that of men. By the end of the women's International Demonstration, the lawyers agreed to place the issue on the agenda in future discussions.

Although she worked cooperatively with women on committees to promote women's right to equality, Macmillan could be very firm in presenting her own view. When the British government, encouraged by the International Federation of University Women, proposed to include a woman delegate to attend the League of Nations discussions on nationality, she turned down the nomination. She explained, 'I would be willing to be nominated by IFUW to prospective Committee but only on following terms: I should not be limited to explaining what the attitude of Federation is and urging the adoption only of the principle to which the Federation has adhered, but should be free to express my own views.'

The post in the delegation was given to Dr Ivy Williams, who described Macmillan as a woman who 'still puts the principle of equality first, whereas I have been saying that we should consider ourselves first as lawyers who would help forward international agreement and only secondarily as women'.

The Council of the League of Nations proposed to consult women's organisations in 1931 on the methods of increasing collaboration with women in the general work of the League. In response, Macmillan suggested that the League employ more women in high-level posts in the Secretariat, and recommend to the States Members of the League that they raise the status of women to that of men, giving women full civil, economic and political rights. Her analysis of the outcomes of gender blindness in the request from The League of Nations is still relevant today.

Full and equal cooperation means a great deal more than being asked to supply information, or mere doing of propaganda and educational work on a policy framed by bodies in which women are not included, or where they are in a very small minority, or inadequately represented. Full and equal cooperation involves the power of directing effective criticism to policies in course of formation, with an effective voice in determining what these policies shall be. It also involves adequate representation among those who administer these policies.

More reading

Bussey, G. and Tims, M., 1965. *Women's International League for Peace and Freedom*. Allen & Unwin.

Kay, H. and Pipes, R., 2020. Chrystal Macmillan, Scottish campaigner for women's equality through law reform. *Women's History Review*, 29(4), pp. 716–736.

Kay, H. and Pipes, R., 2024. *Chrystal Macmillan 1872–1937: Campaigner for Equality, Justice and Peace*. Edinburgh University Press.

Law, C., 2000. *Suffrage and Power: The Women's Movement 1918–1928*. 2nd edn. I. B Tauris.

Leneman, L., 1991. *A Guid Cause: The Women's Suffrage Movement in Scotland*. Aberdeen University Press.

Miller, C., 1992. *Lobbying the League: Women's International Organisations and the League of Nations*. DPhil thesis, University of Oxford. https://ora.ox.ac.uk/objects/uuid:f517ac72-18b3-42b2-9728-31129462bf4a/files/m8a9dc648f42c02edbc e251148cef4f41

LILIAN LENTON:
THE ELUSIVE SUFFRAGETTE

Hilary McCollum

Dr Hilary McCollum is an Irish writer and creative activist. Her award-winning historical novel, *Golddigger*, was published in 2015 by Bella Books. She is currently working on a novel set within the British suffragette movement.

'Whenever I see an empty house I burn it.'

Lilian Lenton was training to be a dancer when she went to a meeting addressed by suffragette leader Mrs Pankhurst. She later said that, 'I made up my mind that night that as soon as I was twenty-one and my own boss . . . I would volunteer.' She went on to become one of the suffragette movement's most prolific and daring arsonists.

Less than two months after her twenty-first birthday, Lilian took part in the mass window-smashing raid in the West End and Westminster on 1 March 1912.

From in front, behind, from every side it came – a hammering, crashing, splintering sound unheard in the annals of shopping . . . At the windows excited crowds collected, shouting, gesticulating. At the centre of each crowd stood a woman, pale, calm and silent.

Lilian was among more than 150 women who were arrested during the raid. She was jailed for two months under the name Ida Inkley, one of several aliases she adopted during her militant career. She served her time in Holloway Prison in a wing entirely populated by suffragette prisoners. Following her release, she was involved in firing pillar-boxes, a tactic developed by Emily Wilding Davison in December 1911, but she had bigger plans in mind.

I was at the Suffragette Headquarters and announced that I didn't want to break any more windows but I did want to burn some buildings, and I was told that a girl named Olive Walley had just been saying the same thing, so we two met, and the real serious fires in this country started.

It seems likely that this was actually Olive Wharry, who also became a well-known suffragette arsonist, rather than the unknown Olive Walley.

The movement's leadership encouraged this escalation of militancy. The strategy was to attack the 'secret idol' of property, in the hope that the insurance companies would bring pressure on the government to give women the vote. Over the next two years, suffragettes set fire to hundreds of buildings across the country, often choosing high-profile targets such as mansions, railway stations, castles, and even churches. Only empty buildings were attacked to make sure that there was no loss of life.

Lilian's first arrest for arson came in February 1913. Around 3 a.m. on 20 February 1913, Lilian and Olive Wharry set fire to the tea pavilion in Kew Gardens, having scaled what the police considered to be an unclimbable fence. The fire brigade fought the flames for two hours, but the building and its contents were destroyed. Lilian and Olive left behind four cards, signed 'Two Voteless Women', which made it clear that this was a politically motivated action. One said, 'Remember, no property will be safe until women are enfranchised . . . You will have to give in, so be sensible, and do so at once.' Another said, 'You can put out a fire, but you cannot put out the militant spirit of women.'

Lilian and Olive were discovered before they could make good their escape. They were pursued by the police across Richmond cricket ground before being captured and arrested. They gave their names as Lilian Lenton and Joyce Locke. As they fled, they had each been seen to throw away a bag. One of the bags contained, 'a hammer, a saw, a bundle of tow, strongly redolent of paraffin and some paper smelling strongly of tar'.

Later that day, Lilian and Olive were charged at Richmond Police Court and remanded for a week. On bail being refused, one of them threw a book and some papers from the clerk's table at the chairman of the bench. They were taken from the court to Holloway Prison where Lilian's conduct was recorded in the prison's daily record as, 'bad, very defiant'. She smashed everything in the cell in which she was first placed, and was removed to a special strong cell. She was kept apart from other prisoners, not allowed to communicate and all her privileges were suspended.

Lilian went on hunger strike. On Sunday 23 February 1913, the prison authorities decided to forcibly feed her. She was tied into a chair and held down by up to seven prison wardens. Two doctors were in attendance and fed a tube up her nostril and down her throat. The pipe should have been pushed down her oesophagus towards her stomach but instead entered her airway. Although Lilian was violently choking, the doctors poured the liquid food down the tube. It entered her left lung. Lilian collapsed in agony. Fearing she would die in prison, the authorities contacted the Home Secretary, Reginald McKenna, who authorised her release. Lilian was carried from prison on a chair and taken by taxi to a friend's house, where she was treated by suffragette sympathiser Charles Mansell-Moulin for septic pneumonia and pleurisy.

As news of Lilian's treatment reached the press over the following days, the Home Secretary initially denied that she had been force-fed and claimed that her condition had resulted from her hunger strike. Lilian Lenton's near death was a key event leading to the government's introduction of the Prisoners (Temporary Discharge for Ill Health) Act, which was rushed through the House of Commons in the weeks following her release, becoming law on 25 April 1913. The so-called Cat and Mouse Act allowed the government to release hunger-striking suffragettes when they grew weak rather than force-feed them. The women were re-arrested as their health started to recover.

Lilian was too ill to attend her next court hearing on 27 February 1913. She then disappeared from London and went on the run from the police, travelling the country setting fire to buildings and burning 'Votes for Women' into golf greens and cricket pitches. On 9 June 1913, she gave herself up at Doncaster court during the trial of Harry Johnson and Augusta Winship for burglary with intent to burn Westfield House, Doncaster. Lilian stood up in court and gave evidence to the effect that she, not Augusta, was the person who had entered Westfield House with the intention of setting it on fire. Augusta Winship was then discharged and Lilian, under the alias May Dennis, was arrested and placed in the dock. She pleaded neither guilty nor not guilty as she refused to recognise the court. On 10 June she was committed for trial at Leeds Assizes. When removed to the cells, she told the police that she would go on hunger strike, be released, abscond, and carry on committing arson until the government was brought to its knees. She said her aim 'was to burn two buildings a week', in order to 'create an absolutely impossible condition of affairs in the country to prove that it was impossible to govern without the consent of the governed'.

Lilian violently resisted finger-printing on admission to Armley jail. She went on hunger strike and was released on licence on 17 June 1913 to the house of a suffragette sympathiser in Westfield Terrace, Leeds. Although the police were watching the house, she managed to escape them by switching places with another suffragette who had come to the house in a van, dressed as a delivery boy.

Lilian went on the run again initially in Harrogate, then in Scarborough and Dundee. The police suspected that she was involved in burning down Ballikinrain Castle in Stirlingshire and Leuchars Junction Station on 30 June 1913. The Chief Constable of Leeds Police wrote to the Home Secretary suggesting that a photograph of Lilian be circulated to all police forces. The Criminal Record Office issued a 'wanted' photo of her. She was described as five feet two inches tall with brown hair and brown eyes.

Lilian escaped to France on a private yacht in July 1913 but returned to Britain again and continued to set fire to buildings. On one occasion, she was given two bombs by a young male sympathiser of the movement. When the woman she was staying with near Edinburgh heard about the bombs, she insisted that Lilian get rid of them in a lake on the estate of a friend. Lilian went into Edinburgh with the two bombs in an attaché case. She asked a policeman for directions. He said he was just coming off duty and offered to show her the way to the tram. Lilian assumed that he had recognised her and would take her to a police station but instead he took her to the tram. To her amusement, he even carried the bomb-filled attaché case for her.

She was nearly caught by the police in Cardiff but escaped dressed as an infirm old lady and got on a train to London. However, on 7 October 1913 Lilian was arrested at Paddington Station while reclaiming a bicycle from left luggage. She went on hunger strike and was initially forcibly fed, but on 15 October 1913 she was released under the Cat and Mouse Act due to concerns about her health. The police kept a strict watch on the house where she was staying, but again she managed to escape. By now she was becoming known as the elusive suffragette.

Lilian was re-arrested on 22 December 1913 and charged with setting fire to an unoccupied mansion in Cheltenham. She went on a hunger-and-thirst strike and was released on Christmas Day to a house in King's Norton. Again, she escaped from under the noses of the watching police.

In March 1914, she made a flying visit to Doncaster WSPU, dressed as a dapper young man, complete with a moustache, cane and Homburg hat. She continued to evade the police until 4 May 1914, when she was arrested in Birkenhead. She appeared at Leeds Assizes on 8 May 1914 but refused to recognise the court and kept up a tirade against the government during the hearing. She was sentenced to twelve months but was released on licence from Armley jail to a house in Harrogate on 12 May 1914 following a hunger strike. As the papers speculated about whether she would escape again the police mounted an extremely close watch on the Harrogate address. Car lamps were trained on the front and back of the house during the hours of darkness and everyone entering and leaving the house was scrutinised. Nevertheless, when the police entered the house to re-arrest Lilian at the end of her licence period, she was nowhere to be found. The police's theory was that she had escaped among a group of veiled women who had left the house together the previous Saturday and then scattered across the moor.

Lilian remained free until the outbreak of war in August 1914 brought a suspension of militant activity. She served with the Scottish Women's Hospitals Unit in Serbia during the war. She was not eligible to vote when women were first granted limited voting rights in 1918, as she did not meet the age and property requirements.

In 1970, as Treasurer of the Suffragette Fellowship, Lilian unveiled a memorial in Christchurch Gardens, Westminster, dedicated to all the women who had fought to get the vote. She died in 1972 at the age of 81.

More reading

Abrams, F., 2003. *Freedom's Cause: Lives of the Suffragettes*. Profile Books.

Kenney, A., 1924. *Memories of a Militant*. Edward Arnold & Co.

Raeburn, A., 1974. *Militant Suffragettes*. New English Library.

Stanley, L., Morley, A. and Culmore, G., 1988. *The Life and Death of Emily Wilding Davison* with *The Life of Emily Davison*. The Women's Press.

ADRIENNE GERHÄUSER AND CORINNA KAWATERS: FEMINISM ON FIRE

Katharina Karcher

Katharina Karcher is Associate Professor in German at the University of Birmingham, UK. Her work focuses on protest movements and political violence in the twentieth and twenty-first centuries. In this context, she is particularly interested in questions of gender, race, class, dis/ability and political ideology. Her research transgresses disciplinary boundaries and draws on a range of theoretical frameworks including feminist theory, cultural studies and critical security studies.

In contrast to Britain, where it is widely accepted that militant and violent protest for female suffrage is a part of the long and varied history of feminist movements, it was long assumed that no such protest existed in the history of German feminism. Although most feminists in the Federal Republic of Germany (FRG) took the stance that only non-violent forms of protest could achieve real social change, some individuals and groups in the German women's movement considered violent tactics imperative to overcome oppression and exploitation on a local and global scale. One of these groups was the Rote Zora (Red Zora, RZ). Between 1977 and 1988, the RZ claimed responsibility for forty-five arson attacks and bombings, most of which took place in the 1980s, and a few more followed in the 1990s.

The West German state classified the RZ as a terrorist organisation. Against the background of Germany's fascist past and a wave of left-wing political violence in the 1970s, many feminist activists in Germany rejected violence of all shapes and forms, and were understandably reluctant to discuss ideas and activities that could associate the women's movement with 'terrorism'. It is important to acknowledge the pivotal role of pacifism and anti-militarism in the history of the German women's movement. However, it would be wrong to limit feminist politics to non-violent activism. A significant part of the existing literature on the New Women's Movement in the FRG reinforces the idea that it is possible to draw a clear-cut line between peaceful feminist protest on the one side, and 'bad' patriarchal violence on the other. The members of the Red Zora were among a small minority of feminist activists who wanted to challenge this dichotomy and have tried to spread militant protest in the German women's movement.

The Red Zora took up central themes in German feminism at the time including violence against women, transnational solidarity, as well as issues around population control, reproductive technologies and genetic engineering. With its attacks, the RZ tried to encourage women and girls to form gangs to fight back against the many forms of violence and abuse that they experienced in their everyday lives. In an interview with the feminist magazine *EMMA* in 1984, two group members explained:

> Our dream is that there are small gangs of women everywhere; and that a rapist, women trafficker, wife beater, porn dealer, creepy gynaecologist must fear that a gang of women finds him, attacks him, and humiliates him in public. (All translations by the author)

Unlike other militant political organisations in West Germany, the RZ focused on small-scale attacks against property and made it a priority not to hurt or kill people in their attacks. When I interviewed three former group members, they told me that their approach to violence was as much the result of personal ethics as of the life-affirming politics of the women's movement. On the one hand, the RZ set itself the objective to convince other women that it was possible to fight back against everyday violence and abuse. On the other hand, the group wanted to challenge the commonly held view that violent tactics were irreconcilable with feminist politics. The RZ took the stance that violent attacks could serve as a form of 'armed propaganda' for feminist struggles. Although the Red Zora did not succeed in spreading violent tactics in the German women's movement on a large scale, its attacks sparked intense debates on the scope and limits of feminist protest.

In April 1977, members of the Red Zora planted a bomb at the headquarters of the German Medical Association to protest against the organisation's insistence on the abortion ban. Shortly after the attack, they released a claim of responsibility that featured, for the first time in history, the name and logo of the Red Zora. The name Red Zora refers to a children's book from 1941, which the group saw as a source of inspiration for its politics. Kurt Kläber's novel *Die Rote Zora und ihre Bande* (translated into English as *The Outsiders of Uskoken Castle*), and which he published under the pseudonym Kurt Held, provided an example of female leadership as the Red Zora envisaged it. The leading character was unconventional, wild and subversive, but also responsible and caring.

In 1978, the RZ carried out a series of attacks against sex shops in Koblenz and Cologne. These attacks caused damage worth 200,000 Deutschmark. Shortly after the incidents, a local newspaper received a letter, in which the Red Zora claimed responsibility for the attacks. In its letter, the group declared that it would no longer accept that women were reduced to their bodies nor were degraded to 'sex-machines' at the disposal of male consumers. With its campaign against the sex industry, the Red Zora sided with anti-porn feminists in the 'sex wars' of the late 1970s and early 1980s. Many feminists in West Germany shared this stance, and some expressed open support for the attacks. A few weeks after the attacks, the feminist magazine *EMMA* published excerpts of the claim of responsibility. A little cartoon figure next to the text, dressed like a suffragette, said: 'Help! – I feel overwhelmed with clandestine joy.'

Retrospectively, members of the RZ admitted that their protest in the 1970s had failed to consider the views of women who worked in the sex industry and had not paid enough attention to less visible forms of sexism and abuse (Die Rote Zora, 1993). Whilst trying to show solidarity with other women, a number of attacks by the Red Zora reinforced forms of hegemonic speech and silence. In its claim of responsibility for a bombing at the Philippine Consulate in Bonn in 1983, the Red Zora accused the Philippine government and other 'corrupt governments' in the 'Third World' of profiting from sex tourism, trafficking and prostitution (ID-Archiv im IISG, 1993, p. 467). The militant feminists declared that they wanted to express solidarity with Philippine women because the sexual objectification of women in 'Third World countries' constituted an offence against all women, including themselves. By emphasising a shared experience of patriarchal oppression, the members of the Red Zora failed to account for the unspoken privileges of their identities.

In December 1993, a group of 'old' and 'new' group members released the brochure *Mili's Tanz auf dem Eis*, which provides the first detailed comment on the history of the RZ. Here, the group stated that discussions with black women, Jewish feminists and lesbian activists had helped them 'to understand that there is more than one experience of sexism' (Die Rote Zora, 1993). Looking back at their campaigns against sex shops and alleged sex traffickers, the authors acknowledged that their living and working conditions as white and predominantly middle-class women in West Germany were very different from those of many of the women they were trying to support. Against the background of widespread poverty, political repression and a lack of job opportunities in the Philippines, the Red Zora admitted in 1993, for example, that marriage with a German man opened a window of opportunity to many local women. While the group has never declared its own dissolution, it carried out its last attack in 1995.

To this day, scholars, journalists and the police know little about the Red Zora and even less about its members. Drawing on previously unconsidered archival material and interviews with former group members, I have written the first detailed study of the history and ideology of the RZ (Karcher, 2017). So far, only three women have been found guilty of membership of the group. They had surrendered to the police voluntarily after years of hiding. Corinna Kawaters stood trial in 1998, Adrienne Gerhäuser in 2007, and Juliane Balke in 2010. The three women were all acquitted due to time limitations on the charges against them.

While the biographies of Kawaters and Gerhäuser are not necessarily representative of those of other group members, they have a lot in common. Born in 1949, Gerhäuser completed a degree in German studies and political sciences. In the early 1970s, she moved to Berlin, where she worked as a teacher. Kawaters was born in 1953 and grew up in Cologne. After studying sociology in Bochum, Kawaters worked as a journalist for the leftist newspaper *Die Tageszeitung* in Bochum. Gerhäuser and Kawaters were actively involved in the women's movement and other political projects. Rather than marrying and settling down, they worked in a range of jobs and moved frequently. In the early 1980s, Gerhäuser moved to Essen, where she completed training as a radio technician. Today, she works as a photographer in Berlin. Kawaters worked in a number of fields ranging from social work to gastronomy. In 1984, she published a detective novel (Kawaters, 1984). Two books with the same protagonist followed. In 2005, Kawaters opened a restaurant in Leipzig.

The main evidence in the proceedings against Kawaters and Gerhäuser was the purchase of small travel alarm clocks. By 1986, the Federal Bureau of Investigation was aware that the Red Zora had a preference for alarm clocks of the brand *Emes sonochron* as incendiary time fuses. In a massive surveillance exercise, prosecuting authorities began to monitor the sale of these clocks throughout Germany. In 1986, employees of the Federal Criminal Police Office confiscated thousands of alarm clocks in watch businesses all over the country, took them apart and engraved code numbers on the back of the clock faces. They then reassembled the alarm clocks and returned them to the shops, which they equipped with video cameras to collect evidence about every purchase of an alarm clock of this type.

On 15 October 1986, Adrienne Gerhäuser fell into the trap. A police camera captured her buying a marked alarm clock that the Red Zora used in a time bomb a few days later. Due to a technical fault, the explosive device failed to detonate and was confiscated by police. Not knowing that all clock stores in West Germany were under police surveillance, Gerhäuser purchased another alarm clock in June 1987. Like Gerhäuser, Kawaters was on a list of suspected terrorists that the Federal Criminal Police Office had produced in 1987. During a raid on 18 December, the police found an alarm clock of the *Emes sonochron* type in her flat in Bochum. Gerhäuser, Kawaters and other suspects on the wanted list of the Federal Criminal Police Office were lucky: due to a timely warning, they narrowly escaped arrest.

Feminist activists in Germany have only begun to document and discuss the history and ideology of the Red Zora. A recent example shows that one does not have to agree with the tactics of the Red Zora to see the activities of this group as part of the long and varied history of feminist movements and to productively engage with their history. Fifteen years ago, a group of feminist activists organised the first 'Red Dawns' [Rdeče zore festival] in Ljubljana, Slovenia, to discuss the challenges that women faced in radical politics, art, and everyday life. Since then, the festival has taken place annually and has become an important platform for feminist art and queer activism in the Balkans, Western Europe, Turkey, and a range of other countries. On their website, the organisers of the festival discuss the history of the Red Zora and state:

> Even though Red Dawns festival refrains itself from political violence, it supports Rote Zora in their belief that the struggle for women's rights is undone, that it goes hand in hand with struggles for social justice, and that we cannot be contented with reformist politics.

The statement by the festival organisers illustrates that there are feminists who take inspiration from the Red Zora without promoting violence. It shows that one does not have to agree with the political views or tactics of militant feminist groups to see their activities as a part of the long and varied history of feminist movements.

More reading

Frauen bildet Banden – eine Spurensuche zur Geschichte der Roten Zora, documentary film by FrauenLesbenFilmCollectif LasOtras, 2019, 77 mins, German with English subtitles.

FrauenLesbenBande, ed., 2023. *Mili Bittet zum Tanz. Auf den Spuren des militanten Feminismus der Roten Zora.* Unrast Verlag: Münster.

Karcher, K., 2015. How (not) to 'Hollaback': Towards a transnational debate on the 'Red Zora' and militant tactics in the feminist struggle against

gender-based violence. *Feminist Media Studies*, 16(1), pp. 70–85. Doi:10.1080/1
4680777.2015.1093099.

Karcher, K., 2019. Violence for a good cause? The role of violent tactics in West
German solidarity campaigns for better working and living conditions in the
Global South in the 1980s. *Contemporary European History*, 28(4), pp. 566–580.
Doi:10.1017/S0960777319000237.

WRITERS

AND

WORDSMITHS

The house at 2 Hope Park Square where the Dangerous Women Project originated was once the childhood home of Dame Rebecca West, who wrote *Black Lamb, Grey Falcon* and covered the Nuremberg trials for *The New Yorker*. A plaque erected in 2022 now marks our proud association with the author, journalist and critic described by *Time* magazine as 'indisputably the world's No 1 woman writer'. Literary links were woven into the Project from its very beginning, and Faith Pullen's biography of West is available on our website.

This section spans almost 1,000 years, from Byzantine historian Anna Komnene to Russian journalist Anna Politkovskaya. It also contains the most entries, reflecting the enormous array of contributions to the Dangerous Women Project about women who used words as their weapon, their means of escape or their livelihood.

Some of the chapters showcase household names such as the Nobel Prize-winning Doris Lessing; others were bestsellers in their home countries but perhaps remain little-known in the UK, such as Flora Nwapa. But we also wanted to widen the lens, to reflect on different ways to make a mark on the world through the written word: diary writers, journalists, advice columnists, editors, memoirists, publishers.

This section therefore gathers together an array of authors from the eleventh century to the twenty-first, offering insights into children's lives in Scotland alongside lesbianism in India. Writing can be, as Louisa Lawson wrote in her first editorial, 'a phonograph to wind out audibly the whispers, pleadings and demands of the sisterhood'.

ANNA KOMNENE: PRINCESS, HISTORIAN, SCHOLAR – AND CONSPIRATOR?

Ioulia Kolovou

Ioulia Kolovou is a Greek-Scottish author and researcher based in Glasgow. She studied classics, history and linguistics in Greece and Argentina, and has an MSc in Creative Writing (University of Edinburgh) and a PhD in English Literature: Creative Writing (University of Glasgow). She has several publications of fiction and non-fiction, including a public academia book on the Byzantine author and historian Anna Komnene (2020).

Who was Anna Komnene?

Most Western people outside the rather narrow circle of Byzantine or Crusades Studies would not be able to say, even if they somehow recognised the name. Yet this twelfth-century Greek Byzantine princess was arguably the first European female historian. A subject for history herself as the first-born child of Emperor Alexios I Komnenos and a power-player for the throne after his death, she was also the author of what Peter Frankopan calls 'the most famous of all the vast range of Byzantine texts', *The Alexiad*. This fifteen-volume account of her father's reign, including a book dedicated to the First Crusade, is, according to Warren Treadgold, a 'lucid, readable, and interesting' narrative, 'a skilful feat of research and synthesis', 'a splendid history'.

Anna was not a completely atypical, one-off phenomenon as a strong, intelligent, educated woman. Her grandmother, Anna Dalassene, was a matriarch who co-ruled the empire with her son Alexios for some time while he was away on military campaign. Anna's mother, Empress Eirene Doukaina, enjoyed reading difficult philosophical or religious texts during dinner and praised them to her teenage daughter. Strong women beget strong women.

In her lifetime Anna was admired for her education, reviled as a conspirator, considered dangerous enough to be forcibly removed from active political life. In her posterity she is unreservedly or grudgingly admired as a historian and her work is regularly cited in scholarly texts, especially on the First Crusade. C. P. Cavafy immortalised her in his poetry. Contemporary literary theorist and psychoanalyst Julia Kristeva called her 'the first female intellectual'. Anna has been fictionalised in historical novels and is the subject of many academic publications.

Why isn't she more visible, more known in Western culture?

Possibly because for a number of influential men, gatekeepers of historical memory and of cultural values, Anna was a dangerous woman. Her intellectual powers, exceptional education and strong confidence created ambivalent feelings in her contemporary men – much as a similarly endowed woman might cause many men to be uneasy, if not hostile, in our own, supposedly more enlightened times.

Byzantine historian Niketas Choniates, writing some fifty years after Anna's death, relates how she and her mother conspired to bring down the legitimate Emperor John II Komnenos, Anna's brother, and install Anna and her husband on the throne. Oscillating between admiration and disapproval, Niketas asserts that Anna 'was ardently devoted to philosophy, the queen of all the sciences, and was educated in every field of learning'.

Yet he has this snippet of gossip to offer his readers about her: when her alleged conspiracy against her brother failed due to her husband's 'frivolous behaviour', Anna 'distraught in her anger, and being a shrew by nature, felt justified in strongly contracting her vagina when Bryennios's penis entered deep inside her, thus causing him great pain'. This unusual comment reveals a great deal about how Niketas (and those who circulated this rumour – whether true or invented it is of course impossible to know) viewed a tough, energetic and ambitious woman: as a frightening shrew who would inflict pain on her sexual partner as punishment for his shortcomings, inverting the usual roles of the sexes, in which the man inflicts pain, while the woman suffers silently.

Recently, scholars are questioning whether Anna really did conspire against her brother. However, Choniates' testimony and negative views on Anna were gleefully adopted by later historians, who represented Anna as an ambitious, bitter, disappointed woman who lost a throne she should have never claimed in the first place. However, none was indifferent to her, for she was a fascinating character and her power was felt perhaps most where it was feared.

Sir Walter Scott is a very good example. His only novel set in Byzantium, *Count Robert of Paris* (1831), was inspired by an episode from *The Alexiad*, and the historian herself (the 'fair authoress' in Scott's own condescending words) became a character in its pages. Scott was apparently smitten by Anna to the point that he considered naming the novel *Anna Comnena*, as he reveals in a letter to his publisher. But the way he treats Anna as a fictional character displays the same mixture of admiration and fear, exorcised with derision, that we saw in Niketas Choniates.

Scott used Edward Gibbon's *History of the Decline and Fall of the Roman Empire*, which he admired greatly, as a source in *Count Robert*. Gibbon's notorious – and totally unfair and undeserved – dismissal of the Byzantine Empire is well known, and although debunked by later scholarship it still informs the ideas of the wider public about Byzantium. In Gibbon's work, Anna is condemned along with her whole cultural milieu, but she also receives that special treatment reserved for those women who dared trespass on the masculine field of authorship. According to Gibbon, in Anna's writing 'an elaborate affectation of rhetoric and science betrays, in every page, the vanity of a female author'.

What Gibbon's statement betrays, on the other hand, is his own casual misogyny. It is interesting to note that immediately after this disparaging statement, Gibbon admits that Anna's opinions were perceptive and judicious. Yet – in his misogynistic overall assertion – by displaying her high education and knowledge in order to confirm her authority Anna is not simply doing what every scholar ever did (and still does), she is being a vain female.

Whether in medieval Byzantium or the enlightened West, a 'female author', particularly one who does not write moral treatises, novels on domestic subjects, and religious or lyrical poetry, was an unsettling phenomenon, for she trespassed on male territory. Bluestockings (i.e. intellectual women) were often the object of mockery in Scott's time. They were considered presumptuous and vain, or total failures as women who could not attract admirers in more conventional feminine ways.

Scott, following on this path, casts Anna as a spoilt, wannabe bluestocking princess, whose self-importance is inflated by professional courtiers, an over-indulgent mother and a long-suffering father. Yet Scott unwittingly reveals how much he admires Anna as a historiographer, and how much he feels threatened by her power, in a telling episode early on in *Count Robert*.

In this episode the protagonist of the novel, Hereward, a young handsome Anglo-Saxon Varangian in Emperor Alexios' personal guard, is introduced to Anna's literary 'salon'. There, Anna is reading extracts from her history to an admiring crowd of family and courtiers. The young hero enters the princess' apartments wielding his battle-axe, which he has refused to hand over at the entrance of the palace; as the folding doors yield to his entrance, we are compelled to think of sexual penetration and male domination. But as Anna reads her account of a battle in which Hereward's brother was killed, Hereward begins to display strange behaviour:

> He lost the rigid and constrained look of a soldier . . . His colour began to come and go; his eyes to fill and to sparkle; his limbs to become more agitated than their owner seemed to assent to; and his whole appearance was changed into that of a listener, highly interested by the recitation which he hears, and insensible, or forgetful, of whatever else was passing before him . . . As the historian proceeded, Hereward became less able to conceal his agitation; and at the moment the Princess looked round, his feelings became so acute, that, forgetting where he was, he dropped his ponderous axe upon the floor, and, clasping his hands together, exclaimed, – 'My unfortunate brother!' (p. 56)

Hereward is so enthralled by Anna's history that he behaves almost like a young heroine from a romantic story. This testament to the power of Anna's historical narrative becomes complete when Hereward drops 'his ponderous axe': his masculinity is subjugated, and the gender roles are reversed. The female historian's powerful narrative disarms and unmans the male warrior, reducing him to an emotional state and dominating him. She has the upper hand in this relationship; she plays the dominant part, the 'masculine' role. Scott very clearly senses the power of the female historiographer as danger, as a threat.

But the male novelist decides that this power must be resisted. As soon as Hereward leaves the palace, he ridicules Anna's history as 'the prolix chat of a lady, who has written about she knows not what'. And when he is reprimanded by his officer for the over-bold manner in which he was looking at the face of the princess throughout the encounter, his answer is charged with sexual entitlement:

> 'So be it, in the name of Heaven', replied Hereward. 'Handsome faces were made to look upon, and the eyes of young men to see withal.' (p. 76)

Anna is not the commanding historian any more, but a mere pretty face; her fearful intellectual abilities are put aside, the emphasis is on her physical charms. Hereward's gaze on Anna's face reduces her to an object existing only for his visual pleasure. The man who was overpowered by Anna's narrative only hours ago, claims that he cannot 'presume to form a judgement' about her history, for he does not understand it, but he will grant that she is beautiful and 'she sings like an angel'. Anna will not be seen on her own terms, as a serious historian who can bring facts to life with her vivid, powerful narrative, but only as a beautiful girl who talks nonsense.

This contradictory portrayal in Scott's *Count Robert* reveals what is at stake in the case of Anna Komnene: in the field of gender relations, which are traditionally power relations of inequality and domination, the self-assured, authoritative female historiographer is dangerous because she is seen as reversing gender roles, challenging the position of authority and power traditionally reserved for male authors only. They, in their turn, feel threatened, emasculated and reduced to passivity by women like Anna Komnene. Although separated by more than six centuries, the Byzantine historian and the Scottish novelist equally felt the danger of Anna's power and tried to resist it.

More reading

Ferris, I., 1991. *The Achievement of Literary Authority: Gender, History, and the Waverley Novels*. Cornell University Press.

Kolovou, I., 2017. Masculine crusaders, effeminate Greeks, and the female historian: Relations of power in Sir Walter Scott's *Count Robert of Paris*. *The Journal of Historical Fictions*, 1(1), pp. 89–110.

Kolovou, I., 2020. *Anna Komnene and the Alexiad: The Byzantine Princess and the First Crusade*. Pen and Sword History.

Kolovou, I., 2020. Reconfiguring the template: Representations of powerful women in historical fiction – the case of Anna Komnene. In A. Bardazzi and A. Bazzone, eds, *Gender and Authority across Disciplines, Space and Time*. Palgrave Macmillan, pp. 313–330.

Neville, L., 2016. *Anna Komnene: The Life and Work of a Medieval Historian*. Oxford University Press.

Perkins, P., 2010. *Women Writers and the Edinburgh Enlightenment*. Editions Rodopi B. V.

HARRIETTE WILSON: PUBLISHED AND DAMNED

Louise Peskett

Louise Peskett is the creator of the Fearless and Fabulous Women of
Brighton and Hove walking tours (previously called Notorious Women of
Brighton), a popular feature of the annual Brighton Fringe festival and, in
2024, nominated for the Audience Choice Award. She lectures on Fearless
and Fabulous Women of Sussex throughout the county as well as holding
down her day job as a museum educator, working with schools and young
people at the Royal Pavilion and other museums in Brighton and Hove.
Her walks have been featured on BBC Radio 4's Women's Hour and her
articles on local women from history have appeared in *Sussex Life*
magazine, the *Brighton and Hove Independent* newspaper, *Jane Austen's
Regency World,* and elsewhere. She blogs at www.historywomenbrighton.
com. Her book *The Fearless and the Fabulous: A Journey through Brighton
and Hove's Women's History* was published in 2020.

A few years ago, heartily tired of talking about the lives of Great Men in
my job as tour guide at Brighton's Royal Pavilion, I started to look into
the women who lurked in the shadows of my home town's history. The
material I uncovered, while pounding the streets and poring over
documents at the local history centre, was nothing short of astonishing.
The discovery that some of Britain's first women doctors and police
officers, the first female barrister, boundary-shifting artists, and
ground-breaking female entrepreneurs have trodden the streets around
me, their voices hidden by Brighton's dominant story that it was
'discovered' by the Prince Regent and set on the road to seaside gaiety
ever since, was a revelation.

Thinking it was about time that people knew this, I put together a
walking tour, visiting the places where some of these intriguing women
were born, lived or just passed through. I called it 'Notorious Women of
Brighton'. The title gave people problems. 'Why "notorious"?', I was asked.
'Aren't you being a bit over-dramatic? I thought these women were sup-
posed to be good. Wouldn't "brilliant" or "celebrated" be more apt?'

But what I didn't want people to forget is that, in the worlds in which
most of these women lived, creating something new, making a success

of yourself, or just demanding an education equal to that of men would have raised eyebrows, stepped on toes, been considered unattractively uppity. Dr Louisa Martindale, Brighton's first GP, for example, courted controversy with her research into STDs. Lawyer Helena Normanton's decision to keep her passport in her maiden name upon her marriage in 1924, becoming the first woman to do so, would not have elicited deafening cries of 'bravo!' When Ellen Nye Chart, a hitherto working-class woman, took on the management of the Theatre Royal in 1876, people were telling her it was no job for a woman even while she was making it into one of the most successful theatres in Britain. Show me a woman who pushed a boundary, however beneficial for society in the long run, and the words 'scandalous' and 'shocking' would have followed close behind.

As for being 'good'? Well, why should only well-behaved and high-achieving women deserve to have their stories remembered? I include some women on my tour simply because they tore up the rule book. Some, despite the promise of an easier life if they just conformed to what a woman should be, brooked no compromise and, against the odds, managed to remain true to themselves.

An excellent example, then, is Harriette Wilson (1786–1845), the cleverest courtesan of Regency London, who captivated, charmed and dazzled her way to the heart of fashionable society, only to shock, anger and terrify her way straight back out again. Far from being anyone's role model, Harriette, spirited, single-minded and a fiendishly good writer as we see in her *Memoirs*, ducked and dived through society making sure, in a world heavily weighted towards men, that she was always on the winning side; her life story, although controversial, set the early nineteenth century alight by holding up a mirror to the double standards that riddled male and female behaviour. Just look, for a start, at the first sentence of those *Memoirs*.

I shall not say how and why I became, at the age of fifteen, the mistress of the Earl of Craven. Whether it was love, or . . . the depravity of my own heart, or the winning arts of the noble Lord, which induced me to leave my paternal roof and place myself under his protection, does not now much signify . . .

From the first paragraph, we know this isn't going to be a staid biography. 'I resided on the Marine Parade at Brighton', she informs us next and goes on to describe how the 'winning arts' of paramour Lord Craven have now dwindled to an annoying habit of drawing cocoa trees for her entertainment. 'It was, in fact, a dead bore.' Only a few sentences in, she moves onto an unflattering description of his sleepwear. 'Surely, I would say, all men do not wear those ugly cotton nightcaps; else all women's illusions had been destroyed in the first night of marriage.' This voice, frank, dry, knowing, allows us to see why Harriette was, in the sprawling Regency demi-monde, a true original.

Far from being sex workers, courtesans like Harriette were not coveted for their sexual availability alone, but for their company, their style, and the cachet they would bring to a man's reputation. For the Regency gentleman around town, having Harriette on your arm was the early nineteenth-century equivalent of dangling the keys to a Ferrari in your friends' faces. The most successful courtesans were clever, accomplished, witty and able to hold their own in conversation; a sort of alpha girlfriend who charged for her time. For a man in pre-Victorian, anything-goes London, there was nothing seedy or shameful about being seen at the opera with a woman like Harriette and, unlike women, men could slip easily between the above-board world of the respectable married family man and the rowdy, gossipy, heavy drinking and gambling milieu of the dandies. Lesley Blanch writes in her introduction to Wilson's *Memoirs*, 'The courtesan was expected to provide all the shades of companionship without the oppressive limitations and implications of marriage. She offered not only the bed but the sofa, the dinner-table and the salon – all save the nursery and the kitchen.' So, all the fun of a relationship without the hard bits. It was a man's world, but, if she negotiated properly and stuck to her guns, a woman could make it work for her.

Like many of her sister courtesans, Harriette had made a decent start in life. She attended a good boarding school and experienced a convent education. Twice she attempted to hold on to a proper job as a music teacher in elegant girls' boarding schools. Twice she ran away, finding the governess' life deadly dull. The second time she came home after her career at a school in Newcastle-upon-Tyne stalled, her father beat her. Too adventurous to reconcile herself to any of the 'decent' options for a woman – either to become a stay-at-home wife for a husband chosen for her or to become a governess – she took her life into her hands and left home, Lord Craven with his night-cap and cocoa trees providing a convenient, if dull, launchpad. If the price of seeing more of life was to play the charming 'bit on the side' to a powerful and vain man, then, I suppose she reasoned, why not? If she played her cards right (as Harriette inevitably and very cleverly did, employing business nous and PR skills far ahead of her time) she could command a lavish lifestyle. Clothes, jewellery, appropriate accommodation at a fashionable address, the latest carriage, even a pension would be forthcoming. Courtesans never solicited; they were sought after, and prospective suitors of Harriette were rigorously 'interviewed'. Contracts were set up, salaries agreed on, terms and conditions set. Harriette aimed high, she was particular in her choices, and understood that creating a mystique around herself would make her the most coveted woman in London.

One man who – initially – didn't make the grade was George, Prince of Wales, the future Prince Regent. Harriette approached him during that first stay in Brighton while the Prince was visiting his new, lavish Pavilion. 'I wonder, thought I, what sort of a nightcap the Prince of Wales wears', she tells us. She began a letter to the Prince, at the time the most eligible bachelor in the country. 'I am told that I am very beautiful, so, perhaps, you would like to see me . . . if you believe you could make me in love with you, write to me.' Amused, the Prince wrote back suggesting a meeting in London. This wasn't good enough for Harriette. 'Sir, to travel fifty-two miles, this bad weather, merely to see a man . . . would, you must admit, be madness, in a girl like myself, surrounded by humble admirers', she wrote in response, 'if you can do anything better, in the way of pleasing a lady, than ordinary men, write directly: if not, adieu, Monsieur le Prince.'

The most shocking thing that Harriette did, however, came much later. In 1825, about to turn forty, she found her fortunes fading. Many of the men who had promised her a pension as part of the deal had conveniently forgotten about her or were busy pulling strings in high places to absolve themselves from their agreed-upon commitments. At her wits' end and with poverty on the doorstep, she hit upon a way to make them pay up. She'd write her memoirs and hold nothing back. She'd give the men concerned notice, and if they were worried about the most minute details of their relationships with her being made public, well, she'd exclude them – at a price. Why not? She'd lived by putting a price on her attractiveness, so why not now charge for her discretion too? A Henry Heath cartoon shows what happened: a positive stampede of men, wanting to pay the £200 that would ensure anonymity, ensued. Barricades had to be erected outside the publishers' premises to keep them at bay. Published in episodes, the men involved would have known when their shaming was nigh. It was one thing being linked to Harriette in the past but people were older, times were becoming less hedonistic, families and respectable dynasties had been forged. No one wanted the warts-and-all details of their relationship with her revealed for all the world to know. Famously, the Duke of Wellington refused to have anything to do with them. 'Publish and be damned!' he declared. Consequently, the hero of Waterloo does not emerge well. 'Rather like a rat-catcher' is how Harriette describes him when they first met. As for his pillow talk, it was 'like sitting up with a corpse'.

What Harriette did, having played power games with men all her life, was to snatch it back – and how – in the world's first ever kiss-and-tell. Harriette grew rich, making £10,000 out of her *Memoirs*, which enjoyed many years as a bestseller before the Victorians relegated them to the top shelf. She was never admitted into polite society again, however. At the time, for a woman to write frankly and unashamedly about sex – and then to do well out of it – was considered depravity of the worst type. I like to think that, perhaps by then, Harriette had had enough of 'polite' society anyway.

If Harriette had been born today, I'd like to think she'd be at the helm of an incredibly successful business. For pluck and entrepreneurial skills, for sticking to her principles, even if they were vastly different from those of everyone else at the time, for making more than a few people consider that, although it was fine for a man to stray from the family home, it wasn't for a woman, sowing the seed for later nineteenth-century feminists to mull over, and simply for telling the most eligible man in Britain she couldn't be bothered to see him because the weather was bad, I think Harriette deserves the acclaim and praise of being one of history's most notorious – and daring – women.

More reading

Blanch, L., 2016. *Regency England Undressed: Harriette Wilson, the Greatest Courtesan of her Age*. BookBlast ePublishing.

Hickman, K., 2011. *Courtesans*. Harper Perennial.

Kelly, I., 2006. *Beau Brummell: The Ultimate Dandy*. Hodder.

Murray, V., 1999. *High Society in the Regency Period 1788–1830*. Penguin Books.

Wilson, F., 2003. *The Courtesan's Revenge*. Faber and Faber.

MARJORIE FLEMING AND EMILY PEPYS: DANGEROUS DIARISING OF NINETEENTH-CENTURY GIRLS

Lois Burke

Lois Burke is Assistant Professor of Critical Heritage, Innovation and Curation in the Department of Culture Studies at Tilburg University in the Netherlands. She is one of the coordinators of the Erasmus Mundus International Masters in Children's Literature, Media and Cultural Entrepreneurship. She has written a book on the writing of late Victorian girls (forthcoming). She has published in the journals *Life Writing*, *International Research in Children's Literature*, *Scottish Literary Review*, *Victorian Periodicals Review*, and in the books *The Edinburgh History of Children's Periodicals* (Edinburgh University Press, 2024) and *The Palgrave Handbook of Digital and Public Humanities* (Palgrave, 2022).

In conduct and medical literature throughout the majority of the nineteenth century, adult writers delineated what was potentially dangerous for growing girls to do and say. Whether this be staying up late, taking hot baths, or even exciting one's passions at the opera, the social and cultural limitations placed on girls during their pre-pubescent and pubescent years seem almost laughable now.

Yet the broadening of girls' minds was no laughing matter for certain nineteenth-century moralists. Precocity was viewed as a particularly dangerous attribute, and was a gender-specific site of anxiety. Extensive knowledge in any subject was deemed to be transgressive for girls, who were expected to stay within the boundaries of acceptable femininity. This was exemplified in John Ruskin's *Sesame and Lilies* (1865), in which he stated that girls should have only a rudimentary knowledge of science and languages, which would enable them to converse with their future husbands. But as this forbidden knowledge was exactly that to girls, the diatribes against it were often of a vague nature; as if British writers were unwilling to engage with the notion that girls would develop curiosity and ambitions beyond their defined lot. For example, in 1855 the conduct writer Mrs Pullan obscurely pleaded that girls should 'be very careful to be always doing something', as if keeping girls busy with feminine accomplishments would keep them away from trouble. Conversely, the girls themselves were obliged to know precisely what was and wasn't deemed to be acceptable conduct and expression – and some knew how to test these imposed limitations through their own writing.

One of the most famous child diarists, Kirkcaldy-born Marjorie Fleming (1803–1811), tested her use of language as well as acceptable topics of conversation through her writing. At six years old, she put pen to paper and described a situation in which she called someone an 'impudent bitch', and how she was chastised for such language.

> To Day I pronounced a word which should never come out of a lady's lips it was that I called John an impudent Bitch and Isabella afterwards told me that I should never say it even in joke but she kindly forgave me because I said that I would not do it again I will tell you what I think made me in so bad a honour is I got 1 or 2 cups of that bad bad sina tea to Day

Victorian editors of Fleming's writing who positioned her as the epitome of childish innocence and artless joy omitted that particular entry in abridged publications of her diary. She also wrote on multiple occasions about how she was specifically not permitted to discuss love, 'heroins' and marriage – yet she still gushed about these subjects.

> In the love novels all the heroins are very desperate Isabella will not alow me to speak about lovers & heroins & is too refined for my taste
>
> [. . .]
>
> I walked to that delightfull place with that a delightfull place young man beloved by all his friends and espacialy by me his loveress but I must not talk any longer about him any longer for Isa said it is not proper for to speak of gentalman
>
> [. . .]
>
> Love I think is in the fasion for every body is marring there is a new novel published named selfcontroul a very good maxam forsooth.

These restricted topics didn't set an embargo on Fleming's curiosity; luckily her manuscripts remain, and such insights which were previously glossed over by Victorian editors can be recovered.

In a similar fashion, ten-year-old English diarist Emily Pepys (1833–1877) documented her quest for the kind of knowledge which was off-limits.

> Herbert and I were left alone, and looked at several nice things in the Encyclopoedia, such as Anatomy, Midwifery etc. etc. etc. but Mama told me

to go to bed 10 minutes before 9 so we had not much time. Herbert and I always go together let one another into all our secrets that we would not tell anybody else for worlds.

As at this point in history there existed no candid medical texts that sought to inform girls about their bodies – their only option was to acquire it covertly, and in Pepys' case divulge that rebellion in their daily writing. Thus, the girl's diary is an invaluable fragment of social history that records this gendered struggle.

Emily Pepys was a collateral descendant of the famous diarist Samuel Pepys, and Fleming's distant relation to Walter Scott was equally used as a marketing ploy when her diaries were published posthumously. It is true that diaries have an androcentric history; those which are generally thought of as the great examples of life writing were penned by figures such as St Augustine, Jean-Jacques Rosseau and Samuel Pepys. Yet feminist life writing scholars from the 1970s onwards have supported the recovery of women's words that have long been buried in archives.

It is high time that this reclaiming imperative was extended to the life writing of girls, too. Carolyn Steedman in *The Tidy House: Little Girls Writing* astutely suggested that 'Writing is a means of growth available to all children, producing artefacts wrought by their own internal rules.' Young diarists who were writing in the nineteenth century deserve credence for their boldness in an age that upheld strict expectations for their conduct. Diarists provoked their own socialisation through life writing, and tested the limits of acceptable behaviour, in preparation for a womanhood that was to be equally steeped in ideology.

More reading

Alexander, C. and McMaster, J., eds, 2005. *The Child Writer from Austen to Woolf.* Cambridge University Press.

Burke, L., 2022. 'A present for my daughter': Gender and posterity in Victorian intergenerational life writing. *Life Writing*, 19(4), pp. 593–612.

Fleming, M. and Macbean, L., 1904. *Marjorie Fleming: The Story of Pet Marjorie: Together with her Journals and her Letters*. Putnam.

Laing, R., 2024. *The Precocious Child in Victorian Literature and Culture: Development and Selfhood from Darwin to Freud.* Palgrave.

Lejeune, P., 2009. *On Diary*. Ed. Jeremy D. Popkin and Julia Rak. Trans. Katherine Durnin. University of Hawaii Press.

LOUISA LAWSON: THE DAWN OF AUSTRALIAN FEMINISM

Sarsha Crawley

Sarsha Crawley completed a Bachelor of Commerce and Bachelor of Arts at Monash University and is a former recipient of the Victoria Young Historian Award. She is an avid reader and in her free time she enjoys painting, pottery and walking with her two dogs.

A defining moment in the Australian women's suffrage movement was the establishment of a newspaper to platform and share women's voices. This formidable step towards enfranchisement was commanded by a bold and dangerous woman. In 1888, against a backdrop of waning gold discoveries and moving towards a federated Australia, uneducated, penniless, single mother Louisa Lawson began Australia's first feminist newspaper. *The Dawn* was to be the 'Australian woman's journal and mouthpiece', championing the rights of women and shaping the way women connected with and inspired one another.

Louisa was forced into domestic labour as a young child, grudgingly caring for her younger siblings, before being unwillingly married at eighteen. There were few alternatives for the daughter of a station-hand. Louisa encountered the toil, violence and financial dependency that life on the goldfields with young children imposed on women. It was from these experiences she wrote, connecting to the untapped, heart-rending soul of women cast into the endless struggle of domestic life.

From its inception, *The Dawn* promised daybreak and a new chapter for women. Louisa began her first editorial declaring *The Dawn* to be 'a phonograph to wind out audibly the whispers, pleadings and demands of the sisterhood'. It was with this spirit that *The Dawn* continued. From writing about suffrage, divorce laws, equal workplace treatment and the upheaval of deep-seated social conventions, *The Dawn* became more than a monthly newspaper. Instead, it embodied a movement of women who, through great and small acts, dangerously challenged late nineteenth-century social norms.

Louisa artfully wove politics into the everyday. Alongside articles about clothing, gardening and housekeeping, rallying political messages eloquently demonstrated that women's very existence was political and should be afforded the same freedoms as men. She plat-formed women's lives and published a perspective of Victorian Australian life neglected by the patriarchal media that diminished and derided women's issues. Her vision was to share that 'there are paths out of most labyrinths . . . fingerposts' guiding women beyond the con-fines of domestic life. She offered women a glimmer of what they could dare to dream.

The Dawn was staffed solely by women at all stages of its operations, from writers to typesetters. Disrupting the male-dominated publishing industry, this defiance led the Typographical Union to boycott the newspaper and canvass advertisers to withdraw their support because they refused membership to women. The Union cited apprehensions about women operating printing presses and male typesetters compet-ing against women's labour. Despite these thinly veiled concerns about staff well-being, *The Dawn* and its team prospered. An astute business-woman, Louisa used this as an opportunity to appeal to and expand her subscriber base, which now reached beyond Sydney into rural New South Wales, the Australian colonies and abroad. The combination of its wide distribution and revolutionary content led *The Dawn* to become the longest-running Australian women's publication of the time. This was a testament to Louisa's ability to realise and articulate her opinions regarding women's rights in ways that resonated broadly, emphasising the importance for women to create platforms to address issues and to create communities that are responsive to change.

This vision impelled Louisa to begin the Dawn Club to further pro-gress the voting rights campaign. This was a fortnightly meeting to unite women by providing opportunities to discuss pertinent issues and develop public speaking skills. Louisa recognised the sore impacts of underdeveloped education in women as yet another barrier to their entrance into politics and the public sphere. These meetings became a melting pot for activists instrumental in the suffrage campaign and typifying Louisa's unwavering belief that women could cross uncharted frontiers. In an editorial entitled 'The Woman of Tomorrow', published in August 1893, Louisa wrote:

> Public speaking is seldom attempted by women unless they have something worthy to be said, and know well how to say it. But man, though he offend the taste of his audience both in matter and manner, still considers it his prerogative to speak.

Such passages connote voices and images we still confront today: dis-plays of condescension and dismissal of women in politics, uneven representation, and women's voices drowned out by male politicians incessant in their misinformed views of women's issues. It conjures an image that continues to reflect women and marginalised voices silenced and spoken over within the political arena.

Louisa's presentation of information refuting societal expectations was a defining feature of *The Dawn*. Her writing was filled with questions and propositions challenging the expectation that women be subdued and subservient, constrained to the private sphere. Probing her readers 'Why should not the mental powers of women have full scope?' and 'Why should one half of the world govern the other?' Louisa's voice was one of the many influential leaders of the Australian Suffrage movement. Yet, what made her contribution unique was that she was able to communicate these ideas and messages into Australian homes. Louisa was able to draw women, who would otherwise be isolated from the reformatory rumblings for women's rights centred throughout cities worldwide, into a campaign that threatened patriarchal reign.

In the June 1890 editorial, Louisa counters the claim that it is 'nonsensical' for women to have the vote by citing the plethora of legal implications to women – to whom the law applies equally, yet of which they have no ability to contest:

> Laws are made upon divorce, the sale of liquor, factory regulations, the employment of children, gambling, education, hours of labour, and scores of subjects upon which women do think, and respecting which they ought to have the power of giving effect to their wishes by the selection of men representing their shade of opinion.

As Louisa herself identified, men represented the lawmakers and law enforcers, they were the heads of communities and the heads of families, they were bequeathed power and rooted into a system that had no space for the voices or opinions of women. To a society that represented and catered for men, Louisa was a fierce and emboldened symbol of danger, threatening upheaval to the wellsprings of power on which men relied.

The 1902 Commonwealth Franchise Act extended white women's rights to both stand for and vote in national elections owing to the bold and dangerous organising of Louisa and her peers. However, it would be nearly another seven decades until true voting equality was achieved, with the 1967 Referendum enfranchising Indigenous Australians. Following the 1903 election, Louisa wrote:

> The sun rose . . . upon the greatest day that ever dawned for woman in Australia, for apart from the pleasure of exercising the just privilege . . . of taking an active and direct part in the election of lawmakers, she had also the blessed satisfaction of being seen as she is – not through the glasses of those interested in her suppression.

Louisa continued her unapologetic examination of women's issues and ceaseless advocacy for a better future in *The Dawn*. One of the most prevalently discussed topics was the treatment of women within marriages. Women were forced into the role of submissive and obedient wives, oftentimes – and in Louisa's own experience – within turbulent relationships. The uneven application of the divorce law for women reflected a society that protected its men from being dishonoured, while legitimising abhorrent conditions for women and condoning violence against them.

Reflecting her own experiences, Louisa defined marriage as 'a position full of work, restricted by many grievous limitations, and implying an abandonment of individuality'. Her message remained cautionary throughout, telling women of the dangers of marriage which required utter dependency and legal absolution of wives to their husbands.

At its heart, *The Dawn* stood for the fulfilment of women, liberating them from dependence of all means. Economically, there was advice on how to create a steady income for one's family as well as domestic tips to reduce the monotonous labour conducive to running a household. She criticised corsets for the way they not only inhibited their wearers from ease of movement, but for their conformity with men's idea of women. Louisa wrote that 'bound, padded, compressed and laced, the modern woman is a highly artificial product', rendering women unable to breathe on her own and seemingly dependent on a corset to keep herself upright. One correspondence from a reader, upon discovering the freedom of corset-less life, said that 'women are not the fools they appear to be: they only need their thought awakened'. Louisa took the mantle to awaken ideas, endangering foregone cornerstones of nineteenth-century life.

The Dawn covered everything, small and large. In October 1896, an informative article provided instructions on how to ride a bicycle, a vital skill that would allow women an independent means of transport. This emphasis on equality and opportunity, even in seemingly infinitesimal domains, reiterates Louisa's unfaltering belief that women should have the same opportunities as men. This extended to personal and academic pursuits, with Louisa ardently encouraging her readers to pursue the new frontiers available to them, declaring in February 1892 that:

> We do not believe the energies of a woman are intended to be spent only in making beds and dusting furniture . . . [women] must have time and encouragement for intellectual efforts too, and they must have outlets for their opinions and their activities, for these are quite necessary and important to a world that contains at least as many women as men!

Alongside this encouragement was the celebration of incredible achievements by women worldwide, of what was once just dreams slowly, but surely, being realised. A regular feature in each instalment was a page of 'News and Notes' celebrating the successes of women everywhere, from the admission of New South Wales' first female physician in 1892, to the first Doctor of Philosophy recipient in Denmark, Anna Hude, to endowments of fellowships for women at Michigan University. Louisa deftly brought women's extraordinary feats into the awareness of seemingly ordinary Australian women's lives. This combination of encouragement and celebration of the possibilities for women made *The Dawn* a dangerous force.

It was this ability to effortlessly integrate the potentially overwhelming and intimidating topic of women's rights into the daily life of its readers that made *The Dawn* stand apart from other publications of the era. *The Dawn* appealed to all the varied machinations of life for women and showed them alternatives through recognition and celebration. As a platform, it was created by women and specifically tailored for women's needs. It was dangerous because it created a community, a network and an arena from which greater issues – legal and political – could be tackled. It needs to be remembered for the incredible legacy it helped foster.

There is a timeless familiarity to the topics covered in *The Dawn*'s editorials. The pay gap, working mothers and incessant pressure from the fashion industry were all features with enduring relevance today. Following a campaign for International Women's Day in 2011, the National Library of Australia digitised *The Dawn*, allowing everyone to appreciate Louisa's incredibly dangerous creation: a platform from which women could address and engage with women's rights, a newspaper of their own.

Louisa Lawson achieved a great deal in her life. She wrote fiction and poetry, raised a family, was an inventor and savvy businesswoman, and was declared 'the Mother of Womanhood Suffrage in New South Wales'. However, her tireless creation and stewardship of *The Dawn* articulately communicated her wholehearted belief in fighting for women's rights. Louisa demonstrated continuously, from the smallest aspects of women's lives to sweeping social reform, that women's interests and voices mattered and deserved to be heard. A powerful and dangerous mission.

In August 1892, Louisa wrote 'In a hundred years [women's] economic dependence will have given way to a recognition and accordance of her proper place in the monetary and social relations of the community.' Over a century later, I hope she would be proud of the multitude of platforms and intersectional communities that continue to share a twenty-first century message with the same dangerous fervour she did in *The Dawn* all those years ago.

More reading

Mahony, I., 2019. A new dawn: Rights for women in Louisa Lawson's *The Dawn*. *ANU Historical Journal*, II, 1, pp. 73–86.

Matthews, B., 1988. *Louisa*. McPhee Gribble/Penguin.

Pearce, S., 1997. From bush battler to city editor: Louisa Lawson and *The Dawn. Journal of Australian Studies*, 21(54–55), pp. 12–21.

Wright, C., 2018. *You Daughters of Freedom: The Australians Who Won the Vote and Inspired the World*. Text Publishing Company.

NELLIE BLY: 'A DANGEROUS WOMAN GONE MAD'

Ashley Orr

Dr Ashley Orr is a Visiting Fellow in the School of Literature, Languages and Linguistics at the Australian National University. Her research focuses on representations of non-normative femininity in neo-Victorian fiction. She is interested in the interplay between nineteenth-century gender ideology and contemporary feminisms in the genre, with a particular focus on gendered embodiment. Ashley is also an Academic Skills Advisor at La Trobe University, where she teaches writing workshops for PhD students.

Nellie Bly's career as a stunt journalist in the late nineteenth century provided the reading public of America with a first-hand insight into the lives of women whose stories might otherwise have remained invisible. Born Elizabeth Jane Cochrane in 1864, she adopted the pen name Nellie Bly in 1885 when she began her career as a journalist. In this same year, *The Pittsburgh Dispatch* published an advice column in response to the plight of a father of five unmarried daughters, in which reporter Erasmus Wilson lamented the lax parenting which failed to prepare women for their roles as wives and mothers. Such views align Wilson with the Victorian-era ideology of separate spheres. Proponents of this ideology clutched to Darwinian evolutionary theory to legitimise women's confinement to the home. Despite its scientific veneer, the ideology was, in fact, little more than a convenient way to neutralise the threat the feminist movement posed to the patriarchal order.

Angered by Wilson's views, Bly penned a response that caught the eye of the *Dispatch*'s editor, who asked her to adapt the letter into a column. Bly's first published piece, 'The Girl Puzzle', served as a public declaration of her status as a dangerous woman. In it, she advocated for women to be offered the same roles and remuneration as men, rather than being confined to low-paying feminised occupations with few opportunities for advancement. Her campaign for equal pay for equal work reflects the ongoing struggle for women to be equally recognised in the workplace. OECD data from 2023 shows that in Bly's home country the gender pay gap was 16.4 per cent, while the UK fared slightly better at

13.3 per cent. Like her suffragette counterparts across the Atlantic, Bly was committed to broadening the scope of women's participation in public life, leading by example in her role as a journalist and, later, as a key management figure in her husband's business enterprises.

Bly's scant formal education and lack of journalistic qualifications made her an unlikely candidate for success in such a male-dominated industry intent, in this period, on professionalisation. However, after getting her 'break' at the *Dispatch*, she went on to have a successful career writing for many publications up until her death in 1922. She was a pioneer in the field of female stunt reporting, a branch of sensational journalism popular in the late nineteenth century. It saw journalists go undercover to expose the underside of Victorian society. Though widely read at the time, these women's contributions have been largely absent from scholarly discussions of the history of journalism in the USA. However, the second-wave feminist movement's burgeoning interest in recovering silenced female voices from the historical record (King, 2005, pp. 3–4), has led to renewed attention towards figures like Bly in recent decades.

Bly's work remained out of print until the early 1990s, when *Around the World in Seventy-Two Days* was reprinted followed by *Ten Days in a Mad-House* in the late 2000s. The former is perhaps Bly's most well-known piece of journalism. Published by *The New York World* in 1890, it chronicled Bly's solo voyage around the world, inspired by Jules Verne's *Around the World in Eighty Days*. While this journey involved considerable risk, her first assignment for the *World*, in 1887, was arguably her most dangerous. For this story, Bly adopted the persona of a madwoman and was subsequently committed to Blackwell's Island Insane Asylum in New York. She went on to publish a series of articles that provided a first-hand insight into the harsh conditions within the asylum, and stressed the humanity (and often sanity) of Blackwell's inhabitants at a time when mental illness was still heavily stigmatised and poorly understood.

While Bly described her assignment as 'a delicate mission', she was nonetheless convinced that the rumours that abounded regarding mistreatment of patients in asylums were inflated. To uncover the truth, she adopted yet another pseudonym, 'Nellie Brown', and sought refuge in a boarding house for women workers, whereupon she began to act insane. Bly's performance involved repeatedly denouncing the other inhabitants of the boarding house as crazy and, in response to questions about her background, feigning amnesia.

Just as Bly had hoped, her erratic behaviour led to the involvement of the police and the presentation of her case before a judge, at which point she was committed to the asylum pending an examination at Bellevue Hospital. At Bellevue, Bly met Anne Neville, a woman committed due to her family's inability to pay for treatment for a medical condition at a Sister's Home. Anne assured Bly that 'I have nothing wrong with my brain . . . but I am unable to do anything. The doctors refuse to listen to me, and it is useless to say anything to the nurses.' Neville's story is echoed by many of the women Bly encountered upon reaching Blackwell's. Many were simply poor, or immigrants who had been unable to communicate and therefore were deemed insane. Others had been tricked or bullied into the asylum. These women's rational entreaties for release – Bly's included – were consistently ignored by medical staff. When Bly herself confronted one of Blackwell's doctors, asking '[h]ow can a doctor judge a woman's sanity by merely bidding her good morning and refusing to hear her pleas for release?' and insisted upon her sanity and that of those around her, the only reply she received was '[t]hey are insane . . . and suffering from delusions'.

Bly's encounters with the medical staff in both Bellevue and Blackwell's – who, apart from one doctor, pronounced her insane – caused her to lose faith in the medical profession. Though she performed the role of a madwoman to be committed, once inside the asylum she 'talked and acted just as I do in ordinary life. Yet strange to say, the more sanely I talked and acted the crazier I was thought to be by all except one physician.' However, the doctors' inability to recognise her sanity led her to believe 'that no doctor could tell whether people were insane or not, so long as the case was not violent'.

The women in Blackwell's were subjected to freezing temperatures, inedible food, routine abuse at the hands of the nurses and bizarre initiation rituals in which new patients were forced to bathe naked in ice-water in front of the other inmates. Complaints were futile, as these were dismissed by the doctors as 'the imagination of our diseased brains' and resulted in even harsher punishments from the nurses. Lamenting the harsh treatment she received in the asylum, Bly mused '[w]hat, excepting torture, would produce insanity quicker than this treatment?' Even for those who were genuinely afflicted by mental illness, the 'treatment' provided at Blackwell's was hardly likely to produce a cure. As such, in an era when 'of all the nervous disorders . . . hysteria was the most strongly identified with the feminist movement', institutionalisation was often little more than a convenient repository for women whose deviant behaviour threatened to disrupt gendered power relations.

After ten days, Bly's release was secured by a lawyer hired by the *World* and she was summoned to testify about her experiences to a grand jury. On a return trip to Blackwell's with the jury in tow, Bly found the conditions much improved, although the sane women she encountered during her stay had been removed, leading her to question '[i]f I was wrong in my judgment of these patients' sanity, why was all this done?' While their fates remain unknown, Bly's determination to 'try by every means to make my mission of benefit to my suffering sisters' was largely successful. By placing herself in danger, she exposed the suffering of women in the public asylum system. The publicity her account attracted resulted in the City of New York allocating a further $1 million per year in resources dedicated to the treatment of the mentally ill. A dangerous woman herself, Bly told the stories of other 'dangerous' women who were powerless to speak for themselves. In so doing, she humanised the experiences of Blackwell's patients. Regardless of their status as victims of circumstance or mental illness, they benefited from improvements to their care as a result of Bly's reporting.

More reading

Norwood, A. and Brandman, M., 2022. *Nellie Bly.* National Women's History Museum. [Online] available at: https://www.womenshistory.org/education-resources/biographies/nellie-bly-0 (accessed 5 October 2024).

Reiss, B., 2008. *Theaters of Madness: Insane Asylums and Nineteenth-Century American Culture.* University of Chicago Press.

Roggenkamp, K., 2016. *Sympathy, Madness, and Crime: How Four Nineteenth-Century Journalists Made the Newspaper Women's Business.* Kent State University Press.

MARIJA JURIĆ ZAGORKA: A THORN IN ONE'S SIDE

Ana Pavlić

Ana Pavlić is a PhD candidate at the University of Zagreb, Faculty of Political Science in Zagreb, with a background in political science and women's studies. In her Master's thesis in Artificial Intelligence for Public Services at the Universidad Politecnica de Madrid and Politecnico di Milano, titled 'Ethics of AI: To Chatbot or Not to Chatbot', she addressed gender bias in AI systems, and gender equality in digital transformation as an important topic for developing and implementing innovative strategies, and policies. In her PhD research, she continues her interest in the ethical governance of AI in education. Her research interests include ethical governance of artificial intelligence, (digital) education, gender, culture, and EU policies.

> Giving up my pen means giving up my life.
>
> From *Kamen na cesti* (*The Stone on the Road*)

Marija Jurić Zagorka was the first professional political journalist in Croatia and South-East Europe, a women's rights advocate, one of the most widely read Croatian writers ever, a co-founder of the Croatian Journalists Association, a novelist, a playwright, a screenwriter, one of the early pioneers of science fiction, the founder of the first women's trade union organisation in Croatia, . . . the list could go on. This is what makes Marija Jurić Zagorka a true feminist icon.

Born on 2 March 1873, and raised in a wealthy family, Zagorka was well educated. Unfortunately, she was forced to marry a Hungarian railway head, over a decade older than she was. After spending three unhappy years in Hungary, she finally escaped her destiny to become a wife and a 'guardian of the hearth', and, returned to Croatia to begin her career as a journalist. Her contribution to the narrative of women as citizens is enormous and, in many ways, unique. The low visibility of Zagorka's work in world literature, journalism and historiography must be corrected due to her feminist standpoint and the politics and policies she advocated for. Her importance in contemporary writing and critical thinking is most valuable.

A statement by M. Vujnović – 'Her past became my future and my story and her story began to merge' – perfectly describes women's position in Zagorka's time and today alike – a position heavily marked by gender inequality. If we want to investigate the reasons behind the growth of women's liberation movements and culture, we must go back to the interwar era, as Mary Louise Roberts notes: 'in all of its interplay between modernity and the challenges towards the same, (that) offered another historical opportunity to challenge the traditional'.

A new class, working women, marked the era, as many women entered the labour market. These were women who challenged both gender and sexual taboos. The new woman was born!

Thankfully, Bishop Josip Juraj Strossmayer supported Zagorka to work as a politically engaged journalist. Her first article 'Egy Percz' ('One moment') was published in 1896 in the journal *Obzor* (*Horizon*), as an instance of political and social revolt against Hungarisation. She reported on political events from the common Budapest Parliament and was a correspondent from Budapest and Vienna. She was the only female political journalist in the South-East European region who reported from the Budapest Parliament within the Austro-Hungarian Empire that Croatia was a part of, due to her critical thinking, objective reasoning and knowledge of Hungarian and Croatian. She was the only journalist who interviewed Heinrich Friedjung during the Friedjung trial. It was hard to imagine a woman working in this traditionally male profession at the time; therefore, she worked hidden in a separate attic room, away from her male journalist colleagues, behind the scenes. As a writer, she could not allow herself the luxury of being discouraged; instead, her situation gave her feminist activism a boost.

Her participation in political struggles resulted in organising the first women's protest in Zagreb in 1903. During the political persecution of the two editors of *Obzor*, she edited the journal herself without recognition from, and despite the political will of, the formal authorities. At the same time, she gave lectures on women in politics, solidarity and the national struggle for women. In 1925, she launched and edited *Ženski list* (*Female Paper*), the first women's magazine in Croatia. In 1938, after leaving *Ženski list*, she founded *Hrvatica* (*Croatian Woman*), a feminist newspaper, as an investment of all her assets.

Zagorka worked from her home at Dolac 8 in Zagreb, where she had the most wonderful sight of the market. She wrote polemical texts that advocated for gender equality and women's rights including women's suffrage, the right to education, and the right to property and profession. Her assets were confiscated during the Second World War and in the censorship era *Hrvatica* stopped being published. She survived the resulting poverty thanks to the help of her subscribers and admirers. She died in her flat in 1957 and was buried in the arcades of Mirogoj Cemetery.

Today, her heritage is preserved in the Marija Jurić Zagorka Memorial Apartment at the same location where she edited *Hrvatica*. Still, there are many women following in her footsteps. The Centre for Women's Studies governs the Marija Jurić Zagorka Memorial Apartment. Founded in 1995 by a group of theoreticians and scientists, feminists, peace activists and artists, the Centre fosters multi- and interdisciplinary studies of women's issues in Croatia, academic discourse, activism, artistic practices, providing education, research, publishing, library activities, cultural events, advocacy of gender equality and women's studies.

Even 152 years after she was born, Zagorka's body of work – comprising comedies, novels, one-act plays, and satires – remains contemporary. Her subversive potential is evident in each move of her quill pen, and she is a widely (re)read author in modern pop culture in Croatia, as well as in women's history and *écriture féminine*. In her literary, journalistic and activist work, she considers the relationship between work and gender, seeing women's right to work as an important factor in pursuing (economic) freedom. Women's work – teaching and writing – represents a way of resistance to the heroines she created – resistance to imposed marriage and a door to liberation.

Her characters are heroines from different social classes. She shows solidarity with working women, aware that the labour division indicates sex/gender roles in society. Anita Dremel reflects on Walby's remark that intersectional changes in economic, family and cultural spheres during the turmoil of modernisation evoked different political answers to production and consumption. Namely, gender equality excluded potentially different interests of diverse groups of women and men, so it is important to reflect upon the values and meaning of labour, and its impact on society.

The subjugation of women was an important part of Zagorka's intimate life. She was mistreated in her childhood and harassed during her professional life, but instead of becoming a martyr she regained her power through knowledge, authorship and, most importantly, work. We might presume that was the reason and inspiration as to why she created characters of strong women – clever and sly, determined and courageous, human rights advocates, and always proactive participants in historical events.

Zagorka's most widely read novel *Grička vještica* (*Witch from Grič*) introduces the female character Countess Nera, a modern superhero with a special power to save women from witch-hunts. Her character and the 'witches' in the novel spring from historical persons, documents and events. Women labelled as witches were peasant women, bakers and beautiful young women who refused sexual offers from men of power, or who were competition to men in the entrepreneurial labour market.

In her novel *Mala revolucionarka (Young Revolutionary)* the main character Zlatica is political, autonomous and actively involved in the national movement during 1903. Noble Dorja is a traveller and fugitive under inquisition in *Plameni inkvizitori (Flaming Inquisition)*. In *Magjari o Strossmayeru (Hungarians about Strossmayer)* a housewife teaches her guest about the importance of women's role in society. Manduša, a character from *Kći Lotrščaka (The Daughter of Lotrščak)*, grows up in a society where she is raised to be married. Her 'wrong breeding' results in excommunication from that same society. Despite the society, she marries an unknown robber to save him from the death penalty. Jadranka, the main character from the novel of the same name, advocates for women's right to work and occupation as a source of economic independence.

Being independent and living restlessly, Zagorka was a thorn in the side of different political systems. Namely, Zagorka was trying to remain loyal to her national roots and women's rights campaigning when Croatia was undergoing the transition from feudal to capitalistic society and during the conversion from one multinational and imperial state (Austro-Hungary) to another multinational and heavily centralised state, the Kingdom of Yugoslavia, along with growing mass culture during the times.

Zagreb, where she lived, was the most developed city in the country at the time. Being a female journalist, provocative and straightforward as she was, exposed her to professional and political degradation from male journalists, editors and the political establishment. Luckily, her voice was supported by the most prominent intellectuals at the time. Interestingly, her tenth anniversary of journalistic work was publicly celebrated during the 1907 Congress of Journalists in Budapest among her male colleagues, and her work was honoured in foreign media for her thirtieth anniversary.

Zagorka was offered money and positions by German and Hungarian media owners to maintain the status quo of political events, and not to advocate for the use of the Croatian language or independence. Instead, during the Interwar Period, she founded female and feminist magazines to defend the Croatian language and promote women's rights. Debates on gender and class were brought to the public sphere because she was brave enough to lead a solitary life. Women in the interwar period were not equal to men. As Vujnovic highlights,

[T]hey were not allowed to be judges, but discriminatory treatment also existed on the levels of civil society and the economy . . . Women living in different geographical areas of the new state were experiencing significantly different legal, social, economic, and cultural conditions . . . Most of the regulations on women's lives were subsumed under marriage laws . . . *Domaće ognjiše* (*Home Fires*), the professional magazine for women teachers published in Croatia, initiated a public discussion about the 1888 Austria-Hungarian law that had installed celibacy for women teachers. This law regulated employment practices until 1929 when the Law on Regulation of Public Education was passed. However, in 1937, an amendment that suggested that all women teachers who entered marriage would be released from their position as teachers evoked the 1888 Austria-Hungary law.

Throughout her literary work, Zagorka wrote about historical events and people, and advocated for everything she believed in: women's right to education, work, economic independence, the right to vote, and equality between men and women. Even though her literary work was considered trivial, it was an empowering means to pull women out of the bedroom and kitchen and into the public domain. This remains her legacy.

More reading

Čale Feldman, L., Dremel, A., Dujić, L., Grdešić, M., Jambrešić-Kirin, R. and Prlenda, S., eds, 2016. *Crveni ocean: Prakse, taktike i strategije rodnog otpora* (*Red Ocean: Practices, Tactics and Strategies of Gender Resistance*). Zagreb Centre for Women's Studies, The Miroslav Krleža Institute of Lexicography.

Dremel, A., Dujić, L., Grdešić, M., Jambrešić-Kirin, R. and Prlenda, S., eds, 2021. *Posebna soba. Žensko nasljeđe: roba, spektakl ili muzej za sve?* (*A Room of Her Own: Women's Heritage, Commodity, Spectacle or Museum for all?*) Zagreb Centre for Women's Studies, Institute for Ethnology and Folklore, University North.

Hrvatski velikani: Marija Jurić Zagorka (*Croatian Greats: Marija Jurić Zagorka*), 2018. https://youtu.be/_jeGQt8PeEo?si=h4CpVa_aPkYfh1W3. [In Croatian]

Jelača, D., 2017. Marija Jurić Zagorka. In J. Gaines, R. Vatsal and M. Dall'Asta, eds, *Women Film Pioneers Project*. Columbia University Libraries.

Jurić, Marija (Zagorka) Hrvatski biografski leksikon (1983–2024), mrežno izdanje. (Croatian biographical lexicon, online edition). The Miroslav Krleža Institute of Lexicography, 2024. https://hbl.lzmk.hr/clanak.aspx?id=155 (accessed 8 October 2024). [In Croatian]

ISMAT CHUGHTAI: AN INTERROGATING DANGEROUS VOICE

Megha Katoria

Megha Katoria is currently pursuing her doctorate in English from Himachal Pradesh University, India. She has previously served as an Assistant Professor of English and Communication Skills at various educational institutions and worked as an assistant editor for newspapers. A passionate reader and writer, she has contributed research papers, poems, articles, stories and book reviews to numerous journals, magazines, books and newspapers. She is also the founder and editor of the *Literary Cocktail Magazine*. In addition to her literary pursuits, she enjoys painting, sketching and engaging in all forms of creative expression.

Ismat Chughtai used her pen as a powerful weapon to interrogate the oppression of women and the patriarchal set-up of Indian society in the 1940s, when themes she wrote about were pushed under the carpet for causing a threat to the social structure of a repressive society. Chughtai posed a threat to the established structure of society, which expected women to sit silently, performing their expected roles without questioning the precincts of the established social paradigm. A potential voice for the silenced and oppressed, she boldly exposed the double standards of society. In the Introduction to *A Life in Words: Memoirs*, M. Asaduddin writes:

> As the subcontinent's foremost feminist writer, she was instinctively aware of the gendered double standard in the largely feudal and patriarchal structure of society she lived in and did everything to expose and subvert it.

Ismat Chughtai was born on 15 August 1911 to a Muslim family in western Uttar Pradesh, India. She was the ninth of ten children born to Mirza Quaseem Beg, her father, who was an honest civil servant. All of her sisters were older than her and got married when she was quite young. She spent her childhood in the company of her brothers, which contributed to her frank nature, visible in her writings. Chughtai's father supported her when her mother and all other relatives opposed her education. The education of women was staunchly resisted during the early twentieth century, to the extent that Chughtai's father was threatened with being ostracised by his relatives for supporting the education of his daughters. In the memoir *Conflict*, Chughtai writes about how her father was advised by friends that he should withdraw his daughters from school as 'to educate a girl was worse than prostituting her'.

In her memoir *Leaving Aligarh Once Again*, she explains how reading had a deep impact on her. She says:

> When I read that the women were the weaker sex and that they were easily corruptible, it had a strange impact on me. I felt angrier with myself rather than the society, thinking there must be something lacking in me. I felt pity, not anger, for my parents. They were trapped in their limited world.

For Chughtai, getting a higher education degree was a battle to be fought. She even threatened to run away if she was not allowed to pursue her education. Her father supported her in her endeavours.

Through her writings, Chughtai does not present women merely as victims and men as oppressors. Instead, she sees society's issues in all their complexity. She shows that women can be as oppressive as men, internalising patriarchal mores and values, which they feel are important to adhere to, and therefore refusing to part with them even when they cause inconvenience to them. In her stories and memoirs, she brings to light different characters from her life. It was from childhood that the rebellious streak was deeply imbued in her personality, and it continued throughout her life. She grew up insisting that she would not play with dolls nor perform other stereotypical roles ascribed to women. Instead, she would do all that the boys did. Chughtai made friends with the daughters of the helpers, who lived in the official bungalow belonging to her family. Her family disapproved of her friendship with the sweeper's and washerman's daughter, labelling her as a 'chamari' (a woman of low caste in India, who does menial jobs). Shanta Gokhale highlights Chughtai's sharp wit in responding to anything she disagreed with. To emphasise this, he references her own words when she responded to being called a 'chamari':

> Yes, I was a chamari in my last life and I will be a chamari in my next life. It is only in this one that something has gone wrong.

Chughtai was significantly influenced by an open-minded and bold woman named Rasheed Jahan, who was a doctor by profession and a writer and political revolutionary. In the words of Tahira Naqvi, Rasheed

Jahan was 'a woman of a particularly strong-willed, liberated sort'. In 1936, while Chughtai was completing her bachelor's degree, she attended the first meeting of the Progressive Writers Movement in Lucknow where she met Rasheed Jahan for the first time. She admired Jahan's bold character and wanted to be like her, and it was through her that Ismat Chughtai was able to see the stark reality of life. Shanta Gokhale notes that after getting in touch with Rasheed Jahan, the beautiful and crimson red dresses of her own stories 'vanished into thin air' and all her 'ivory idol pieces were shattered' as 'life stark naked' stood before her.

People were often scandalised by Ismat Chughtai's writings and said that no woman could pen down such 'indecent' work. She used to receive dozens of insulting and abusive letters and she often tore them up and continued to write the truth of society, which existed but remained hidden. In 1941, she wrote a brilliantly crafted story, 'The Quilt' ('Lihaaf'), which produced a storm of controversy landing her in the quagmire of the court. The story brings forth the lesbian relationship between the wife of a rich landlord and her maid servant. The narrator is a child, who tells all that happens with a childlike innocence, unaware of the inhibitions posed by society. While the wealthy landlord remains busy in his homosexual pursuits, the wife feels ignored and is gripped by a sense of loneliness. She turns to Rabbo, her maid, for the fulfilment of her desires. Chughtai delineates a woman's sexual desires and longings – a subject considered forbidden in patriarchal society. The British government tried her in court in Lahore on charges of obscenity, but in the end she won the case.

According to her own account, the story was based on the real life of the wife of Nawab Swale Khan of Aligarh, who was gay. In an interview recalled by M. Asaduddin, she said:

> In my stories I've put down everything with objectivity. Now if some people find them obscene, let them go to hell. It's my belief that experiences can never be obscene if they are based on authentic realities of life. These people think that there is nothing wrong if they can do things behind the curtains . . . All of them are halfwits.

At a time when such issues were unthinkable, Chughtai's writings proved to be a breakthrough in Urdu literature. The gender-class interface is well portrayed in her story 'Lingering Fragrance' ('Badan ki Khushboo'). This story depicts the system of concubinage, where the poor village girls are employed in palaces to train the princes sexually and it is none other than the elder women of the household who provide 'healthy maids for their sons'. Thereby, they become perpetrators of injustice, demolishing 'sisterhood' as a myth. As Kudchedkar highlights, Chughtai introduces us to a social setting, where 'women are turned into commodities, totally disposable, totally dispensable, to be used and discarded'.

'Tiny's Granny' ('Nanhi ki Nani') highlights the hypocrisy and false religiosity of upper-class people. It exposes the harsh realities of society that make it challenging for lower-class girls to lead respectable lives. It also highlights Granny's pitiable, lonely existence and her lifelong struggle for identity. 'A Pair of Hands' ('Do Haath') focuses on the plight of poor people for whom morality is not important. Their only concern is working and earning enough for life's basic necessities. Ram Autar is a sweeper who returns from the army and is happy to see the child born to his wife. People try to make Ram Autar aware of the fact that the child has been born to his wife after two years after he left the village. He is not concerned whether the child born to his wife is his or some-body else's. He is just happy that the child will support him in his old age. The story exposes the hypocrisy of the upper class, who overlook their own flaws while blaming the poor for society's problems. The story also foregrounds the issue of women being no more than a commodity – bought or sold at the convenience of all other members of the family. 'By the Grace of God' ('Allah ka Fazl') narrates a mother's obsession to get her daughters married, and how she marries her twenty-two-year-old daughter Farhat to a sixty-year-old man. Farhat is in love with a young man, Anwar, but instead of letting Farhat marry Anwar, her mother forces Farhat to stay in an incompatible marriage with a rich old man. Farhat is sacrificed at the altar of marriage for the convenience of other members of the family, as Farhat's staying with the old man provides them with economic security.

Chughtai talks of all the happenings in the 'home' and focuses her attention on this enclosed space. These happenings otherwise remain hidden from the outer world. She brings to the fore the plight of women who are compelled to dance to the beats of tradition. 'The Wedding Shroud' ('Chauthi ka Jora') presents the desperation of a mother to marry off her elder daughter to a cousin who has come to stay with them. In order to woo him, they lavish hospitality on him, even at the cost of selling off their meagre belongings. This cousin robs the younger sister of her dignity. He extracts all the physical labour from the elder daughter without acknowledgement, and then leaves as his marriage has been fixed elsewhere. The elder daughter is heartbroken and dies soon after. On many occasions in the story, the younger daughter ques-tions patriarchal notions, but is silenced.

In her memoir *Leaving Aligarh Once Again*, Chughtai questions her own identity, individuality and existence. She interrogates society:

Who decides what is right in this world? Who were the makers of my life? If it is my parents then why did God endow me with intelligence? What can I do with it?

Chughtai was influenced by the works of Fyodor Dostoyevsky, W. Somerset Maugham, Anton Chekhov, O. Henry and Premchand. A major early influence in her life was also her brother, Azeem Beg Chughtai, a well-known writer of his time. She somehow managed to escape from being tied into wedlock at the age of fifteen and married Shahid Latif at the age of twenty-nine. She met Latif while he was pursuing his Master's degree and they became good friends. Later, Shahid Latif took up the path of a film director. Marrying at the age of twenty-nine was different to the expectations of her time, when girls were married at a young age. Gokhale notes that Chughtai knew of her friends being 'married off around the age of twelve' and she 'saw their lives . . . the whole business of marriage seemed to be dreadful – sex, cooking, beatings from the mother-in-law and all the other in-laws'.

Sometimes referred to as a 'tehri lakeer' (crooked line), which is also the title of her semi-autobiographical work, Ismat Chughtai died on 24 October 1991. Here too there was a thread of controversy, as she had asked to be cremated, which goes against the Muslim tradition whereby a person is buried, not cremated as are Hindus. The instructions she left regarding her cremation rather than burial caused a furore in India and Pakistan. Naqvi labels Chughtai as an 'indomitable spirit' and a 'Grande Dame of Urdu fiction' and amply illustrates that she was a rebel, much ahead of her times. She courageously and fearlessly interrogated patriarchal practices and brought to the fore the grave injustices being perpetrated in society, making her a 'dangerous' woman for those who would like patriarchy to reign supreme.

More reading

Chughtai, I., 1984. Tiny's granny. Trans. Ralph Russell. *Contemporary Indian Short Stories*. 1959. Sahitya Akademi, pp. 117–129.

Chughtai, I., 1995. *The Crooked Line*. Trans. Tahira Naqvi. Kali.

Kumar, S. P. and Sadique, eds, 2000. *Ismat: Her Life, Her Times*. Katha.

DORIS LESSING: 'THAT EPICIST OF THE FEMALE EXPERIENCE'

Jane Rogers

Jane Rogers FRSL writes novels, stories and radio drama. She has set books in the present (*Island*), the past (*Mr Wroe's Virgins*, which she adapted as an award-winning TV serial for BBC 2) and the future. *The Testament of Jessie Lamb* won the Arthur C. Clarke Award and was Man Booker longlisted. Her most recent novel is *Body Tourists*, set in 2045. Her classic serial adaptation of Anita Desai's *Clear Light of Day* was broadcast on BBC Radio 4 in 2024. She has taught writing at all levels, and she is Emerita Professor of Writing at Sheffield Hallam University.

The writer Doris Lessing was dangerous in quite a number of ways. As a 'political agitator' and former communist she was deported from South Africa in 1956. She was only allowed to continue her visit to Rhodesia (now Zimbabwe) the same year because the authorities had made a mistake with her records. The UK government considered her sufficiently dangerous to keep her under surveillance by MI5 and MI6 for twenty years, on account of her communism and anti-racism activism.

She was certainly dangerous personally. Her idealism, combined with her sense that her life had a mission, led to behaviour that was scandalous in the 1940s, and which must have been emotionally damaging, both to herself and those who loved her. For example, she left her husband of four years and their two young children to work for the Party and then to permanently quit Rhodesia for England.

She was dangerous as a writer. Above all, as a writer. Because she was fearless in her determination to explore and dissect the history she lived through; apartheid, the fall of communism, the effects of the Second World War, and the changing relationship between women and men. In her writing, she also dissected herself; her dreams, her past, her motives, her mistakes. She was dangerous because she was seeking the truth and did not take prisoners.

Born in 1919 in Persia, Lessing and her family moved to Rhodesia in 1925. She grew up on a large but impoverished farm on the high Karroo, and developed a love of the country and of Africans, which radiates through all her work. Lacking much formal education, she read voraciously and quickly began to despise the hypocrisy and racism of white settler society. She joined the Communist Party in 1944 and first came to the UK in 1949, bearing her third child and the manuscript of her first novel. *The Grass is Singing* was published in 1950 to international acclaim, and Doris was launched as a writer. She was also an impoverished single mother, living by her journalism and her fiction, struggling to retain her belief in communism in the face of increasing evidence of Stalin's atrocities, and eventually leaving the party in 1956 after the Soviet invasion of Hungary. She moved on to explore a range of other belief systems and ways of interpreting the world, through psychoanalysis, Buddhism and Sufism, in a continually developing attempt to make sense of her experience. At every stage of her life, she wrote prolifically and with intense emotional and political involvement. When she was awarded the Nobel Prize for Literature in 2007, the Swedish Academy described her as 'that epicist of the female experience, who with scepticism, fire and visionary power has subjected a divided civilisation to scrutiny'.

For me, as a young feminist writer in the 1980s, Lessing was a role model – an incredible adventurer through fictional forms and structures. She wrote novels: realist-autobiographical (the *Martha Quest* books); present-day political (*The Good Terrorist*); dystopian science fiction (*The Memoirs of a Survivor*); space fiction (*The Canopus in Argos* quintet); and unclassifiable (*The Fifth Child*). Under her own name and pseudonyms, she published more than fifty novels. She wrote plays that were staged at the Royal Court; she wrote some of the best short stories of the twentieth century. She wrote journalism and reportage, and the two volumes of her autobiography, *Under My Skin* and *Walking in the Shade*, offer a penetrating investigation into her own life and work.

She was the first woman writer I read who wrote about sex as if it was an interesting but perfectly normal part of life, which deserves discussion as much as any other human experience. To certain types of men, I think Lessing must have seemed extremely dangerous. The collapse of conventional prohibitions about sex in the face of global war, followed by the sexual emancipation of women in the 1950s and 1960s, gave her plenty of scope. Her entirely reasonable belief that women and men are equal enabled her to take and discard lovers in a way that some men undoubtedly found unromantic. But she was neither heartless nor complacent. The book that many consider her greatest, *The Golden Notebook*, sets out to analyse, amongst other themes, precisely what the differences are between men and women, in what they want from sexual relationships.

The protagonist, Anna Freeman (note the name) is interested in exploring her own contradictions. She is a 'free' woman, who has rejected the idea of marriage, yet she is heartbroken when her lover of five years, Michael, leaves her. She sleeps with a range of other men, but some are patronising, some are inadequate lovers due to their fears and misconceptions about women, and some are purely trophy-hunting. She finds herself having to play the role of mother, saintly counsellor, wise woman. Some of these men treat her as if she has no feelings at all, so that they can betray or insult her at will. Sexual liberation is both freedom and misery. Anna does not want to believe, politically or ideologically, in monogamy, so her lasting grief over the loss of Michael is something she tries to dismiss, and even blames herself for. There is no answer.

Anna is a writer who cannot write and has scant respect for the successful book she has written. She is a communist at the moment when the truth about Stalin emerges. She is also a single mother. The novel's structure reflects the deep divisions in her life; it consists of four notebooks, black for her writing life, red for her political life, yellow for stories where she tries to make sense of her experience, and blue for her diary. Her greatest struggle is to keep herself open to every experience and to be willing to be changed by it. Anna is a character in transition – or in breakdown, some would argue. It would be impossible to refer to her as a victim or an innocent or a career woman, though she contains elements of all three of these. What is striking is the honesty with which her often conflicting lives (physical, emotional, intellectual) are portrayed, and this is surely why so many women revere this book.

Lessing was never afraid to push into dangerous subject matter. It is well documented (not least by Lessing herself) that she didn't get on with her mother, and that she felt horribly impatient with her mother's hypocrisy, self-pity and ineffectualness. When Doris became a mother herself, she had no compunction about abandoning her own children, who were being brought up with all the privileges and prejudices of white settler society. She writes about this in *Under My Skin*:

> It was the way of life I had to leave . . . I explained to the babies that they would understand later why I had left. I was going to change this ugly world, they would live in a beautiful and perfect world where there would be no race hatred, injustice, and so forth . . . I carried, like a defective gene, a kind of doom or fatality, which would trap them as it had me, if I stayed. Leaving, I would break some ancient chain of repetition. One day they would thank me for it.
>
> I was absolutely sincere. There isn't much to be said for sincerity, in itself.

Oh, but there is! There is a very great deal to be said for sincerity. And how many of us could publicly expose and acknowledge our deepest mistakes? Knowing Lessing's own history, I found the topic of mother-hood revisited in a very moving way in *The Good Terrorist* (1985).

This novel is ostensibly about IRA terrorism in London. But it is really about the relationship between a mother and daughter. The daughter, Alice, is pig-headed and blinkered by revolutionary political ideals which are not in the least thought-through. She feels contempt for her bourgeois mother, but her mother is a useful source of money. The mother loves her, supports her to the point of financial ruin, disagrees profoundly with her politics, tries repeatedly and considerately to help her in a whole range of ways, and is rejected. The mother is the voice of sanity in the book, the person who sacrifices herself for the sake of a relationship which is quite impossible, but not because of the fault of the older woman. The mother is the tragic heroine whom the reader loves.

This is one of Lessing's greatest achievements; that she was not afraid to change her mind. To keep on striving passionately for what she believed in, in life as in literature, but always to keep a beady critical eye on herself, on what she had done and become. To be dangerous to herself. She continually renewed herself through interrogation.

Dangerous, difficult, brilliant, honest; one of the towering writers of our times.

More reading

Brazil, K., ed., 2016. *Doris Lessing and the Forming of History*. Edinburgh University Press.

Diski, J., 2016. *In Gratitude*. Bloomsbury.

Feigel, L., 2019. *Free Woman: Life, Liberation and Doris Lessing*. Bloomsbury.

Frick, T., 1988. Doris Lessing – The art of fiction no. 102. *The Paris Review*, 106, spring.

Guttridge, P., 2013. Doris Lessing obituary. *The Independent*, 17 November.

FLORA NWAPA: PIONEERING NIGERIAN ADMINISTRATOR, ACADEMIC AND AUTHOR

Ejine Olga Nzeribe and Ebere Okereke

Ejine Olga Nzeribe is the first daughter of Flora Nwapa. A British Chevening Scholar, she has an MBA from Durham Business School, an LLB Honours degree from the University of Buckingham, and a Bachelor of Arts degree in Theatre Arts from the University of Jos, Nigeria. She was a practising lawyer and company secretary before concentrating on her chosen field: customer care, training and development, and management leadership. Ejine has a passion to develop people to reach their highest potential and bring out the best in themselves through practical learning solutions. Ejine has a skill for telling and writing stories. She is the writer and publisher of a corporate biography, *Inspiring Growth: The History of Red Star Express* (2012) and has recently published a biography of her mother, *Flora Nwapa: This Book Must Be Written* (2024).

Dr Ebere Okereke is a global health physician and has held pivotal roles in esteemed organisations, including Public Health England, the Tony Blair Institute for Global Change, and Africa CDC. She is a Fellow of the UK Faculty of Public Health and an Associate Fellow at the Chatham House Institute London. She was recognised by the British Medical Association as an outstanding role model for women in academic medicine. She is a graduate of the University of Nigeria College of Medicine, and she holds a Master's in Public Health from Newcastle University and an honorary Doctor of Science degree from the Liverpool School of Tropical Medicine.

To Nigerians, who would be considered a dangerous woman?

Flora Nwapa (1931–1993), considered Africa's first internationally published female novelist, fits this bill.

The two leading characters in Flora's books, *Efuru* and *One is Enough*, live in a society dominated by the male and by gender issues. A dangerous woman is one who elopes from her father's house to live with her poor lover, who could not afford to pay the customary bride price necessary for a marriage contract, bringing shame to her successful warrior father and family name. The character Efuru in the book *Efuru* knows she has committed a taboo; she does it irrespective of the consequences and has no apologies for following her heart. Amaka in *One is Enough* escapes from being beaten by her husband for her utterances (nearly killing him in self-defence). She walks out of the marriage to start life afresh in a new city rather than be insulted and maligned just because she has not conceived a child, and is considered persona non grata within the community.

A dangerous woman is enterprising. She can do what men do and do it even better with a quiet and dogged personality, holding her own in matters concerning the home and business. Efuru refuses to go to the farm with her husband – preferring to trade instead because, as she succinctly explains, she is not cut out for farm work. Her first husband Adizua, in deference to her (or for his own personal and selfish needs) abandons the farm and joins her in trading, thereby committing an act that is anathema to the norm. Her second husband, Gilbert, trades with Efuru as a partner and equal. He does not lord it over her; she has a say in how the business will be run and takes decisions even when these put her on a direct warpath with Gilbert.

One Is Enough's Amaka is not only enterprising but a dangerously ambitious woman. She is a contractor, one of the female traders who had sprung up during and at the end of the Nigerian Civil War. With others, she had taken part in the 'attack trade' – going behind enemy lines to buy products from the enemy who were killing her people. Her ambition is to become an economically independent woman, which she believes will insulate her from the whims and caprices of rapacious males parading as husbands or lovers and provide her with the recognition and respect that she is being denied because of her perceived predicament.

A dangerous woman excels in everything she does to the detriment of her male counterparts. Adizua can no longer work successfully on the farm as he is intoxicated with his love for Efuru. Indeed, the full Igbo language meaning of Efuru is 'Nwanefuru': a child who everyone loves. It is not surprising that Adizua gives up farming to the total consternation of his fellow farmers. Clearly the 'dangerousness' of Efuru has overpowered his authority over the home and the ability to focus on what appears to have been a clear-cut profession. Amaka also sets out to excel in everything she lays her hands on – contracts, business, acquisition of wealth and relationships – irrespective of her misfortunes, in a bid to gain the respect she craves so much as compensation for her childlessness; and to prove that she could be successful despite her situation.

A dangerous woman is opportunistic, devious and cunning. Amaka moves to Lagos to start life afresh and uses the association of her sisters' friends to find out information for getting contracts. A dangerous woman is also one who uses what she has ('bottom power') to get what she wants. She sets out to lure a Catholic priest with everything she has, including sexual gratification for material gain. She knows she has made an impression on the man of God from the first day she meets him and sets out to exploit the situation. Her personal assertion is that she would go for the kill because a priest is firstly a man capable of feelings and like any other man could be tempted. She does the same with Alhaji and the many others that come after him; never for love and always for her own material needs – to survive and excel on her own terms.

A dangerous woman is one who totally annihilates a man. The Catholic priest falls head over heels in love with Amaka. She becomes pregnant, and when he decides to be accountable and own up to his deeds, she rebuffs him. This is not part of her plan. She wants to prove to the entire world that she is not barren; she wants to continue her life as is, without the trappings of a marriage. She is sure the priest would not contemplate leaving the priesthood for her sake. And she is happy with this regardless of the stigma of being the mother of nameless children. Indeed, as a dangerous woman, she takes the decision to name her twins after her own father and is bent on hiding their paternity.

A dangerous woman is one who wants to be a mistress rather than a wife because she wants to be free to express herself and do the things she wants to do. This is seen in *One is Enough*'s Amaka. Being a mistress is unheard of, but as a dangerous woman she does not care what people will think; she does not care about the shame to her name and family; she does not care what or how society would label her. She declares to her mother and sister that she is through with marriage and is not shaken into submission despite all her mother's entreaties to marry the priest.

In the characters of Efuru and Amaka we see different dimensions of what it means to be a dangerous woman in the Nigerian context. Flora Nwapa depicted these women as dangerous, not because of who they are but because of what the masculine society they lived in had turned them into being. Who is a dangerous woman? A dangerous woman is one who dares to survive in a man's world and does so successfully to the utter consternation of her male counterparts. A dangerous woman is one who does the unthinkable, irrespective of culture and tradition. She takes ownership and accountability for her actions, be they positive or negative, without fear, without even a fear of the unknown. A dangerous woman is a woman who literally declares to the whole world: 'I am who I am.'

Florence Nwanzuruahu Nkeiru Nwapa, popularly known as Flora Nwapa, was born into two prominent families in Eastern Nigeria – those of Nwapa Nduka and Onumonu Uzoaru. The latter, her maternal grandfather and Madam Ruth, his influential wife, established the Anglican Church in Oguta. Flora's father worked as a UAC agent in Nigeria while her mother was the first local woman to achieve a standard 6 pass at St Monica's School Ogbunike.

Flora's secondary school education was at the famous Archdeacon Crowther Memorial Girl's School in Elelenwa, followed by CMS Girls School and Queen's College Lagos. She attended University College Ibadan in 1953, where she was President of the Queen's Hall, meeting Queen Elizabeth II and the Duke of Edinburgh during their visit to Nigeria. After her BA degree, she attended the University of Edinburgh and obtained a Diploma in Education.

Nwapa started her career as a Woman Education Officer in the Ministry of Education, Calabar, from where she moved to Queen's School Enugu as a teacher. She soon left for the University of Lagos where she rose to the position of Assistant Registrar in charge of Public Administration in 1966. *Efuru* was published the same year. Flora had sent the manuscript to Chinua Achebe who sent it on to Heinemann Educational Books London. Upon its publication, Flora became the first African female writer to be published internationally. Heinemann published *Idu* in 1970. *This Is Lagos and Other Stories* and *Never Again* were subsequently published by Nwamife Publishers Enugu. Other books, essays and articles followed in quick succession, across a writing career of thirty years.

During the Nigerian Civil War, she married Chief Gogo Nwakuche, who became an industrialist. At the end of the war, Flora was appointed the first woman Commissioner for Health and Social Welfare of the newly created East Central State. After stints as Commissioner for Lands and Survey and Commissioner for Establishments, she set up Tana Press Limited and Flora Nwapa Books Limited to print and publish books. She still found time to lecture in creative writing or literature in Nigeria and abroad. Consequently, she was at various times a visiting lecturer at the Alvan Ikoku College of Education Owerri, Imo State Nigeria and Visiting Professor of Creative Writing at the University of Maiduguri Borno State Nigeria, and she gave lectures in many universities in the United States. She was billed to travel to East Carolina University, North Carolina as an Associate Professor in Creative Writing for one year when she died in 1993.

Apart from *Efuru, Idu, This Is Lagos and Other Stories* and *Never Again*, Flora wrote *One is Enough, Women are Different, Wives at War, Cassava Song & Rice Song, Emeka – Driver's Guard*, and other stories. Her children's books included *Mammywater, Journey to Space* and *Miracle Kittens*; these were written to preserve the oral tradition of storytelling that she had experienced while growing up, and to provide books that would make sense to Nigerian and African children.

Flora Nwapa's last novel, *The Lake Goddess*, was published posthumously in 2020 and was republished in the United Kingdom in 2023. *Conversations*, consisting of two plays – *The Sycophants* and *Two Women in Conversation*, first published in 1993 – was republished in 2023.

Flora never set out to be a writer. She maintained that the feeling came from within based on a particular interest in both rural and urban women in their quest for survival in a fast-changing world dominated by men. She was not a feminist. She proclaimed herself a womanist, believing that a woman must be economically independent in her own right.

She was truly a dangerous woman.

More reading

Nwapa, F., 1966. *Efuru*. Heinemann Educational Books.

Nwapa, F., 1981. *One is Enough*. Flora Nwapa Books Limited.

Nwapa, F., 2023. *The Lake Goddess*. Abibiman Publishing.

Nzeribe, E. O., 2024. *Flora Nwapa: This Book Must Be Written*. Kraft Books Limited.

ANNA POLITKOVSKAYA: WHO ORDERED THE KILLING?

Lucy Popescu

Lucy Popescu worked with the English Centre of PEN, the international
association of writers, for over twenty years and was Director of its Writers
in Prison Committee from 1991 to 2006. She co-edited the PEN anthology
Another Sky (Profile Books, 2007). *The Good Tourist*, her book about human
rights and ethical travel, was published by Arcadia Books in 2008. She is
the editor of the refugee anthologies *A Country of Refuge* (Unbound, 2016)
and *A Country to Call Home* (Unbound, 2018).

On 7 October 2006, award-winning Russian journalist Anna Politkovskaya was shot dead outside her Moscow apartment. She was deemed
a dangerous woman by many for her investigative work, and paid for it
with her life. Her body was found slumped in the lift of her apartment
block, together with a gun and four bullets. Her murder had all the
hallmarks of a contract killing, down to the *kontrolnyi vystrel* (the
control shot), a final bullet into the head at close range. There is little
doubt that her death was in retribution for her fearless reporting,
particularly on human rights abuses in Chechnya.

Born in 1958 in New York, Politkovskaya studied journalism at
Moscow State University. She worked on the Soviet newspaper *Izvestiya*
for over ten years, before joining *Novaya Gazeta* in 1999, one of the few
newspapers to be openly critical of the Kremlin, its policies in Chechnya
and corruption in the armed forces. She worked as a special correspondent for the Moscow newspaper and wrote extensively about Chechnya
and human rights abuses in Russia. English translations of her books
include *A Dirty War: A Russian Reporter in Chechnya* (2001), *Putin's
Russia* (2004) and *A Russian Diary*, published posthumously in 2008. At
the time of her death, she was working on an article about torture in
Chechnya that implicated Ramzan Kadyrov, then the Chechen Prime
Minister appointed by President Putin. After her murder, rumours
began to circulate that Kadyrov himself was responsible and had
ordered the contract killing to coincide with Putin's birthday.

Politkovskaya was recognised worldwide for her championing of
human rights, but her reporting had brought her enemies from various

quarters. In the early noughties, I was working as Director of English PEN's Writers in Prison Committee and we regularly held campaigns protesting against the intimidation of this courageous journalist. In 2001 Politkovskaya was forced to flee to Vienna, after receiving death threats from a military officer accused of committing atrocities against civilians in Chechnya. She acted as a mediator in the Nord-Ost theatre siege in Moscow in 2002. Two years later, we learned that Politkovskaya had fallen seriously ill as she attempted to fly to Beslan to cover the hostage crisis there. After drinking tea on the flight to the region, she lost consciousness and was hospitalised, but the suspected toxin was never identified. The results of her blood tests were reportedly destroyed. This led to speculation that she had been deliberately poisoned to stop her from reporting on the siege. Politkovskaya was shaken by this, but continued to write, despite the death threats. One of her enemies was undoubtedly the Chechen leader Kadyrov who, she claimed, had vowed to kill her.

I met the journalist in 2004 when she was in the UK for the launch of her book, *Putin's Russia*. She spoke little English, and I spoke no Russian, but her commitment and compassion were clear. Two years later, I was working on the PEN anthology, *Another Sky*, featuring the works of persecuted writers, and I commissioned a piece from Politkovskaya. Her English translator, Arch Tait, sent her contribution to me just a few weeks before her brutal murder. As it turned out, it was the last piece she wrote for a foreign readership and her words were disturbingly prescient of her death. She writes of being a condemned woman:

> Kadyrov's government has publicly vowed to murder me. It was actually said at a meeting that his government had had enough, and I was a condemned woman . . . What for? For not writing the way Kadyrov wanted?

She also succinctly expresses the dangers and challenges facing journalists like herself, and the pervasive climate of fear that silences so many of them:

> I loathe the Kremlin line . . . dividing people into those who are 'on our side', 'not on our side', or even 'on the other side' . . . if a journalist is 'not on our side', however, he or she will be deemed a supporter of the European democracies, of European values and automatically become a pariah . . . So what is the crime that has earned me this label of not being 'one of us'? I have merely reported what I have witnessed, no more than that . . . somebody who describes the life around us for those who cannot see it for themselves, because what is shown on television and written about in the overwhelming majority of newspapers is emasculated and doused in ideology.

When the news came through of her murder, I remember the shock we all felt that she had been gunned down in cold blood. Newspapers all over the world reported Politkovskaya's death and her funeral was attended by thousands of mourners. It was terrible to think that all of us at PEN, and Politkovskaya herself, had dreaded the possibility that she would meet a violent end. Her untitled final essay, published in *Another Sky*, also demonstrated that she remained dedicated to her profession as a campaigning journalist until the very end.

Putin was markedly silent immediately after Politkovskaya's murder. When he finally condemned the murder, in an interview with a German newspaper, his parting shot was that 'her political influence inside of Russia was negligible'. At the time of her death, Alexander Litvinenko, a former FSB agent exiled in the UK, claimed Putin was responsible. A month later, he was also dead.

On 14 June 2014, five Chechen men were convicted of Politkovskaya's murder. Rustam Makhmudov was found guilty of firing the shots and his uncle Lom-Ali Gaitukayev – already serving a prison term for another contract killing – was charged with organising the crime. Both men were sentenced to life imprisonment. Former policeman Sergei Khadzhikurbanov, who had allegedly organised surveillance of Politkovskaya's movements prior to her death, was sentenced to twenty years in prison, and Gaitukayev's other two nephews, Ibragim and Dzhabrail Makhmudov, were accused of driving the getaway car and received fourteen and twelve years respectively. Another former police officer, Dmitry Pavlyuchenkov, had earlier received eleven years for his part in the murder.

Even if these men are guilty, the question remains: Who ordered the killing?

NB: Since writing this, Khadzhikurbanov has been pardoned after fighting in Ukraine, according to his lawyer, Alexei Mikhalchik. He received the presidential pardon in 2023 after completing a six-month military contract.

More reading

Politkovskaya, A., 2001. *A Dirty War: A Russian Reporter in Chechnya.* Trans. Thomas Crowfoot. Harvill Press.

Politkovskaya, A., 2004. *Putin's Russia.* Harvill Press.

Politkovskaya, A., 2008. *A Russian Diary.* Trans. Arch Tait. Harvill Secker.

MONARCHS

AND

MYSTICS

Female rulers exert a special fascination for many. In Edinburgh, for example, the chambers of Mary, Queen of Scots are preserved at the Palace of Holyroodhouse, their floors tramped by centuries of tourists.

Yet opposition to women's power has always been present: Protestant reformer John Knox blasted Mary and other members of his so-called Monstrous Regiment of Women, declaiming that for a woman to 'sit in the seat of God, that is, to teach, to judge, or to reign above a man' made her 'a monster in nature'. Less vitriolic but no less damaging are contemporary attitudes to historical women, as seen in Marianne Moen's essay on the two Viking women unearthed at Oseburg, whose leading roles in their society were repeatedly downplayed by twentieth-century male scholars.

Knox's perception of divine right cuts to the heart of this section. A woman ordained to rule by the gods, or God, is seen as a woman inherently dangerous. Those who dare to seek power, such as the Empress Matilda in Lucy Flannery's chapter, who acted as regent in both Italy and Normandy as well as waging an eighteen-year civil war for England's throne, have been tarred as unnatural viragos. Despite this, all around the world, women have reigned over us, sometimes as wives and consorts, or regents acting on behalf of a relative, but often as ruling queens whose legitimacy stems from their lineage.

Speaking with holy authority was viewed as acceptable in some communities, where an abbess instructed her flock or a devotee of the *orisas* led Yoruba societies. Yet as Jill E. Marshall notes of the Pythia at Delphi, when a female prophet acted as conduit for the divine – especially where the enquirer is male – then disbelief or violence could follow. Lower-status women such as widows and folk healers did not even have the protection of a religious order, meaning that accusations of witchcraft were often deadly. Both Sarah L. King in her chapter on the Pendle witch trials and Sara Sheridan in the Foreword to this volume point out that the marginalised suffer most when supernatural threats are perceived.

This next part therefore links together those who risked everything at the intersection of faith and power: not only the faces preserved in statues and portraits in stately palaces, but saints and mystics too, and most importantly perhaps, the women whose names are lost to time.

HATSHEPSUT: A FEMALE KING

Stephanie Aulsebrook

Stephanie Aulsebrook is a former Postdoctoral Research Fellow at IASH
and is now an Assistant Professor at the Faculty of Archaeology, University
of Warsaw, Poland. She specialises in the archaeology of Late Bronze Age
Greece, in particular the production, use and social significance of metal
artefacts, as well as the prehistoric community at the UNESCO-listed site
of Mycenae. Her research interests also include the wider East
Mediterranean during the same period. She shares with the Ancient
Egyptians a love of cats.

In Ancient Egypt, the fifth pharaoh of the 18th Dynasty was a woman,
Hatshepsut. Clever and ambitious, she overcame the difficulty of being
a female king by combining her acknowledged femininity with
traditional (male) pharaonic representation. As the embodiment of
Egyptian state power, she was without doubt a formidably dangerous
woman. A campaign of violent destruction to eradicate her memory
led to suggestions that the existence of this female king was considered
transgressive. But was it her gender that led Hatshepsut to be
considered a danger to the cherished cosmological order of Ancient
Egypt?

Hatshepsut, born around 1507 BC, was the daughter of pharaoh Thutmose I and Ahmose, who amongst his many wives was the official queen
or Great Royal Wife. Hatshepsut was Great Royal Wife to her father's
successor, Thutmose II. Thutmose II was also Hatshepsut's half-brother,
the son of one of her father's less prestigious wives. During her father's
reign, Hatshepsut was made the highest-ranked priestess in the cult of
one of the chief Egyptian deities, Amun. With these titles came associated duties and privileges, and as a royal, Hatshepsut would have owned
and controlled large estates and workshops. Therefore, Hatshepsut held
a high position in the political and religious hierarchy of the Ancient
Egyptian royal court, and she had a substantial input into the governance of the state even before she became pharaoh.

Hatshepsut's husband's reign was brief, but they did have a daughter
together, Neferure. Upon the death of Thutmose II, his very young son,
by another wife, was declared Thutmose III and Hatshepsut was
appointed co-regent. A contemporary stele stated:

> [The King] went up to heaven and was united with the gods. His son took his place as King of the Two Lands (Egypt) and he was the sovereign on the throne of his father. His sister, the God's Wife Hatshepsut, dealt with the affairs of the state: the Two Lands were under her government and taxes were paid to her.

This arrangement was uncommon, but not unprecedented. Co-regency was used to protect the succession. Usually, the incumbent pharaoh promoted their chosen successor to rule alongside them, ensuring an orderly transition; the co-regent was treated as a second pharaoh. Appointing a co-regent while the pharaoh was a child was accepted practice, although infrequently required. In this case, the co-regent was not made pharaoh and stepped down when the child-pharaoh reached maturity. It is not known whether Hatshepsut already harboured further ambitions when declared as co-regent. Yet, within the first seven years of her co-regency Hatshepsut had become pharaoh.

Hatshepsut was not the first female pharaoh. Three centuries earlier, Queen Sobekneferu of the 12th Dynasty became pharaoh. Her reign was short, and unfortunately very little is known about her. Other earlier female pharaohs have been postulated, but the evidence for their status and even existence is scant. Hatshepsut stands out because of the way she inserted herself into the succession by bending political norms and because of her subsequent treatment after death.

To be pharaoh was not simply to rule the Egyptian state. There was more to it than making policy decisions or public appearances. Egyptians believed the pharaoh's chief role was to maintain *ma'at*. This complex concept of cosmological order encompasses truth, goodness and justice, and was embodied by Egypt itself as well as by the goddess named *ma'at*. All Egyptians were charged with this responsibility, but only the pharaoh, through their divine nature, could intercede directly with the gods. To be pharaoh was to be Egypt's spiritual protector, guarding its people against chaos. By declaring herself pharaoh, Hatshepsut moved beyond the considerable power she already wielded as co-regent to assume the mantle of ultimate divine authority.

Hatshepsut needed to legitimise her claim. We can see how she achieved this through the reliefs, steles and sculptures commissioned for her impressive monuments. Moving away from her initial use of her husband as the basis for her claim, she declared herself chosen by the god Amun and her father, Thutmose I. Hatshepsut rewrote history by inventing a co-regency between herself and her father. She also adopted for herself the standard pharaonic fiction of a divine procreation.

Upon accession, pharaohs acquired several new names. Hatshepsut's new pharaonic names were carefully selected to incorporate references to her father and various goddesses, especially *ma'at*. For example, part of her new prenomen, 'true one of the ka (spirit) of Re', was, due to its gendered feminine word construction, spelt in the same way as the word 'ma'at'. This clever wordplay was impossible for male pharaohs. It repeated the structure used by Sobekneferu, for her prenomen, and may have been a deliberate nod to this previous female king.

Hatshepsut was a prolific monument builder. Pharaohs used this type of self-aggrandisement to justify their rule. Hatshepsut used forms popularised by earlier kings and placed her monuments by those of particularly celebrated pharaohs, grounding her status within Egypt's architectural traditions. Her main focus was elaborating the religious complex at Karnak, dedicated to the god she regarded as her divine father, Amun.

Perhaps the most famous material expression of Hatshepsut's concept of the female king is how she chose to visually represent her physical form. Early depictions of her followed pre-existing conventions for queens. Then came a significant shift: Hatshepsut's female body was given male pharaonic accoutrements including headdress and beard. Her later statues are indistinguishable from those of male pharaohs, but their inscriptions use feminine forms. Hatshepsut was not pretending to be male; however, she had become confident enough to use the classic tropes of pharaonic imagery. It was a statement that she was at the height of her power. This male/female dualism was not new. Male pharaohs incorporated visual aspects of female goddesses when appropriate. The pharaoh embodied unity, whether that was the union between Upper and Lower Egypt (hence the reference to Egypt as the Two Lands) or male and female. Hatshepsut combined the latter in a unique fashion still firmly set within traditional Egyptian imagery.

Hatshepsut continued the pharaonic tradition of military and diplomatic expeditions. She used an expedition to the Kingdom of Punt as an opportunity to bring back exotic materials and goods, such as myrrh trees, for dedication to her divine father Amun. Reliefs of Hatshepsut showed her as a sphinx trampling her enemies. Potential internal enemies were also warned of the dangers of opposing Hatshepsut:

> He who shall do her homage shall live, he who shall speak evil in blasphemy of her Majesty shall die.

Loyalty to the pharaoh was obligatory to maintain *ma'at*. To judge by the splendour of some of her officials' tombs, Hatshepsut also generously rewarded those with faith in her kingship. It seems that, although Hatshepsut's actions meant Thutmose III played a junior role, their relationship was amicable. Hatshepsut trusted him enough to make him head of the army. Yet, her monuments emphasised his inferior role. She was mentioned more frequently, shown standing in front of him, depicted with the prestigious 'double crown' more often, and, in one scene, he is shown worshipping her and the powerful goddess Hathor. At no time did Hatshepsut deny that Thutmose III was co-regent nor seek to replace him but, by becoming pharaoh, she rejected the expected path for temporary co-regents.

Hatshepsut died in her fifties. Originally buried alongside her father, Thutmose I, her body was moved when a new tomb was created for him. A mummy, which preliminary research has identified as Hatshepsut, is currently on display at the recently opened National Museum of Egyptian Civilization (NMEC) in Cairo.

After her death, Thutmose III had a long and successful reign. Hatshepsut's legacy was accepted for two decades without difficulty. Attitudes changed when Thutmose III appointed his son, Amenhotep II, as co-regent. Hatshepsut was suddenly recast as a dangerous liability. Documents relating to her reign were destroyed. A brutal campaign of destruction and mutilation took place at many of her greatest monuments. Her cartouche was hacked out of inscriptions, her image chipped off reliefs and sculptures of her were either toppled or had the male pharaonic elements removed. This assault on her physical memory was not extensive. Many smaller monuments were left intact. They targeted the largest and most impressive of Hatshepsut's architectural achievements where she was most publicly visible, and therefore at her most dangerous. The severity of this action was only matched by the treatment meted out two centuries later to the heretic king, Akhenaten, whose religious reforms shook Ancient Egyptian society.

For a while, many Egyptologists assumed this vindictive action was undertaken by Thutmose III in retaliation for being forced into what these scholars regarded as the humiliating position of junior co-regent to a woman. However, this theory doesn't account for the timing of the destructions. Why would he wait all those years? It also doesn't fit with the apparently amicable relationship between Hatshepsut and Thutmose III throughout the co-regency.

Generally, scholars, particularly during the mid-twentieth century, interpreted this campaign of destruction as evidence that Ancient Egyptians considered Hatshepsut's reign to have been a failure, and they were quick to blame her gender as the underlying reason. Her use of male body imagery was suggested to have been an attempt to deceive

Ancient Egyptian society, in an apparently analogous way to the Pope Joan legend. Some scholars depicted her as scheming and overly ambitious, wrestling power away from the rightful king. Hatshepsut was even criticised for failing to pursue suitably militaristic policies due to her femininity. Others focused on finding the 'real' (male) power behind the throne – a favourite candidate was her Royal Steward, Senenmut.

Some arguments were made from a position of ignorance. Further excavations since then have uncovered much more evidence concerning Hatshepsut's reign. This has demonstrated that Hatshepsut followed a path of kingship very similar to the most celebrated male pharaohs, and Egypt prospered under her rule. Other arguments, however, betray preconceptions about the role of women in Ancient Egypt, ideas not borne out by the evidence. In comparison to contemporary societies, women in Ancient Egypt had better legal rights, a greater role in public life, participated more widely in economic activities and were given the same payments or privileges as men for performing the same task. Female overseers, governors and judges are attested. Of course, Ancient Egypt was not a utopia of gender equality, but neither can it be shown that a female pharaoh was considered inherently dangerous. No equivalent measures were taken to erase the name of Sobekneferu or any other female pharaoh. Sons were favoured over daughters for the succession, but a male pharaoh was clearly highly desirable, not essential.

So, why was so much effort taken to desecrate Hatshepsut's achievements and obliterate her name? During her reign, Hatshepsut had wielded royal power while Thutmose III held a junior role. Yet, Hatshepsut only became a specific danger to Thutmose III when it was time for him to choose and secure the legitimacy of his successor, Amenhotep II. This danger did not arise because of her gender. Rather, she had demonstrated the power non-pharaonic royals could wield. Amenhotep II was, like his father and grandfather, also the son of a less prestigious wife, and his mother was not royal. His legitimacy had to be secured against family rivals. This fear may explain why Amenhotep II decided against recording his queens' names. He hoped such an action could prevent the same problem arising for his own successor. The reality of this threat is proven by events after the death of Amenhotep II, as one of his younger sons (Thutmose IV) usurped his chosen successor. The actions of Thutmose III and Amenhotep II also did not prevent the accession of another female pharaoh just over a century after the reign of Hatshepsut.

That the eradication of Hatshepsut's legacy was intended to protect Amenhotep II explains why the campaign of destruction happened after he became co-regent with Thutmose III. This drastic measure was taken to strengthen his position and thus maintain *ma'at* by ensuring an orderly transition. Hatshepsut's officials were probably deceased by this point, removing a possible source of dissent. The destruction of her memory was a coldly calculated and carefully targeted political act, advantageous to her immediate successors. The previous characterisation of this action by some scholars simply as a vindictive meaningless frenzy borne of misogyny perhaps reflects their underestimation of Hatshepsut herself. A dangerous woman, yes, but more significantly a skilful stateswoman who set a dangerous precedent. She drew upon her talents and ambition to successfully build a power base that enabled her to defy established conventions governing royal succession and ascend the throne in her own right. In her own words, as attributed to her in an inscription from Karnak, 'I became conscious of myself as efficient king, and I seized what he (Amun) has put in front of me.'

Hatshepsut's modern reception remains mixed. On many occasions her life is judged by standards not applied to male pharaohs. For example, in 2016 Hatshepsut's Wikipedia entry almost immediately commenced with speculation about her relationship with her Royal Steward, presented as a motive for her rise to power (now removed). Others have been able to celebrate her achievements on their own merit and accept Hatshepsut as one of the most successful pharaohs to rule Ancient Egypt, male or female. For instance, during the Cairo metro construction project, her name was used for the tunnel-boring machine in honour of her grand infrastructure developments. Forced to confront the dual ideological challenges of ascending to the throne through unconventional means and of being a female king, Hatshepsut proved herself dangerously capable of controlling the complex politics of Ancient Egypt to fulfil the role of the pharaoh with great success.

More reading

Baum, M. and Thomas, S., 2017. *Hatshepsut*. Leaders of the Ancient World Series. Rosen.

Cooney, K., 2014. *The Woman who would be King: Hatshepsut's Rise to Power in Ancient Egypt*. Oneworld.

Grimal, N., 1992. *A History of Ancient Egypt*. Trans. I. Shaw. Blackwell.

Shaw, I., ed., 2000. *The Oxford History of Ancient Egypt*. Oxford University Press.

Tyldesley, J. A., 1994. *Daughters of Isis: Women of Ancient Egypt*. Penguin.

THE ORACLE AT DELPHI: PREDICTING AND ENDURING DANGER

Jill E. Marshall

Jill E. Marshall earned her PhD in the History of Religion from Emory University. Her research focused on women's religious activities in the ancient Mediterranean world, particularly prophecy and divination, and she has published *Women Praying and Prophesying: Gender and Inspired Speech in First Corinthians* (Mohr Siebeck, 2017). She works as lead instructional designer at Artisan Learning, where she creates e-learning and curriculum for workforce education. In her free time, she writes fiction that draws on her historical research.

What's more dangerous than a woman who speaks for God?

In ancient Mediterranean religions, inspired prophecy, especially when voiced by a woman, could be a dangerous process. In Greek traditions, women held the title 'prophet' (in Greek, *prophêtis* or *mantis*) at the oracular Temples of Apollo at Delphi and Didyma, and the Temple of Zeus at Dodona. Cassandra and the Sibyl, legendary prophets who were not connected to temples but who prophesied when the spirit came to them, loomed large in the collective imagination of the Greeks and Romans. These women prophets were acknowledged and esteemed conduits for the gods' will, but the men who sought oracular advice often suspected that they were corrupt or mad. Herein lies the danger. It is precarious to ignore the words of a god, yet, in the eyes of men, women's words were inherently deceptive, frivolous or worthless.

The subject of oracular predictions, moreover, raised the stakes of the process and increased the danger that the women both posed and endured. Prophecy sanctioned and/or predicted political upheaval and violence. From its earliest literary depiction in Herodotus' *Histories*, the oracle at Delphi addressed questions about conquests, wars and settlements of foreign lands, and provided divine sanction for violent actions. According to Plutarch, the Sibyl prophesied 'the numerous desolations and migrations of Greek cities, the numerous descents of barbarian hordes, and the overthrow of empires' (*Pyth. orac.*, 398D).

This anxiety-filled political situation led to challenges and violence during oracular enquiries or extemporaneous prophecy. In temple-based prophecy, male enquirers sometimes threatened, assaulted or killed a priestess who refused to prophesy or who gave unfavourable oracles. In Sibylline traditions and legends about Cassandra, violence upon the prophet more often came from the god who inspired her. The prophetic process, therefore, was dangerous on two levels: prophets spoke divine words that foretold precarious situations, and in turn they experienced verbal, judicial and physical challenges from gods and men.

In one of the earliest literary portrayals of female prophecy, Herodotus depicts the Delphic prophet as one means by which the gods directed human history. She is not mad or raving. Rather, she gives clear yet ambiguous oracles and interprets them when asked to do so. *The Histories* does not include episodes in which enquirers, priests or gods violate the prophet. Instead, they test and question her integrity. These challenges emerge from human anxiety over two things: first, the truth and interpretation of oracles about the future, and, second, their own roles in dangerous political manoeuvres. For instance, in his interactions with the oracle, King Croesus of Lydia first tested several temples, determined that Delphi was a true oracle, and became increasingly confident in the oracles of the Pythia (the female prophet at Delphi) and in his ability to interpret them. When he failed in his campaign against the Persians, he challenged the prophet and asked why she led him astray. She subdued his challenge by correctly interpreting the oracles for him (1.46–91). This anxiety over receiving true prophecy manifests in other early stories in which enquirers are concerned that someone else has bribed the prophet or that she is in cahoots with their enemies in order to trick them (5.63; 5.90; 6.66). In Herodotus' account, the enquirers who make these accusations do not use physical force.

In later texts, the anxiety over falsehood and future transforms into violence upon the prophet. For instance, Strabo records an episode at a different temple, Dodona, in which enquirers killed the prophet. When the warring Boeotians and Pelasgians consulted the oracle, the prophet told the Boeotians that 'they would prosper if they committed sacrilege'. They suspected that the prophet favoured their enemies, so they

> seized the woman and threw her upon a burning pile, for they considered that, whether she had acted falsely or not, they were right . . . since, if she uttered a false oracle, she had her punishment, whereas, if she did not act falsely, they had only obeyed the order of the oracle. (*Geography*, 9.2)

The Boeotians' violence caused the male temple leadership to bring them to trial before the two living priestesses, but the offenders objected to women judging them and requested two men to judge alongside the priestesses. The verdict broke along gender lines: the men voted for acquittal and the women for conviction. The episode shows a struggle between enquirers and temple officials, male and female, over sacrilegious violence and interpretation of oracles.

In an episode recorded by Plutarch, who was a priest at Delphi in the late first century CE, Alexander the Great and the Delphic temple officials similarly struggled over control of the institution. On a day that the oracle was not functioning, Alexander demanded a consultation, and the priestess refused, citing the law as support. Alexander then dragged her into the temple, which caused her to exclaim, 'You are invincible, my son!' He took this statement as his oracle, 'the oracle that he wanted from her' (*Alexander*, 14). This narrative demonstrates the ability of the prophet to refuse enquiries, but the enquirer responded with violence so that he could interpret her words as he wished and nullify any danger introduced by a negative oracle.

So far, the aggressors in these stories have been human, driven by their anxieties over false oracles and their own roles in war. In other episodes, the aggressor is divine. Plutarch records an incident at Delphi in which a man forced the prophet to prophesy, and the god Apollo violently possessed her (*Def. orac.*, 438A–C). For Plutarch, who interprets prophecy through a philosophical lens, the point of the story is the necessity of the proper state of body and soul before an oracular session. Disturbances of the prophet's body 'filter into her soul' (*Def. orac.*, 437D). In this case, the sacrifices before the session did not produce the proper results, which caused the Pythia's reluctance, but the priests forced her into the temple. Her emotional agitation resulted in 'harshness of her voice', erratic movements and death. Plutarch is clear that this is an unusual case: her inspiration was 'misleading, abnormal, and confusing' (438A). Frenzy and erratic responses are not normal, despite the common perception, both ancient and modern, that the prophets experienced 'madness' (*mania*; see Plato, *Phaedr.*, 244A–B). These responses are dangerous because they show that something has gone wrong in the meeting between prophet and god. Divine contact requires caution.

In poetic portrayals of Cassandra, the Sibyl and the Pythia, authors vividly describe the intense inspiration of the god, which reflects the prophet's visions of future danger. In Aeschylus' *Agamemnon*, Cassandra prophesies the murder of Agamemnon and the downfall of his family. Her prophecy occurs in waves that she cannot control and is visual and agonising. She sees violent action unfold (1072–1177), and describes her mental state: 'The pain! The terrible agony of true prophecy is coming over me again and again, whirling me around and deranging me in the fierce storm of its onset' (1215–1217). An intermission in her prophecy occurs, and she tells how she gained prophetic ability from a sexual encounter with Apollo (1202–1213). Apollo 'wrestled' with her and 'breathed delight' (1206), but her refusal of him doomed her to be a prophet who would never be believed.

In the Latin epic tradition, Virgil's *Aeneid* likewise portrays Cassandra as a victim of violence and disbelief. She was 'torn from the sacred depths of Minerva's shrine, dragged by her hair' (2.504–505). Cassandra is followed by another female 'prophet of doom', Calaeno, who shrieks oracles and instils dread in those who hear her (3.295–312). Finally, when the Sibyl guides Aeneas in the underworld, she experiences uncontrolled, violent inspiration. Visible and audible signs mark her possession:

> Suddenly all her features, all her colour changes, her braided hair flies loose, and her breast heaves, her heart bursts with frenzy, she seems to rise in height, the ring of her voice no longer human. (6.46–50)

Virgil portrays inspiration as though Apollo and the Sibyl were a rider and horse. She 'tries to pitch the great god' but 'his bridle exhausts her raving lips' (6.79–80). The god 'whips her on in all her frenzy, twisting his spurs below her breast' (6.100–101).

Another Latin poet, Lucan, in his *Civil War*, owes much to Virgil's Sibyl in his violent portrayal of a Delphic session. In the dark epic about the foundation of the Roman Empire, the general Appius Claudius is afraid of entering the war, so he consults the oracle at Delphi (5.65–70). She is afraid of entering the shrine, because contact with Apollo is damaging: 'the human framework falls apart under the frenzy's goad and surge, and the beatings of the gods shake their brittle lives' (5.116–120). But Appius forces her into the temple, where the god 'mastered her breast and never more completely invaded his priestess' frame, drove out her former mind, and told the mortal part to leave her breast to him entirely' (5.165–169). She 'boils with a mighty fire', and Apollo 'plunges flames into her guts' (5.173–175). She sees a vision of all of time at once, which physically weighs her down (5.177–181). Her initial fear of Apollo was correct: 'the beatings of the gods' caused her death. This most violent story about female prophecy fits firmly into Lucan's view of the Roman civil war: human violence, rather than divine ordination, established the political situation in which Rome found itself.

In these accounts, the god violently possesses the prophet. She experiences internal physical pain in fire and whips, and god driving her out of her body or weighing her down. Prophecy occurs in uncontrollable cycles, compelled by the god. The danger that she faces reflects the danger of her visions and the nature of the prophetic process. Likewise, the danger that prophets encounter at the hands of men reflects their fear of the future and their discomfort in placing their lives and fortunes in the hands of a woman who could be mad, corrupt or simply wrong. At stake in depicting prophecy in these violent terms is the questions of who has control over the prophet and her speech within the fear-ridden situation – the god, the men who interpret the oracles, or the prophet herself.

More reading

Hagedorn, A. C., 2013. The role of the female seer/prophet in ancient Greece. In J. Stökl and C. L. Carvalho, eds, *Prophets Male and Female: Gender and Prophecy in the Hebrew Bible, the Eastern Mediterranean, and the Ancient Near East.* SBL Press, pp. 101–125.

Johnston, S. I., 2008. *Ancient Greek Divination.* Wiley-Blackwell.

Marshall, J. E., 2017. *Women Praying and Prophesying: Gender and Inspired Speech in First Corinthians.* Mohr Siebeck.

WU ZETIAN: SHE, THE EMPEROR

Suria Tei

Suria Tei's work ranges from prose fiction to scripts for screen and stage. She is the author of two novels. The first, *Little Hut of Leaping Fishes* (Picador, 2008), was listed for the inaugural Man Asian Literary Prize and Best Scottish Fiction and won Malaysia's Readers' Choice Award. Her second book, *The Mouse Deer Kingdom* (Picador, 2013), came third in the same award. The short film she wrote the script for, *Night Swimmer*, won Best Short Film at Vendome International Film Festival. She has also published two memoirs: *Unspoken: Living with Mental Illness* (2021) and *The Zen Cat* (2022). Suria came to Scotland in 2002 to study, which led to a doctorate in creative writing and film from the University of Glasgow. She now lives in Glasgow.

The woman, Wu, who has falsely usurped the throne, is by nature obdurate and unyielding, by origin truly obscure . . . With her mouth concealed behind her sleeve, she skilfully slandered other women; with crafty flattery and perverse talents she deluded the ruler. She then usurped the pheasant regalia of empress and entrapped our ruler into an incestuous relationship.

And then with a heart like a serpent and a nature like that of a wolf, she favoured evil sycophants while destroying her loyal and good officials. She has killed her own children, butchered her elder brothers, murdered the ruler, poisoned her mother . . .

The woman in question is Wu Zetian (also named Wu Zhao; 625–705 AD) – of the Tang Dynasty. She is the first and only woman emperor in the history of China. In 690 AD she declared herself 'Emperor' and started a new dynasty – Chou (690–701 AD) – at a time when aristocratic men were the only respected voice in Confucian society, and when, according to philosophers such as Mencius, a 'woman's greatest duty is to produce a son'.

Wu first entered the court as the Emperor Taizong's (599–649 AD) concubine in her early teens and, after his death, was taken by his son and successor, Gaozong (628–683 AD), to become his consort. Wu's rise from concubine to the highest position in one of Chinese history's most splendid periods has created interest not only within academia but also the creative industry. Theatre, films and television dramas depicting different accounts of her life from different perspectives have been developed: some sympathetic, but mostly critical. Today, 1,300 years after her death, Wu remains a controversial figure, dividing opinion among researchers.

Most arguments with regard to Wu, predominantly around her wrongdoings and accomplishments, originate in the exploration of truthfulness and fairness in her portrayal in archival texts. For all the tales associated with Wu, one thing stands out – most comments centre upon an image of a cruel, calculating and shrewd woman. Putting aside dramatic presentations of her in creative media, historical records concerning Wu are dubious. While the former often prioritise audience ratings over truth, the latter largely focus on her 'evil deeds'. This notion is highlighted in the *Cambridge History of China*:

> Everything concerning this remarkable woman is surrounded by doubts, for she stood for everything to which the ideals of the Confucian scholar-official class opposed – feminine interference in public affairs, government by arbitrary personal whim, the deliberate exploitation of factionalism, ruthless personal vendettas, political manipulation in complete disregard of ethics and principles. From the very first the historical record of her reign has been hostile, biased and curiously fragmentary and incomplete. (pp. 244–245)

A lack of unbiased historical documentations of Wu exists. Her historical record is 'incomplete', because historians and critiques were so preoccupied with demonising her that,

> less is known of the details of political life during her half century of dominance than of any comparable period of the Tang. (p. 245)

This phenomenon is suspected to be the result of resentment towards her, for no other reason than her being a woman. My opening quotation, abstracted from a manifesto written by Lo Ping Wang in support of a rebel leader who attempted to ouster Emperor Wu, lists the crimes allegedly committed by Wu in her quest for power and, later, to consolidate her position. Criticism of her was echoed by many during her time, from court officials to the gentry class, and through to the grassroots, whose knowledge of her was shaped by the former two groups. It also represents the traditional view of historians in the past towards Wu. Those historians, undoubtedly, were men of the elite class.

In a society that believed men are superior to women, and that 'a woman's duty is not to control or take charge' (according to Liu Xiang's *Biographies of Exemplary Women*), Wu's control of the state unsettled them. As Yang Lian Sheng, a historian of the twentieth century, pointed out, 'The severity of Confucian injunctions against female rule means she could never be accepted in her position.' While attempting to implement new policies and reformation, Wu had to put in more effort to consolidate her power during her reign.

Those efforts inevitably invited further criticism. Firstly, in order to convince people and to be accepted by them, Wu turned to archaic rituals to demonstrate her temporal power and harmonious relationship with heaven. Religious symbolism and ceremonies were used to legitimise her elevation to Gaozong's empress at the initial stage and, later, her own regime, in the hope of silencing her opponents. Secondly, she was said to have established a secret police force, to maintain surveillance on her enemies. This so-called 'secret secretariat' was in fact a group of scholars employed by Wu,

> to process for the empress memorials addressed to the throne, and to make decisions on the policy which were properly the functions of the chief ministers. (Wang, 1957, p. 977)

Thirdly, it is not difficult to understand that the strong security she set up for self-protection was prompted by constant threats from her many male rivals – the aristocrat court-officials – who continually sought opportunities to dethrone her.

Ironically, for all the criticism against her from Confucian men of her time, it was the system created by them that had prepared Wu for entering the court, thus allowing her the opportunity to open a path for herself.

Born in a family that had a close connection with the imperial court, Wu is said to have been prepared by her father Wu Shihou, a chancellor of the Tang court, to join the emperor's harem. At a time when a woman's greatest achievement was to be married well, to be selected as a concubine would bring pride, status and wealth to a family, and in the case of Wu's clan, a more formidable relationship with the emperor. From a young age, Wu had been specially trained in literary, musical and intellectual skills, which were traditionally exclusive to men. The effort paid off. She was recruited into the palace of the Emperor Taizong at the age of fourteen.

It was also those skills and this knowledge that enchanted the Emperor Taizong. Impressed by Wu's intellectual take on the history of China, the emperor promoted his new favourite from a lowly concubine who took care of the royal laundry, to his secretary. This exposed Wu to state affairs at the highest level.

However, that all ended with the death of the emperor in 649 AD. Abiding by tradition, Wu, as with other wives and concubines of Taizong, was sent to live in a temple as a nun. Stories of how she later became a concubine of Gaozong – the new emperor and Taizong's youngest son – are varied. Some said Wu had begun an incestuous affair with the young prince while under the former emperor's roof. Others described a 'chance encounter' – orchestrated by Wu – in the temple where Wu served her duty as a widow to the emperor, during which Gaozong was struck by her beauty and intelligence, and arranged for her return to the palace. There began Wu's gradual rise to power.

As the third-ranking concubine, Wu is said to have eliminated the empress and the emperor's favourite consort by extremely brutal means, including sacrificing her own newborn daughter and, later, having her two rivals killed.

Now the new empress, Wu, trusted by her husband – who was sickly and weak – became actively involved in state affairs. Shielded by a screen, she would sit with Gaozong in court sessions, and supervise the emperor on matters ranging from the country's most petty to most vital policies. Her political dominance was summed up by the prominent Sung historian, Si Magqian:

> The great power of the empire all devolved on the empress. Promotion and demotion, life or death, were settled by her word. The emperor sat with folded arms.

It was during this period that Wu began to take unprecedented measures to elevate the status of women, who had long been suppressed in the male-dominant Confucian society. Among her efforts were extending the mourning period for a mother to equal that of a father, sending a male 'bride' to the Turks, in opposition to the tradition of sacrificing a woman for political kinship, and raising the positions of her mother's clan by honouring her relatives with high posts in court. Most drastically, Wu defied traditions. This was evident during a rare and complicated ritual, which was vital to lend legitimacy to her status as equal partner to the emperor. She led the first-ever procession of women – consorts and women related to the imperial clan – in a sacred ceremony at the foot of Mount Tai (Taishan). It aimed, symbolically, to be close to heaven, granting divine acceptance. Recent archaeological finds, from murals depicting women riding on horseback, reveal that women of Wu's times had the freedom to travel, assume outdoor activities and become involved in trade, all of which were once exclusive to men.

In addition, while Wu is accused of bringing to an end the literati patronage of Gaozong during the early years of his reign, she sponsored scholars to produce *Lienu Zhuan*, a collection of biographies of famous women in Chinese history. At the same time, a book that amassed a large work of music and rituals, *Yue Shu*, was produced. Buddhism enjoyed state patronage, and later in her reign was made the official religion, resulting in buildings and carvings of images of great aesthetic value and grandeur.

Wu's other achievements include giving opportunities to scholars from non-aristocratic backgrounds to sit the court-official entry examinations and to be recruited based on their talent rather than family connections and background. During Wu's reign in the Chou Dynasty, 40 per cent of non-aristocratic candidates were successful. While some of them were called to court, others served in education and administration at a local level.

Wu's support of the system promoted social and economic mobility, according to the institutional history known as the Tong Dian. This was only one of the many reform programmes established by Wu for the well-being of the lower classes. Others, for example, included tax reductions, bestowing heavy rewards on the elderly, and offering relief to the poor. All these accomplishments were ignored by historians of her period, especially Yuan Shu, whose take on her – a 'calamity' – represents the attitude of traditional historiography towards Wu's rule (Twitchett, 1979, p. 329).

In conclusion, I have no intention to whitewash Wu, as, for whatever reason, brutality of any kind is intolerable, had she committed it. The aim of this chapter is to point out the prejudice of the historians towards a woman who was ahead of her time, unafraid to be anti-Confucianism, and who campaigned for gender and social equalities.

THE OSEBERG BURIALS: WOMEN OF THE VIKING AGE THEN AND NOW

Marianne Moen

Marianne Moen is currently Head of Department of Archaeology at the Museum of Cultural History, University of Oslo. Her research focuses on the interrelationship of past and present from a feminist viewpoint, gender in the Viking Age and modern understandings of the same, the role of violence in Viking Age identities and on mortuary archaeology and expressions of past ways of being and living, amongst other topics. Her PhD explored perceptions of gender relating to the Viking Age, and this article was written in the early stages of that project.

What makes a woman dangerous a thousand years after her death?

How much of a threat can the dead and decayed body of a nameless woman pose?

Judging from the academic treatment of the Viking Age female double burial found at Oseberg in Norway, the answer seems to be quite a substantial one. It is large enough at least to have occasioned an academic discourse about the role of the two buried women in the hundred years since the burial was excavated that tends towards removing the women from positions of political power, and instead places them outside the public sphere. The reasons behind this form a complicated web of biases and prejudice, both conscious and unconscious.

Mention the word 'Vikings' and a score of images spring to mind. The Viking Age has seen sustained interest from academic quarters and popular culture over the last 150 years. Consequently, a great deal is known about the culture and beliefs of the time. However, with this degree of knowledge comes a real danger of assuming the Viking Age to be a known entity. There is a tendency to think of it as a time with values and ideologies closely resembling our own, when instead it was a different world entirely.

Representations of the Viking Age often focus on doughty men who go out and conquer, pillage, trade and settle in foreign parts of the world. These men run, order and lead society, taking care of public speaking, politics and leadership. Women, when discussed at all, are placed in the background. They happily tend the hearth and remain within the boundaries of the home. Or they may feature in stories of male endeavour as a motivating reason for male action. Very occasionally, we encounter a shield maiden, a feisty young girl who almost inevitably eventually gives up her violent ways to settle down as a wife and mother. The Viking Age man can be anything he wants, but the Viking Age woman is usually a housewife, and a content one at that.

Yet a great deal of evidence does not support this image. Both written and archaeological sources show women trading, travelling, fighting and taking on leading roles in religious activities. There is even evidence of women as chieftains. This evidence is not hard to find, nor is it scarce. Nevertheless, scholars of the Viking Age, both historians and archaeologists, often confidently state that women did not lead active public lives and were bound to the homestead, whilst positions of power were nearly invariably held by men. We can still read confident statements to the effect that women were not allowed to carry weapons, nor participate at legal gatherings at the Þing. Such statements are directly contradicted by substantial amounts of written and archaeological evidence, and there is plenty of research which highlights this, but still these ideas somehow remain generally accepted in academic discourse.

We are looking at a real divide here, between the Viking Age as we're told it was, and the Viking Age as it appears in the evidence. This divide naturally begs the question: Why? Why is evidence of powerful women in the Viking Age still downplayed or ignored in modern scholarship?

In order to answer this, I believe we need to look to the naturalisation of modern, Western, gendered value divisions, and how they are justified in part by a belief in their longevity. However, I will first show an example of the different treatments of men and women in academic interpretations of the Viking Age.

It is commonly thought that Viking Age populations used large burial mounds to symbolise status and ownership. When these burials contain ships, they are usually termed chieftains' burials, and used to support theories of local power structures. Much is made of how such burials show the elite's ability to display wealth and influence in order to exert dominance and control – unless, of course, the burial in question is shown to have been constructed for a woman. In such cases, scholars will cast about for alternative explanations that allow them to continue placing women firmly outside the sphere of public power. Where a woman is buried, there is no talk of dominance or power. Women with power, we are made to understand, do not fit the entrenched Eurocentric gendered ordering of society, which the Vikings supposedly shared with us. Thus, female burials are treated differently from male ones, even when they are directly comparable, as the case below illustrates.

In the 1860s, a magnificent ship burial was excavated at Gokstad in Vestfold, Norway. It was covered by a barrow of monumental size, and contained a great wealth of grave goods. Then, in 1904, an even more spectacular find was uncovered at Oseburg, also in Vestfold. The burial at Oseberg was similarly covered by a monumental barrow, and contained grave goods even more wealthy than the burial at Gokstad. The Gokstad burial is nearly always talked about as containing a chieftain; the Oseberg burial, on the other hand, is hardly ever discussed in the same terms. Instead, interpretations range from the women being a religious sacrifice, or that one of them was a young lady sent in marriage from Denmark to a Norwegian chieftain, or that they were ritual specialists, or that one of them was the mother of a well-known (male) Viking, or even that there was a third, male, body in the original burial that has since gone missing. In common to all these different interpretations is that the women themselves are not the main agents, but instead relegated to supporting players in stories about men. The difference between these two burials is of course the gender of the interred. Gokstad contains one man; Oseberg contains two women. Other than this, the burials are comparable in almost every way. The grave goods have more similarities than differences: the ships are both large, seagoing vessels, the barrows are of comparable size, they are placed in comparable locations and are dated to within seventy years of each other. The evidence here speaks very clearly in favour of women with political power, and yet interpretations consistently shy away from this explanation, presumably because it does not fit with what we think we know about women and men in the Viking Age.

If we strip away the 'knowledge' that women did not have political power in the Viking Age, what we're left with is strong evidence that they actually did. Oseberg is, apart from the gender of those buried, comparable to other mounds from the same period (as discussed by Unn Pedersen). The mounds are argued to be an integral part of the political power play at the time. We do not actually know of any reasons why women could not be chieftains in the Viking Age. We just have an assumption that they could not, which has become so firmly fixed as to be upheld even in the face of contradictory evidence.

The logical conclusion to be drawn from Oseberg would be that this is the burial of two women who were likely leaders or chieftains. But this conclusion is not what we see in the prevailing interpretations. As seen above, these explanations tend to try and remove the women from any role of direct power, and place them somewhere where they do not threaten male-dominated power structures. To see the reasons behind this, we need to cast back to the foundations of our current knowledge.

Across Europe, archaeology became a discipline in its own right in the course of the nineteenth century. Ideas about human progress and evolution therefore coloured many early theories. Significantly, Victorian values of gendered divisions of labour were applied to the past without necessarily considering if evidence supported this (Elisabeth Arwill-Nordbladh provides a detailed review). It would have been highly inappropriate for the wives and daughters of scholars of the time to have worked, hunted or fought in battle, and because this morality and gender ideology was seen as natural, these things were equally unthinkable when considering past societies. And so, the Viking Age became a world that shared Victorian ideals of appropriate occupations for men and women, and these ideas have been perpetuated throughout the last 150 years.

Voices of dissent have been raised, pointing out that the evidence doesn't support such a model, as well as saying that we need to stop projecting our own ideology on to the past unquestioningly. Yet, these voices are still in the opposition, struggling to become part of the mainstream academic debate. One must ask the question whether this is because a past that shares the view that women were somehow 'other', always outside of society and never the driving factors of progress and change, is maintained because it justifies social injustices in today's society. Diminishing the importance of women in the past is a useful tool in upholding a social structure that fears and ridicules women in the present. Essentially, if women have always held a secondary role in society, this must be because it is the natural order of things.

Of course, the Oseberg burial was excavated over a century ago. It's not unreasonable to suppose that early theories were coloured by a worldview in which women were not considered adults on a par with men. This is indeed reflected in early scholarship, as can be seen in a publication from 1928 which described the burial as 'naturally limited, as it lacks male artefacts'. Unfortunately, such bias has not been left behind in the distant past, but is instead perpetuated into modern scholarship. For example, in 1995 a theory was put forward that Oseberg was a religious sacrifice. This was a theory influenced by the sex of the interred, since other burials of a comparable nature were not given the same interpretation. In 2005, an article suggested that there was a third, male burial, which has since disappeared without a trace. In 2007, the suggestion was made that the burial was that of a young Danish woman, sent in marriage to a Norwegian chieftain. This final theory builds on the evidence that the ship's timbers originated in Denmark, and that the ship was built some fifteen years before its final depositioning. Setting aside the obvious sexism of the interpretation, which robs the buried women of any agency, this theory also falls short, as the youngest of the women was fifty years old when buried. In other words, she was hardly a young bride.

What we can take away from these examples is a sense that these two powerful women, buried such a long time ago, are still dangerous enough to sustain a need for them to be discounted and discredited by poorly reasoned arguments.

The example of Oseberg shows that there were powerful women in the Viking Age, and that they could wield symbols of power, command resources and be worthy of burials on a monumental scale alongside men. From other sources, we can conjecture that such women were not considered a threat to their male contemporaries. But to modern scholars, such powerful women become dangerous, subversive and threatening. This has resulted in consistent attempts to diminish the role of women and make them less than their male counterparts.

Our problem is not that we don't have evidence of powerful women in the Viking Age. It is instead that such evidence as we do have tends to be distorted to fit in with what scholars seem to feel is appropriate. Is it really so dangerous to allow women a place in prehistory that isn't tied to the kitchen sink? Judging from the treatment of the Oseberg women, it must be. Threatening gendered values and ideologies 1,000 years after their death, they are indeed dangerous women.

More reading

Coleman, N. L. and Løkka, N., 2014. Vikingtidens kvinner i ettertidens lys. *Kvinner i Vikingtid*. Scandinavian Academic Press.

Moen, M., 2019. Challenging gender: A reconsideration of gender in the Viking Age using the mortuary landscape. *IAKH*. University of Oslo.

Pedersen, U., Moen, M. and Skogstrand, L., eds, forthcoming. *Gendering the Nordic Past: Dialogues between Perspectives*. Brepols.

Price, N. S., 2019. *The Viking Way: Magic and Mind in Late Iron Age Scandinavia*. Oxbow.

ST MARGARET OF SCOTLAND: A DANGEROUS SAINT

Claire Harrill

Claire Harrill is a former Lecturer in English at the University of Birmingham, where she specialised in medieval literature. Her research focused on how female power was understood and constructed, taking St Margaret of Scotland as a case study. Claire now works for an educational equalities charity and lives in Wales with her family and cat, Chaucer.

Dangerous women come in unexpected forms. At first glance, St Margaret of Scotland (c. 1045–1093) does not radiate danger. As a pious woman and dutiful queen who had eight children and apparently spent her life in fasting and prayer, Margaret is easy to dismiss as a woman who posed little danger to the male establishment.

However, that is far from the case. Margaret was an English princess, born in exile in Hungary to a son of Edmund Ironside and a woman about whom we know nothing for sure, but her name: Agatha. Margaret returned to England with her family following the death of Edward the Confessor since her father was a potential heir to the throne. However, that throne was famously taken by William the Conqueror, at which point Margaret, her brother Edgar and her sister Christine became very dangerous.

Margaret was, at that point, most likely safely stowed away in an abbey, probably Wilton, far from the opportunity to make a political marriage that could challenge the Conqueror's power. But this wasn't long-lasting. Either Margaret's brother Edgar or the whole family became involved in a Northern English anti-Norman uprising. When this uprising failed, Margaret and her family fled to Scotland where they were welcomed by King Malcolm III, on the condition that Margaret would accept him as her husband.

The arrangement of this marriage is shrouded in mystery and the medieval conventions of writing about saints' lives. Margaret's twelfth-century biographer would have it that Margaret was unwilling, but conceded grudgingly because she knew it would help her family and their supporters. The *Anglo-Saxon Chronicle* tells a different story, in which Margaret's brother refused to agree to the marriage, but Malcolm forced him to comply. According to the medieval chronicle tradition, Malcolm fell deeply in love with Margaret on sight, yet it was still three years from Margaret's arrival to their marriage. What caused this delay? Perhaps it was Margaret's or her brother's reluctance, or perhaps it was the complication that Malcolm was already married. We do not know if this marriage was dissolved, if Malcolm's wife died or if, as plenty of Anglo-Saxon kings had done before him, Malcolm proceeded with two simultaneous wives. We only know that history remembers Margaret in great detail and makes very little mention of Malcolm's first wife, Ingeborg.

When Margaret married Malcolm, she did not just become the wife of the King of Scots. She became the first-ever Queen of Scots. As the last of the Anglo-Saxon royal line, Margaret – or her family – were politically significant enough to demand a place for her as consecrated queen, not just royal bed mate. As Queen of Scots, Margaret posed a very real danger to the new Anglo-Norman dynasty in England. Support for her and her family was strong in the north of England, recently rocked by anti-Norman rebellion as it was, and Margaret's swift and copious production of sons not only secured the place of her and her family in Scotland but also formed an implicit threat to the Conqueror's royal place in the south. Margaret's sons had a strong claim to the English throne as well as the Scottish one, and there was no way for the Conqueror to discredit Margaret without discrediting himself. His own claim to the English throne was based on his relation to Margaret's uncle, Edward the Confessor.

During her time as Queen of Scots, Margaret, most likely in conjunction with Malcolm, reportedly reformed the Scottish Church so that it conformed to Roman practice rather than the practice of the Church of St Columba. Margaret seems, in fact, to have been so insubordinate to native Church authority that a legend arose around the Church of St Laurence. In this legend, Margaret's wicked female body was struck down with horrible pains because she dared enter the aforementioned church, which was only for men. In the legend, Margaret is compelled to beg the church clerics to heal her.

Margaret also reportedly led Malcolm's reform of secular law. One of those she is said to have abolished is a law that allowed the king to be adopted by the rich, old and childless in order to inherit their money. The widespread reports of Margaret's reform (always emphatically undertaken under the aegis of Margaret's adherence to Scripture) also served the political purpose of making Scotland appear religiously and legally unassailable. Under Margaret's influence, her twelfth-century biographer-confessor Turgot of Durham argued, Scotland was no longer an uncivilised backwater. Instead, it was a modern, European, religiously orthodox country ruled by a powerful royal couple and heartily approved of by God himself. If the Conqueror wanted to turn his land-acquiring ambitions to Scotland, he would get no approval from the Church.

Of course, our surviving picture of Margaret is coloured by the political concerns of her day, but even so, it seems likely that Margaret was an influential queen. If she did not manage the reforms herself, she appears to have worked cooperatively with her husband in order to bolster Scotland's place on the European political stage. Her two most politically active children, her son who later became David I and her daughter Matilda who married Henry I of England, also consciously followed her example in their own negotiations of royal power, and both were powerful and influential monarchs. They are both often compared with or likened to their mother in literary and chronicle works, perhaps as a way of seeking or confirming the legitimacy of their power.

But Margaret's enduring danger is borne out in the texts written about her, each of which seeks to co-opt her into a political cause. In the eleventh century, that was the attempt to preserve the Anglo-Saxon royal line the face of the Norman Conquest. In the twelfth and thirteenth centuries, Margaret was used in England to protect the dubious royal position of her daughter, who, some claimed, had run away from the life of a nun to marry Henry I. Similarly, Margaret had to protect the place of her sons as Kings of Scots in a hotly contested succession.

Margaret is described as a saint almost from the moment she dies. Yet, in the years following her death, it is her political role as queen, not her religious role as saint, that draws the attention of the writers who use her potentially dangerous icon for political ends. By the fifteenth century, the Scottish chronicler Walter Bower deployed Margaret in his nationalist history, the *Scotichronicon*, as a kind of hybrid between the Virgin Mary and Scotland's mythical foundress, the Egyptian princess Scota. She was portrayed as a figure who combined a real connection to the earth and the people of Scotland with an unassailable and Church-sanctioned divine right not only to the Scottish throne but to Scottish political independence. It was in Margaret's dual identity, as English princess and Scottish queen, that her potential danger and usefulness lay. But Margaret was not just a potent political symbol. Her life suggests that she was also a real political actor.

Margaret of Scotland was a dangerous woman. That danger might have been cloaked in a seemly veil of obedience to Scripture and divine duty, but Margaret not only embodied the threat of the Anglo-Saxon royal line to Anglo-Norman power in England, she also made a real material difference to the Scottish royal line in the Middle Ages. Of course, many historians dismiss this as nothing more than her motherhood, nothing more than the addition of royal blood and the idea that her sons might be heirs to England as well. However, it seems more likely to me that the various reports of Margaret's real political impact on Scotland are based in some kind of truth. Margaret (most likely in conjunction with Malcolm) managed what few other medieval women have ever managed. She managed to wield real power and take political action, yet to come out of it with a glowing posthumous report. And are they not twice as dangerous, those who can do as they please while persuading others that they have acted only for everyone's else's good?

More reading

Earenfight, T., 2013. *Queenship in Medieval Europe*. Palgrave Macmillan.

Gameson, R., 1997. The Gospels of Margaret of Scotland and the literacy of an eleventh-century queen. In L. Smith and J. H. M. Taylor, eds, *Women and the Book: Assessing the Visual Evidence*. British Library and University of Toronto Press, pp. 149–171.

Groag Bell, S., 1988. Medieval women book owners: Arbiters of lay piety and ambassadors of culture. In M. Erler and M. Kowaleski, eds, *Women and Power in the Middle Ages*. University of Georgia Press, pp. 149–187.

Harrill, C. L., 2016. 'Ego Sum Margarita, Olim Scotorum Regina': St Margaret and the idea of the Scottish nation in Walter Bower's *Scotichronicon*. *Medievalia et Humanistica*, 41, pp. 65–79.

Harrill, C. L., 2023. Mater Sanctissima: Sanctity and motherhood in the Miracula of St Margaret of Scotland. In J. P. Pazdzoria, ed., *Christianity in Scottish Literature*. Scottish Literature International, pp. 16 –34.

Huneycutt, L. L., 1989. The idea of the perfect princess: The life of St Margaret in the reign of Matilda II (1100–1118). *Anglo-Norman Studies*, 12, pp. 81–97.

Keene, C., 2013. *Saint Margaret, Queen of the Scots: A Life in Perspective*. Palgrave Macmillan.

THE EMPRESS MATILDA:
LADY OF THE ENGLISH

Lucy Flannery

Lucy Flannery is an award-winning writer who works in radio, theatre, film, TV, fiction and non-fiction. Credits include *A Business Affair* (with Christopher Walken), *Like a Daughter* (with Alison Steadman), *The Story of Tracey Beaker*, *Tomorrow Will Be Too Late* and *Poisoned Beds*. Her radio sitcoms *Rent* and *Any Other Business* are regularly broadcast on BBC Radio 4 Extra. Lucy was the creator of the Havant Literary Festival and 2020 Writer-in-Residence at the University of Plymouth. She currently teaches playwriting at Chichester Festival Theatre and is a member of the Writer's Guild of Great Britain Audio Committee.

Great by birth, greater by marriage, greatest in her offspring – here lies the daughter, wife and mother of Henry.

What a miserable epitaph for one of the bravest, strongest, toughest, most resourceful and most uncompromising women of the twelfth century – the Empress Matilda, Lady of the English.

Henry I, the youngest son of William the Conqueror, had over twenty children but only two of them were legitimate – the twins William and Matilda. William was his heir to both the throne of England and the Dukedom of Normandy, but for his daughter he negotiated a splendid match. At the age of nine, she became the wife of the future Holy Roman Emperor, Henry V.

Matilda, who is also known by the Norman Mahaut or the Anglicised Maud or Maude, completed her education at her husband's court, acquiring regnal, military and diplomatic skills in abundance. However, there was no issue from this first marriage and, after Henry's death in 1125, no role for her at the German court either. Recalled to her father's side at Rouen, the twenty-five-year-old Matilda was appalled to find herself betrothed to Geoffrey, son of the Comte d'Anjou. The woman, who had been an Empress and acted as her husband's Regent in Italy, was now ordered to marry a callow seventeen-year-old. Henry I squandered his daughter's formidable gifts in an attempt to secure the south-east boundaries of the Duchy of Normandy and subdue the often disloyal Fulk of Anjou. It was a massive error of judgement by him and one which was to have repercussions for all his subjects.

Matilda's brother William drowned on the *White Ship* in 1120. After the deaths of his son and his first wife, Henry remarried, confident of producing more children. But the longed-for boy did not materialise, leaving Matilda as his only legitimate heir. Spotting the danger a little late, Henry gathered his court together and forced them to swear allegiance to his daughter. Although the nobles went through the motions, they weren't really about to allow themselves to be governed by an upstart count like Anjou. Nobody even countenanced the notion of Matilda actually ruling in her own right.

In 1134, Henry I died, famously, of a surfeit of lampreys and his nephew, Stephen of Blois, hurriedly crossed the Channel, secured the backing of the Church and seized the throne for himself. Matilda, pregnant in Anjou with her second son, was powerless to act. And that might very well have been that if it hadn't been for one thing: the character of the Empress Matilda herself.

Five years later, this most dangerous of women crossed the Channel at the head of a force that included her redoubtable half-brother, Robert of Gloucester. Leaving behind her husband Geoffrey, now Comte d'Anjou, to capture Normandy, she enlisted the support of a number of English nobles and that of her uncle, David I of Scotland, and began a campaign against her usurping cousin.

This vicious but relatively unknown civil war raged for eighteen years. The *Anglo-Saxon Chronicle* described it as a time when 'Christ and his saints slept'. The peasants bore the brunt of the damage caused by the interminable hostilities. Apart from the deaths sustained in battle, there were frequent famines caused by the destruction of crops and stock to prevent them falling into enemy hands. This was one of the grimmest periods of the entire Middle Ages, surpassed only by the plague-ridden fourteenth century and the bloodshed of the Wars of the Roses.

In 1141, Matilda's forces won a brilliant victory at Lincoln, capturing King Stephen. Now effective monarch, Matilda entered London in triumph and began planning her coronation at Westminster. But it was not to be. The City of London would not accept her and rose up in revolt, citing her arrogance and inflexibility. They also did not take kindly to the tax that Matilda proposed to levy upon them to bolster the royal revenues, sadly depleted after years of plunder as Stephen's war chest. Matilda and her retinue had no choice but to flee for their lives.

This wasn't the only time she escaped by the skin of her teeth. An uprising in Winchester led by Stephen's queen resulted in the Empress having to retreat to Devizes. Her brother Robert was captured in a desperate battle, fought as a decoy to divert attention away from her flight. Matilda agreed to free Stephen in exchange for his return. The advantage was lost but the war was far from over.

Her most astonishing exploit was at Oxford. Robert returned briefly to Normandy to render support to Geoffrey, who demanded this aid as the price for his continuing fealty. Taking advantage of his absence, Stephen managed to surround Matilda's castle. Recognising its near-impregnability, he settled in for a long winter siege. The weather favoured him, soon turning to icy conditions. The snow lay deep around the castle, a vivid glistening backdrop to the relentless blockade.

Just before Christmas, Matilda ordered white habits to be sewn for herself and a handful of companions. Her servants were distressed as they looked like winding sheets. The Empress and her liegemen wore the white-hooded garments over their normal clothes as they escaped – some accounts say via the postern gate, some claim they were lowered from a window into the town. Camouflaged against the snow, they galloped away with Matilda riding astride for the first time in her life. A blizzard overtook them but still they carried on to Wallingford, a distance of some fifteen miles. It was an extraordinary achievement.

Following the death of her brother, never beaten but never wholly victorious, Matilda finally relinquished her claim to the throne in favour of that of her eldest son, Henry. She left England in 1148 following astute negotiations with the Bishop of Winchester that ensured that King Stephen recognised Henry as his official heir. After Stephen's unexpected and sudden death, her diplomatic and administrative skills were fully exploited once more when she regularly acted as her son's Regent in Normandy. Henry II was the founder of the Plantagenet dynasty and was a strikingly powerful monarch in his own lifetime, controlling an enormous territory which included England, Ireland, Wales, Normandy, Brittany and Aquitaine.

Matilda never set foot in England again.

Her strength of character, uncompromising pride and single-mindedness – those same qualities that made her father, grandfather and son outstandingly successful – made Matilda unnatural, shrewish and a harridan. Even her financial acumen was turned into a weapon against her. But despite the disappointments and betrayals she was forced to weather, her legacy is enduring. Thanks to her skill and shrewdness in securing the succession for her son, her dynasty ruled unopposed for centuries. It may have taken 400 years before England saw a female monarch, Mary I, governing in her own right, but five years later, Mary's half-sister Elizabeth was crowned queen. And so began a Tudor reign that, partly due to those same characteristics of strength of mind and determination displayed by the Empress Matilda, plus a shared ability to command unwavering loyalty from fiercely intelligent men, is still looked upon as one of the most successful in British history. Her great-to-the-power-of-eleven-grandmother would have been proud.

More reading

Follett, K., 1989. *The Pillars of the Earth.* William Morrow & Co.
Hanley, C., 2019. *Matilda: Empress, Queen, Warrior.* Yale University Press.

MARGUERITE PORETE: FAKE WOMAN AND DANGEROUS MYSTIC

Laura Moncion

Laura Moncion received her PhD from the University of Toronto. She reads and writes in Canada, the USA and Germany.

Sometimes, being a dangerous woman means doing what men do freely but being harshly punished for it. In the fourteenth century, Marguerite Porete did so by writing a mystical text that pushed the boundaries of the human, challenged ecclesiastical authorities, and would eventually cost her her life.

Not much is known about Marguerite's early life, except that she was from the region of Valenciennes in what is now Belgium, and was likely a beguine, pursuing a type of non-cloistered religious life that was popular among women in late medieval Europe. Porete is best remembered, however, as the author of the *Mirror of Simple Souls* (*Mirouer des simples ames anienties*), written near the end of the thirteenth century. The *Mirror* is a mystical text structured as a dialogue between the personified figures of Love and Reason. Reason asks Love a series of questions about the soul's journey to unite with God.

Reason's nit-picking enquiries and Love's simple, swooping answers allow Marguerite to both answer questions that the reader might have and establish the authority of Love over Reason. This type of dialogue is a fairly common trope in didactic medieval religious texts; where the *Mirror* becomes mystical is in Love's answers. Through the person of Love, Marguerite explores the idea of total annihilation of the self in mystical union. At the peak of the mystical experience, according to the *Mirror*, the mystic can cease to exist and become instead a piece of God.

This is the key to the spiritual anarchy that laces all mystical texts: the idea that a person can experience the divine while still alive. This is the claim that calls into question the limits of what humans can know and what they can be.

Marguerite's text claims that humans can become God by unbecoming themselves. By stripping away human anxieties, ambitions and that bugbear of medieval theology, the human will, a person can cease to be a person and can actually become the divine – for a few moments only – before being plopped back into their earthly body. The *Mirror* describes the human becoming lost in God as a river flowing into and getting lost in the sea. This claim to having not only known but been a part of the divine gives Marguerite the spiritual authority to write her text.

It also gives her the spiritual authority to reject other sources of authority – namely, the Church. She refers to the medieval Church as 'Holy Church the Little', subordinate to 'Holy Church the Great', which is made up of those mystics who have had contact with God's divine eternity. While Holy Church the Great is the domain of Love, Holy Church the Little is ruled over by Reason – that same Reason who 'leaps to conclusions and neglects the sweet kernel of meaning'. By extension, Marguerite's personal, affective experience of God has greater authority than Church doctrine.

This all sounds very dangerous – and it is – but Marguerite was not the only one writing about such sublimation of the self in the 1300s, nor was she the only one questioning Church doctrine. Meister Eckhart, a male German theologian writing at the same time as Marguerite, preached very similar ideas to his followers. In fact, there is reason to believe that Eckhart was influenced by Marguerite's *Mirror*, or vice versa. Eckhart's Sermon 52 advises those who desire the spiritual path to make themselves so 'poor in spirit' that they cease to exist and become one with God. In the same sermon he challenges the Church's authority, and the idea that the best way of reaching divine illumination is through reason.

Marguerite's and Eckhart's ideas are very similar and similarly dangerous – but they were treated very differently. Although they walked the same spiritual tightrope, and were both under suspicion for most of their lives, Marguerite paid for it with her life. Sometime between 1296 and 1306, the Bishop of Cambrai declared the *Mirror* heretical and had copies of it burned in the public square of Valenciennes. Marguerite caught wind of this and objected. She sent the *Mirror* to three other theological authorities for approval. Even though they all agreed that the *Mirror* was technically orthodox, Marguerite and her book were brought before the papal general inquisitor of France, the king's confessor, William of Paris. She was eventually found guilty of being a 'relapsed heretic', and burned on 1 June 1310 in the Place de Grève in Paris.

There are a couple of reasons why the inquisition made Marguerite pay with her life for a book that clearly could have been considered orthodox. First, the inquisition examined the *Mirror* in its standard way, by extracting sections from the text and having theologians assess these snippets for theological correctness. When read in this way, bits of the

Mirror that seem to mock or denigrate Reason taken out of context can make the whole text seem like a rant against the Church's authority, or a spiritual programme intending to dismantle Holy Church the Little.

Marguerite also lacked the institutional protection that saved Meister Eckhart when he was later put on the spot for his writings. Marguerite had likely begun her religious life as a beguine. She would have lived in a communal dwelling with other women devoted to a life of prayer and service, but not necessarily having taken formal vows of poverty or chastity. Beguines were often associated with local parishes and received the sacraments from local priests, but beguines were not formally regulated or administrated by the Church. These women lived dangerously independent lives, not directly ruled by a male authority. Their way of life sometimes appeared as tenuously orthodox as Marguerite's *Mirror*.

By the time the *Mirror* was put on trial, it seems that Marguerite had gone rogue even from her group of beguines. She did not have a male confessor to advocate for her, which had saved other women mystics who had previously come under scrutiny. At the trial, allegedly she neither defended nor recanted her *Mirror*, but sat in silence as the twenty-one theologians of the inquisition argued. Buoyed by her conviction in her right to live her life and conduct her religion as she saw fit, Marguerite refused to submit to the Church's idea of what proper female piety should be. A man like Meister Eckhart could just about get away with this kind of spiritual anarchy; for a woman, the stakes were much higher. Her transgression was so much linked to her gender that the inquisitors called her 'pseudo-mulier' – fake woman.

The inquisition found Marguerite guilty of being a dangerous woman, a heretic in both religion and gender. Women today still run the risk of being labelled 'pseudo-mulier' in a number of situations. In a boardroom, women who speak up are called bossy and mannish. In the media, female politicians are critiqued on their clothing or personal life while male politicians are questioned on their policies. As well as having their gender identity called into question, women are consistently under-recognised or even punished for doing the same work as men. In almost every country, women are paid less than men of the same group for the same type and the same amount of work. Marguerite, although she lived and died in a world much different from our own, is one of a long line of dangerous women that extends into the present day – women who stare down inquisitions, women who refuse to allow their inner and outer lives to be regulated by patriarchal logic.

More reading

Carson, Anne, 2005. *Decreation: Poetry, Essays, Opera*. Knopf.

Grundmann, H., 1995. *Religious Movements in the Middle Ages*. Trans. Steven Rowan. University of Notre Dame Press.

Kocher, S., 2008. *Allegories of Love in Marguerite Porete's* Mirror of Simple Souls. Brepols Publishers.

McGinn, B., 2001. *The Mystical Thought of Meister Eckhart: The Man From Whom God Hid Nothing*. Crossroad.

Porete, M., 1993. *The Mirror of Simple Souls*. Ed. E. L. Babinsky. Paulist Press.

Terry, W. R. and Stauffer, R., eds, 2017. *A Companion to Marguerite Porete and the Mirror of Simple Souls*. Brill.

Trombley, J. L., 2023. *A Diabolical Voice: Heresy and the Reception of the Latin Mirror of Simple Souls in Late Medieval Europe*. Cornell University Press.

ANNE ASKEW: RE-FORMING DANGEROUS WOMEN

Debapriya Basu

Debapriya Basu is Associate Professor in English in the Department of
Humanities and Social Sciences, Indian Institute of Technology, Guwahati,
India. Her doctoral research (jointly funded by a Government of India
University Grants Commission Research Fellowship and an Inlaks
Research Travel Grant to King's College London) was on Renaissance
English women poets. She teaches classical and Renaissance drama,
digital humanities, and detective fiction. Her academic interests are
scholarly editing and bibliographical studies, digital archiving, and early
modern English women's writing. Her recent publications include an essay
titled 'Here doth shee mourne: Epitaphic Compulsion in Isabella Whitney's
Lament upon William Gruffith's Death' in *Women's Writing* in 2024. Her
online edition of *Anne Askew* (work in progress) was initially funded by an
Erasmus Mundus Postdoctoral Fellowship (2014–2015) and is hosted by the
University of Amsterdam.

The sixteenth-century gospeller and female preacher Anne Askew lived a
dangerous life in dangerous times and was made to pay the ultimate price
for her headstrong will. She was a contemporary of Anne Boleyn, who
died a short decade before her. But unlike the most unfortunate of Henry
VIII's queens, Askew's death has largely been forgotten by the modern
world. She was a remarkable woman, passionate about her faith and rashly
courageous in proclaiming it in a world fraught with religious dissent and
state-sanctioned violence. Her quiet radical Protestantism so disturbed
both the monarchical government and the English Church that she had
to be turned into an example and a spectacle. She was repeatedly
imprisoned, illegally tortured in the Tower of London because she would
not betray her reformist sisters, and burnt at the stake for heresy in 1546.

Her life, although sparsely documented, is fascinating. But her life
beyond death is even more compelling. While in prison, she was persuaded by her co-religionists to write an account of her interrogations,
and bear testimony to the hitherto unheard-of and grossly illegal racking of a woman of gentle birth. After her death, her life and her words
were appropriated by two firebrand reformers: the martyrologist John

Foxe (he of the *Book of Martyrs* of 1563 fame) and John Bale (known to modern readers primarily as the writer of the earliest extant verse play in English, *Kynge Johan*, c. 1538). Barely were her ashes cold when the first-person account of Askew's trials was published with copious glosses and fire-and-brimstone editorial rhetoric by Bale in two books titled *The First Examination of Anne Askew* (1546) and *The Latter Examination of Anne Askew* (1547). These unique testimonies of a female martyr sold so well that several editions were printed throughout the century. Almost two decades later, Foxe printed Askew's words without Bale's commentary. But he too added interpolations and concluding remarks describing the site of her burning at Smithfield and intensified the emotional impact of his retelling with a powerful woodcut illustration. In one of the frequent ironies of history, these masculine textual manipulations of the dangerously wilful twenty-five-year-old Anne turned her into the last word in persecuted Protestant victimhood.

Anne Askew was born in Lincolnshire in 1521 to Sir William Askew and Elizabeth Wrottesley. Sir William was knighted in 1513 and became high sheriff of Lincolnshire around the time of Anne's birth. Her brother Edward was Henry VII's cup-bearer, her half-brother Christopher was gentleman of the privy chamber, and her sister Anne married a lawyer in the employ of the Duke of Suffolk. If not demonstrably reformist, her family background was therefore privileged gentry with close connections to the court. It is generally accepted that Anne received a good education, possibly from tutors. She married Thomas Kyme, only to seek divorce, startlingly, on grounds of scriptural incompatibility. Responding to the mention of 'mastre kyme' in Askew's account of her examination before the king's council at Greenwich in *The Latter Examination*, Bale is inspired to provide an account (derived from unnamed sources) of her marriage. According to him, Askew's father had negotiated for a match between his eldest daughter Martha and a rich neighbour's son, the said Thomas Kyme. Unfortunately, Martha died before the marriage could take place and Sir William forced Anne to marry Thomas against her will. Bale describes her union with Kyme as 'ungodly,' 'unlawful' and 'coacted' or coerced. He nevertheless notes that she despatched her wifely duties in a Christian manner and had two children but, 'In processe of tyme by oft readynge of the sacred Bible' she converted to Protestantism.

Askew's love for non-conformist and risky behaviour is witnessed by the corroborative record, independent of Bale, of Askew's examination in the Privy Council. The proceedings show that on 19 June 1546 one Thomas Kyme appeared in court with his wife, but she is said to have refused to acknowledge him as her husband. This subversive behaviour is looked at askance by the Council, which lets Kyme go but detains Anne because

> she was obstinate and heady in reasoning of matters of religion, wherein she showed herself to be of naughty opinion . . .

As though issuing a gentle rebuke and not a rigorous punishment, the recorder sighs,

> seeing no persuasion of good reason could take place, she was sent to Newgate, to remain there to answer to the law.

Askew's headstrong and confrontational personality, which Bale does his best to suppress by shifting the focus onto the alleged wrongs committed by father and husband, is evident from her own words too. She often states that she refused to answer questions put to her by her inquisitors. When she is told that the priests of Lincoln would 'assault me and put me to great trouble', she 'not being afraid' made it a point to go there 'to see what would be said unto me'. For six days she sat reading the Bible in Lincoln Minster in what amounted to an act of civil disobedience, openly flouting the legislation of the Act for the Advancement of True Religion (1543).

After having forced all churches to keep a copy of the 'chained' Great Bible on the premises, Henry VIII had sought to regain lost control through this Act by restricting 'women, artificers, apprentices, journeymen, serving-men of the rank of yeoman and under, husbandmen and laborers' from reading it. In an added clause, women of the gentry were allowed to read the Bible, but only in private. Askew's public performance in Lincoln Minster was surely sufficient for her to be noted among the lay preachers who disseminated 'pestiferous and noisome teachings and instructions' in underground churches and heretical conventicles and against whom this Act was ultimately directed. Indeed, the Queen herself was not immune to charges of heresy, as John Foxe recounts in his *Acts and Monuments*. In the summer of the same year that Askew was to die, a warrant for Queen Catherine Parr's arrest for Protestant sympathies was issued by two of Askew's interrogators Stephen Gardiner, the Bishop of Winchester, and Lord Chancellor Wriothesley. Although the crisis was avoided and Catherine became famous in history as the one who survived marriage to Henry VIII, this fraught atmosphere at court rendered Anne Askew's connections to the Duchess of Suffolk and other Protestant women a strong vulnerability in the face of her unconventionally expressed Protestant beliefs.

The process of Askew's condemnation and burning was instigated with an interrogation (leading to twelve days imprisonment in the Counter) at Saddler's Hall by the Lord Mayor of London and the Bishop of London's chancellor, Edmund Bonner, under the *Act of Six Articles* (1539). The first article of this Act concerned the Eucharist, which was a deeply controversial issue at the time. The Six Articles Act adopted the Catholic position in the debate, asserting that 'the natural body and blood of our Saviour Jesus Christ' is present 'really' in the bread and wine consecrated by the words uttered by a priest. It went on to claim that 'after the consecration there remaineth no substance of bread or wine, nor any other substance, but the substance of Christ, God and man'. Dissent in this matter was heresy and those who did not agree would

> suffer judgment, execution, pain, and pains of death by way of burning, without any abjuration, clergy, or sanctuary to be therefore permitted.

Askew strongly defies this injunction in her writing. 'I believe [the Eucharist] to be a most necessary remembrance of his glorious sufferings and death', she declares confidently as she invokes the words of the Bible, that other kind of powerful word accessible to the laity thanks to the Reformation. Her arguments and rejoinders, which together slant into the dangerous area of women's preaching, are firmly based upon the Protestant tenet of *sola scriptura*: if it is not in Scripture, it is not under discussion. Her memory is remarkably retentive and, in a cryptic style that is succinct and spare, she throws biblical chapter citations in her interrogators' teeth without deigning to quote or explicate. Her writing shows remarkable stylistic control, reconciling the reformist value of plain speaking with a highly evolved sense of drama and rhetorical impact. The description of her racking is almost poetic in the way in which economy of expression is balanced with depth of feeling:

> Then they did put me on the rack, because I confessed no ladies nor gentlewomen to be of my opinion, and thereon they kept me a long time. And because I lay still and did not cry, my lord Chancellor and master Rich took pains to rack me their own hands, till I was nigh dead.

Askew's pointed silences, however, are defused by Bale's clamour. Not for nothing was he nicknamed 'bilious Bale' by his contemporaries. Where she remains silent in irony or for dramatic effect, he senses a dangerously powerful statement that must be defused with quotation and, sometimes, bitter and personal abuse. Foxe's strategy in reforming Askew is slightly different. After presenting Askew's account with minimum intervention, he pens a moving eyewitness account of the scene of her execution, pointing out the martyr's youth and beauty and milking the tragedy and pathos of the moment for his own partisan purposes. This, along with the woodcut, historicises Askew completely, turning her into just another model of female virtue whose life was to be emulated by female Protestants of his day. The other camp in the war of religion, however, was vocal about the threat posed by obstreperous women like Anne Askew. The Jesuit Robert Parsons, for instance, wrote a vitriolic diatribe in 1640, challenging her inclusion in Foxe's *Calendar of Martyrs*. He calls Anne 'a yong heaffer [heifer] or steere that abideth no yoke . . . a coy dame, and of very evill wantonnesse' for leaving her husband and taking upon herself 'to gad up and downe the country a ghospelling and ghossipinge'.

Harassment, arraignment, imprisonment, unthinkable torture and painful death notwithstanding, Anne Askew's words and recorded actions give the lie to her portrayal by her male co-religionists as the last word in victimhood. Reading Bale's commentary now, it is glaringly obvious that his constant and unrelenting interventions subtly mould the impact of Anne's own voice, and the way in which both he, and later Foxe, portray the dead girl tries to diffuse a lot of the tensions that her very unconventional life choices had the potential to generate. Bale upholds her as a mascot of subversion in his own fight against religious hegemony but paradoxically tries to erase those aspects of her personality that pose challenges to the patriarchal order. While the authorities turned Askew into one kind of spectacle, her male co-religionists as well as their religious opponents turned her into another. This is usually the way in which masculine authority seeks to control and contain the unruly energies unleashed by dangerous women who cannot, for historical, strategic or personal reasons, simply be ignored.

Bale's rhetoric reveals once more the fact that subversion is not necessarily coterminous with radicalism. Askew was undoubtedly as deeply religious, as thoroughly virtuous, and as godly as Bale and Foxe would have her be. But she was also arrogant, reckless, brilliant, a poet and a writer, and a woman on a mission. As her texts make clear, her death was the result of a series of informed choices. Anne Askew intentionally challenged the established order with the only weapon a woman in her time and circumstances could effectively wield. She used her religion to acquire power, which both endangered her and made her dangerous. By reforming Askew in the image of the helpless victim of state cruelty both Bale and Foxe silently acknowledge her power and disruptive potential as a dangerous woman.

More reading

Coles, K. A., 2008. *Religion, Reform, and Women's Writing in Early Modern England*. Cambridge University Press.

Hickerson, M. L., 2005. *Making Women Martyrs in Tudor England*. Springer.

Highley, C. and King, J. N., eds, 2017. *John Foxe and His World*. Taylor & Francis.

Kennedy, G., 2000. *Just Anger: Representing Women's Anger in Early Modern England*. SIU Press.

Pender, P., 2012. *Early Modern Women's Writing and the Rhetoric of Modesty*. Springer.

The Religious Tract Society, n.d., 1831, 1836, 1840, 186[?]. *Writings of Edward the Sixth, William Hugh, Queen Catherine Parr, Anne Askew, Lady Jane Grey, Hamilton and Balnaves*. Republished in *British Reformers*. Presbyterian Board of Publication, 1842, volume 3.

Watt, D., 1997. *Secretaries of God: Women Prophets in Late Medieval and Early Modern England*. Boydell & Brewer.

Wilson, D., 2018. *The Queen and the Heretic: How Two Women Changed the Religion of England*. Lion Books.

THE WOMEN OF THE PENDLE WITCH TRIALS: 'WHORES AND WITCHES'

Sarah L. King

Sarah L. King is a writer living in West Lothian, Scotland with her husband and children. A childhood spent in Lancashire listening to stories of the notorious Pendle witches inspired an interest in the history of witchcraft, leading her to complete her undergraduate dissertation on the subject at Lancaster University in 2006. She is the author of a historical fiction trilogy about the Pendle witches: *The Gisburn Witch*, *A Woman Named Sellers*, and *The Pendle Witch Girl*. Sarah also writes historical romance as Sadie King.

'Get out of my ground, whores and witches, I will burn one of you, and hang the other!' Richard Baldwin, a miller, is reputed to have called out to some unwelcome visitors to his mill-house. In his account of the trials, the court clerk Thomas Potts tells us that the subjects of his angry words were Elizabeth Southerns, alias Old Demdike, an old woman of around eighty years, and her granddaughter, Alizon Device.

'Revenge thee either of him, or his', the aged woman uttered in reply. Potts tells us that she later confessed that these words were spoken to a familiar spirit named Tibb.

Shortly after this angry exchange the miller's daughter fell ill, and a year later she died. In 1612, Elizabeth Southerns, her granddaughter and countless others in the Forest of Pendle found themselves accused of witchcraft. By the summer of the same year, Elizabeth Southerns had died in prison, while her daughter and two of her grandchildren had been sent to the gallows.

Academic study of the history of witchcraft accusations has already painted a vivid picture of the sorts of women who were vulnerable to the cry of 'witch!' For example, it is those who were impoverished and living on the edges of their community, those who practised folk medicine, and those who were widowed. Such women were often regarded as suspicious, malevolent and dangerous.

However, the miller's choice of words, his furious blending of insults which suggest both sexual promiscuity and devilish practices, underscore a theme that is prevalent throughout the story of the Pendle Witch

Trials in 1612. His association of these two words, although doubtlessly uttered angrily and in the heat of the moment, nonetheless betrays a psychological link between two forms of unacceptable and threatening behaviour.

It is an unsurprising find. After all, even nowadays the language used to characterise feminine seductive behaviour is often intrinsically linked to witchcraft. If a woman is considered attractive and charming then she is also bewitching, beguiling and capable of putting men under her spell. In modern Western culture, such language might seem whimsical or, at the very worst, irritatingly objectifying. However, a closer examination of some of the women caught up in the 1612 trials reveals that in the early modern period perceptions of their sexual behaviour were used to both ridicule and condemn them, contributing to the idea that these women posed a danger to their communities.

One of the 'whores' to whom Richard Baldwin referred was probably Elizabeth Southerns. We know from Potts' account of the trial that she had two children – a daughter, Elizabeth Device, and a son called Christopher Holgate – and that by 1612 Elizabeth was an elderly widow. In his research into Elizabeth Southerns' family history, John A. Clayton suggests the possibility that her elder child, Christopher, was born out of wedlock prior to her marriage to Thomas Ingham in 1563. If this was the case, this would have been well known around the small communities of Pendle; a source of gossip at the time and for many years to come, recalled easily to mind as it was by the miller during that angry exchange.

To the further detriment of the family reputation, her daughter Elizabeth Device appears to have followed suit. As John A. Clayton has outlined, Elizabeth married John Device in 1590, and together they had three children; James, Alizon, and Henry, the last of whom died in childhood. John Device seems to have died in 1600 and, in the same year, Elizabeth gave birth to another daughter, Jennet. Whilst it is mathematically possible for Jennet to have been John's child, it does seem more likely that the child was the product of an extra-marital affair. Certainly, this seems to have been the prevalent belief amongst their neighbours. In Potts' account of the trial we are told that when questioned by the local Justice of the Peace, Roger Nowell, in spring 1612, Elizabeth confessed that she had bewitched John Robinson to death because 'the said Robinson had chidden and becalled [her] for having a bastard-child with one Seller'.

In 1612, mother, daughter and grandchildren lived together in an isolated cottage, teetering on the edge of dire poverty, a substantial part of their small income coming from begging. Through the insults and mockery levelled at them by their neighbours, we see a picture emerging of an undesirable family, and the emphasis placed upon their sexual morality plays a significant part in this. If they were so morally bankrupt that they would lie with men outside of marriage and bear illegitimate children, what else were they capable of? How exactly did they ensnare these men? Was it simply their feminine wiles or something more malign? We can imagine the gossiping tongues wagging.

Another pertinent example of how this underlying concern with improper sexual conduct played a role in the 1612 trials is found in the case against Jennet Preston. Jennet lived in Gisburn, now in Lancashire but at the time in Craven, Yorkshire. As a result, she was tried separately from the other so-called witches, her trial taking place in York a month before the Assizes in Lancaster.

Jennet was accused of bewitching to death Master Thomas Lister, a gentleman of Westby Hall, Gisburn, and of plotting to kill Master Lister's son and brother, to which end she was alleged to have enlisted the help of her friends, the Devices. She was found guilty and hanged at Knavesmire, York in July 1612.

Unlike Elizabeth Southerns and Elizabeth Device, there are no examples of Jennet being mocked or ostracised by her community for her sexual conduct. There are no accusations of bearing illegitimate children or having illicit affairs. Nonetheless, a careful read between the lines of the court transcripts paints a picture of the undesirable, even dangerous behaviour that probably contributed to Jennet's downfall.

The court clerk, Thomas Potts, takes great pains to stress that Jennet 'was for many years well thought of and esteemed by Master Lister' and 'had access to his house, kind respect and entertainment'. Indeed, Potts says, 'nothing [was] denied her [that] she stood in need of'. Everyone knew it, he says: 'which of you that dwelleth near them in Craven but can and will witness it?'

Potts' words were intended to demonstrate how a kindly gentleman was cruelly tricked by an evil witch who repaid his generosity with her callous and ungodly actions. Yet, as Jonathan Lumby has outlined in his research into Jennet's case, they betray something much deeper; behind Potts' moral posturing, we get a sense of a close, long-standing relationship between Master Lister and Jennet. This begs an inevitable question: Was this simply a wealthy man doting on a servant, or something more? Was Jennet, in fact, his mistress? The plot thickens when we consider Master Lister's dying words, as reported by Potts:

When Master Lister lay upon his death-bed, he cried out in great extremity: Jennet Preston lays heavy upon me, Preston's wife lays heavy upon me.

In front of the York Assizes, these words were interpreted as an accusation. Master Lister, as he lay dying, had told everyone exactly who had caused his demise. But was that his real meaning? Or, as Jonathan Lumby suggests, could he have been calling out for the one he loved, the one he wanted to lay his weakening eyes upon just one last time? Or, was he stricken with guilt at conducting an extra-marital affair with Jennet, his panicked words forming a sort of dying confession?

Whatever it was, we can imagine the public humiliation for his family; his wife and his children, when news of his dying words spread. In his community, it would have been far more comfortable to interpret them as the denouncement of a witch than as the long-held affection for an absent lover.

Of course, we will never know for certain. But what is interesting is that whilst this evidence may point to a sexual relationship between the two, it is never explicitly expressed in Potts' record of the trial. Unlike some of her counterparts, any reference to Jennet's sexual behaviour is skilfully avoided, undoubtedly due to the sensitivities around the fact that there was an esteemed gentleman involved in this case. Poor, uneducated women were reasonable targets to be scorned for their sexual conduct. Wealthy men were another matter entirely.

There are many reasons why a woman was considered dangerous enough to be suspected of witchcraft in the sixteenth and seventeenth centuries. As we have seen in the case of the Pendle witches, perceptions of a woman's sexual morality undoubtedly played a part in this. At the very least, it was another stick with which to beat them, another way in which their character could be called into question. To the early modern mind, their behaviour was undesirable, even ungodly: Did their loose morals mean that they were in league with the devil? At worst, their sexual behaviour became a motive to scorn them as a witch – a convenient, convincing accusation when no other might do.

In the early modern period, women who bore children outside of wedlock, or had affairs with other men, or indeed with gentlemen, were seen to be subverting the normal social order. Their behaviour challenged an accepted view of how the world should be, and how women should behave within it.

This made them dangerous, and for onlookers in their communities, it begged the question: *If they could do this, what else were they capable of?*

More reading

Froome, J., 2010. *Wicked Enchantments: A History of the Pendle Witches and their Magic*. Palatine Books.

MacFarlane, A., 1970. *Witchcraft in Tudor and Stuart England*. Routledge.

Thomas, K., 1971. *Religion and the Decline of Magic*. Weidenfeld & Nicolson.

TRAVELLERS

AND

TRAILBLAZERS

Pioneers, both in the sense of exploration and of innovation, leave an indelible mark on the world. For many of our contributors back in 2016, the opportunity to celebrate their favourite adventurers or visionaries was too good to pass up, and we proudly published myriad biographies of women who dared to break boundaries. From the 'queen of science' to the 'Madonna of the Townships', these chapters offer a selection of those who changed the world by pushing boundaries in fields as varied as cinema, medicine, sport, music, science, aviation and geography.

Exploration in particular has traditionally been seen as a masculine preserve, steeped in conquest and empire-building. Our authors overturn this narrative, showing how 'female globe-trotters' could instead take nuanced positions at odds with the colonialist mission; for Mary Kingsley, as Jo Woolf shows, travels through west Africa leavened her overt imperialism, as when she campaigned against property taxes imposed by the British in Sierra Leone, or opposed prejudice against the people of Africa in the pages of *The Spectator*. Similarly, Isabella Bird took part in colonial reconnaissance in Persia as a means of protection – safety in numbers – but her passion for wildernesses stemmed in part from impatience with the Westernising influence she saw in so many places. Jenni Calder's chapter on Bird shows how she battled the strictures of Victorian society, seeking escape through travel.

For each of these pioneers, male opposition had to be overcome, but hardship proved a spur to even greater achievement. In the case of Sophia Jex-Blake and the rest of the Edinburgh Seven, for instance, their attempt to sit an anatomy exam at the University of Edinburgh culminated in a riot by more than 200 students and local citizens. But the abuse outraged the wider student body, and indeed the nation, leading eventually to formal admission to university for women. In the words of Jo Spiller, 'they met with an equal, opposite and determined resistance. However, the "chariot wheels of progress" were in motion and the momentum would prove unstoppable.'

In an age when 90 per cent of Nobel Prizes still go to men, Women's World Cup winners receive a third of the prize money of their male counterparts, and fewer than 10 per cent of pilots are women, these trailblazers show the need to keep fighting for equality – to make the momentum unstoppable.

MARY SOMERVILLE: QUEEN OF SCIENCE

Ruth Boreham

Ruth Boreham was the John Murray Archive Project Curator for the National Library of Scotland when she first came across Mary Somerville in 2005 and has been fascinated by her ever since. Now working at the Scottish Book Trust, as well as running walking tours in Edinburgh exploring women's history, she is also researching and writing a biography on Mary.

A definition for me of a dangerous woman is someone who is not prepared to put up with the role society gave her. In the nineteenth century Queen Victoria represented the most powerful model of womanhood. She established the ideal figure of the Victorian wife and mother and the image of the devoted, home-loving female was used in fiction and by the journalists and politicians of the time. Women, therefore, did not need much education and would do nothing beyond the home. Now and then, however, a woman from the past surprises you with her intellect, her ability and the fact that she was able to use these in a world dominated by men. Mary Somerville was one such woman:

> I was annoyed that my turn for reading was so much disapproved of, and thought it unjust that women should have been given a desire for knowledge if it were wrong to acquire it.

Mary was born in 1780 at Jedburgh in the Scottish Borders, the home of her maternal aunt. Her father was a naval captain and, having waved him off in London on his latest voyage, her mother was making her way home to Burntisland, Fife, when she got 'caught short' and gave birth at her sister's house. In a twist to Mary's story, her mother was laid so low after the birth that Mary was suckled by her aunt – this lady later became her mother-in-law as well!

Mary was brought up in the coastal town of Burntisland. With a largely absent father and a mother who did not believe in education beyond what was needed for church, young Mary was allowed to run wild and free, spending much time observing the flora and fauna. When her father did return from one of his voyages, he was disappointed to see she lacked education and so he sent her to a fashionable and expensive boarding school near Edinburgh. She described her stay in her autobiography:

> A few days after my arrival, although perfectly straight and well made, I was enclosed in stiff stays with a steel busk in front, while above my frock, bands drew my shoulders back until the shoulder-blades met. Then a steel rod, with semi-circle which went under the chin, was clasped to the steel busk on my stays. In this constrained state, I and most of the younger girls, had to prepare our lessons.

Although she stated that she finished her time there 'like a wild animal escaped out of a cage', she had at least developed a taste for reading, and had some notion of simple arithmetic, grammar and French. She also had poor handwriting and spelling. Mary wasn't unintelligent though, and took great pains to educate herself. She saw an algebra equation in a ladies' magazine, which intrigued her and set her on her future path. The family were relatively poor and she was forbidden to stay up all night with a candle reading – so she used to memorise problems from her brother's books and then work them out while she laid on her bed in the dark, checking the next morning to see if she had got them right.

> I had to take part in the household affairs, and to make and mend my own clothes. I rose early, played on the piano, and painted during the time I could spare in the daylight hours, but I sat up very late reading Euclid. The servants, however, told my mother, 'It was no wonder the stock of candles was soon exhausted, for Miss Mary sat up reading till a very late hour;' whereupon an order was given to take away my candle as soon as I was in bed. I had, however, already gone through the first six books of Euclid, and now I was thrown on my memory, which I exercised by beginning at the first book, and demonstrating in my mind a certain number of problems every night, till I could nearly go through the whole.

She also read those books deemed acceptable for women at the time. For example, she read the writings of Hannah More and other evangelicals. Yet, she later stated, 'I detested their books for they imposed such restraints and duties that they seemed to have been written to please men.' And Mary received an education most females at the time did, designed to make her appealing as a wife. She received some lessons from a local schoolmaster, and spent winters in Edinburgh learning to paint (from Alexander Nasmyth), dance, play the piano, etc. Her maternal uncle also proved crucial in expanding her knowledge, helping her to learn Latin for example by reading Virgil with her.

At the age of twenty-four Mary married her first husband, Captain Samuel Greig, who was a cousin of Mary's mother. His father was Admiral of the Russian Baltic Fleet. Samuel was also an officer in the Russian Navy, but left active service on marriage to Mary, whose parents were reluctant for her to move to Russia. Instead, the couple moved to London, where Samuel took up the position of Commissioner of the Russian Navy and Russian Consul. Here, Mary spent much of her time alone. She continued her mathematical and scientific studies through reading as much as she could, although her husband 'had a very low opinion of the capacity of my sex, and had neither knowledge of nor interest in science of any kind'. If things had continued this way, her name would mean nothing in the twenty-first century.

But widowhood came after Mary gave birth to her second child in 1807, and with it came a sense of freedom, both financially and socially. She moved back to Scotland with her two young sons and was able to study more openly, although her family often considered her both eccentric and foolish.

In the 1810s, Dr William Wallace, Professor of Mathematics at the University of Edinburgh, set a mathematical puzzle. Mary found out and immediately set to solving it, and in so doing won a prize medal. She impressed Wallace to the extent that he offered her further instruction and a reading list, and also introduced her to his brother John, with whom she read mathematics. This important relationship with the Wallace brothers was the start of Mary's move into the scientific and mathematical world as an adult.

In 1812, Mary married for a second time. Her new husband, her cousin, was an army doctor called William Somerville. He had a liberal outlook more suited to Mary and was also interested in science (it was his mother who had suckled Mary as a baby). William was very keen for Mary to continue her studies and, when they had to move to London for work reasons, he supported her attendance of lectures at the Royal Institution, studying and eventually writing her books. William also visited libraries and institutions which were not open to women, helped with proof-reading, and arranged for Mary to meet important scientific men. Although many women regarded science as an acceptable pastime, Mary's intellectual enthusiasm for science and obvious talent led to her acceptance by the 'serious' scientific men in London.

Mary's first publication appeared in the Royal Society's journal, *Philosophical Transactions*, in 1826. It was a report of her observations on the magnetising power of sunlight. In fact, she can be seen discussing some of this with J. M. W. Turner in the 2014 film, *Mr Turner*. Although her deductions were later proved to be incorrect, and she felt 'heartily ashamed' for publishing her results, this article is of great importance. It was the first experimental paper by a woman to be published in the journal under her own name. Yet, as women were barred from entering the Society's premises, William had to go and present her paper instead. It was this publication that helped to establish her reputation as a serious scientist.

Not long after this paper appeared, Mary was approached to translate Pierre Laplace's *Mécanique céleste*, in which Laplace had presented his nebula hypothesis of the solar system. Mary agreed and it appeared as *The Mechanism of the Heavens* in 1831, followed by the largely non-mathematical *Preliminary Dissertation to the Mechanism of the Heavens*.

Although not a bestseller, it was generally well received and adopted as a textbook at Cambridge University in 1837. She and her husband were also entertained as official guests for a week at the university. Other accolades came as well: the Royal Society commissioned a marble bust of her, the Royal Irish Academy made her a member, and in 1835 she and Caroline Herschel were made the first female honorary members of the Royal Astronomical Society.

Mary also became a friend and tutor to Ada Lovelace, daughter of Lord Byron, whose mother insisted she had a mathematical education rather than one concerning the arts, for fear she would turn out like her father. Mary introduced Ada to her friend Charles Babbage, and the two of them worked together on Babbage's differential machine.

Mary became the breadwinner of her household when William retired on ill-health. To improve his well-being, and to live more cheaply after a number of financial crises, the family moved to Italy, where Mary spent the last almost forty years of her life. Distance was not a problem though, and she continued to correspond with the leading scientific men of the day, for example Charles Babbage, John Herschel, Michael Faraday and David Brewster. She also continued to correspond and send manuscripts to her publisher John Murray. Her letters talk about the life she was leading in Italy, her writings and gossip about mutual acquaintances.

Mary's third book, her most popular work, was her two-volume *Physical Geography*, which appeared in 1848. It was an immense success, appearing on university textbook lists for many years. It eventually went through seven editions, many of them revised by Mary herself, who was keen to ensure it was as up to date as possible.

Mary continued to write books until her death. The last book published during her lifetime was *On Molecular and Microscopic Science*, in 1869. Even after its publication, she continued to work, spending four or five hours every morning studying the latest mathematical theories. She died in 1872.

Whatever difficulty we might experience in the middle of the nineteenth century in choosing a king of science, there could be no question whatever as to the queen of science. (*The Morning Post*, Monday, 2 December 1872)

In some ways Mary behaved just as all women were told they should. She married, had children, and spent a lot of time looking after her family. But, to me, she is dangerous because she wasn't prepared for this to be the sum total of her life. She had a thirst for knowledge, which led her to educate herself as much as possible. She was someone who wrote to the leading scientific men of the day and fully expected a reply. Mary was dangerous because she didn't stop, working right up until her death at the age of ninety-one. More than that, she was dangerous because she inspired others to follow in her footsteps. Perhaps the greatest memorial to her can be found at the University of Oxford. Somerville College was founded in 1879 to provide an opportunity for women to gain a higher education, who were at that time excluded from membership of the university. The name Somerville was chosen in honour of a formidable role model.

More reading

Arianrhod, R., 2012. *Seduced by Logic: Émilie Du Châtelet, Mary Somerville and the Newtonian Revolution.* Oxford University Press.

Neeley, K. A., 2001. *Mary Somerville: Science, Illumination, and the Female Mind.* Cambridge University Press.

Patterson, E. C., 1983. *Mary Somerville and the Cultivation of Science, 1815–1840.* Springer.

Stenhouse, B., 2021. Mister Mary Somerville: Husband and Secretary. *The Mathematical Intelligencer,* 43(3), March, pp. 7–18.

Strickland, E., 2016. *The Ascent of Mary Somerville in 19th Century Society.* Springer Cham.

ISABELLA BIRD: WRITER, EXPLORER, TRAILBLAZER

Jenni Calder

> **Jenni Calder** is the author of many books on literary and historical subjects
> and writes fiction and poetry as Jenni Daiches. After twenty-three years at
> the National Museum of Scotland she returned to freelance writing and
> lecturing. Non-fiction includes *Lost in the Backwoods: Scots and the North
> American Wilderness* (Edinburgh University Press, 2013) and *The Burning
> Glass: The Life of Naomi Mitchison* (Sandstone Press, 2019). Her most
> recent fiction is *Somewhere Else* (Scotland Street Press, 2024).

When she was thirty-three years old Isabella Bird, the Yorkshire-born
daughter of an Anglican clergyman, wrote:

> I feel as if my life were spent in the very ignoble occupation of taking care of
> myself, and that unless some disturbing influences arise I am in great danger
> of becoming perfectly encrusted with selfishness, and . . . of living to make
> life agreeable and its path smooth to myself alone.

The year was 1864. Isabella was living in Castle Terrace, Edinburgh, with
her mother and sister, where they had moved after the death of her
father. She had been an intermittent invalid since childhood, and felt
herself cocooned in a comfortable but stifling, respectable existence.
But she had some experience of a different life, and it was perhaps this
experience that enabled her to understand the danger to herself of
'becoming perfectly encrusted with selfishness'.

She was one of a generation growing up when the expectations of
women were repressively limiting, and when illness, lethargy, insomnia
and depression were often the consequence. Isabella experienced all of
these, and recognised the potential of women being dangerous to themselves. Years later she wrote: 'I shall always in the future as in the past
have to contest constitutional depression by earnest work and by trying
to lose myself in the interest of others.'

Her first experience of liberation came in 1854 when she was sent off
to North America to stay with cousins, in the hope that the change of
environment would be good for her health. Eighteen years later she was
ready for another, much more ambitious, expedition. She was now

forty-one, unmarried, and uninterested in marriage and the conventional life marriage implied. She set off alone on travels that took her to Australia, Hawaii and America's Pacific Coast.

In San Francisco she boarded a train to head east. California had been connected by rail to the east coast since 1869, but Isabella was going only as far as Truckee in the Sierra Nevada. She stepped out into the seething turmoil of a makeshift mining town and made her way unconcerned through streets crowded with drunk prospectors, gamblers and prostitutes. She was going to hire a horse and ride alone to Lake Tahoe. She was going to ride astride in an outfit she had specially adapted for the purpose. Yet, no one in Truckee cared much about this revolutionary step. Tahoe, with its 'brilliancy of sky and atmosphere' and 'elasticity of air' and an alarming encounter with a bear, didn't disappoint but it was just a prelude. The real adventure was to come.

Back on the train she continued to Denver. Her destination was Estes Park, in the Front Range of the Rocky Mountains north-west of Denver, the railroad terminus. Estes Park was an unsurveyed wilderness, barely inhabited by humans, but teeming with wildlife.

Isabella bought a horse and acquired a guide, Jim Nugent or Mountain Jim, a one-eyed former Indian scout, dressed in tattered deerskin and heavily armed – 'as awful looking a ruffian as one could see', she commented cheerfully in a letter to her sister Henrietta at home in Edinburgh. The cheerfulness is indicative. Her response to wildness, natural and human, was enthusiasm, although when Mountain Jim made overtures of affection she turned him down, and not all the wild men she encountered were as accommodating. Jim met a violent end, shot by Griffith Evans, a cattleman in whose cabin Isabella stayed while in the valley.

Isabella spent months in the Rockies, and would return to Estes Park, but this time, running out of money, she earned her keep by cooking and cleaning for the cowboys. She relished the labour. 'I cleaned the parlour and the kitchen, washed up, baked and then made 4 lbs of sweet biscuits and baked them after which I had to clean all my tins and pans and do my own room and haul water.' Her willingness to work was, in a sense, a passport to safety. The men clearly did not feel threatened by her, and she retained her confidence in the 'habit of respectful courtesy to women', which she believed characterised the frontier.

She was often alone when she travelled in the Rockies, sometimes getting lost and always acutely aware of isolation and vulnerability. On one occasion she was engulfed in a snowstorm that obliterated the track.

I cannot describe my feelings on this ride, produced by utter loneliness, the silence and dumbness of all things, the snow falling quietly without wind, the obliterated mountains, the darkness, the intense cold, and the unusual and appalling aspect of nature. All life was in a shroud, all work and travel suspended.

But throughout her writing, it is implied that potential danger was vital to her avoidance of being a danger to herself. Of another occasion, when she lost her way, she wrote: 'I felt very eerie and made up my mind to trudge on all night steering by the pole star . . . it was gruesome.' Baking bread for cowboys, a gruesome trudge through the night – a far cry from the drawing rooms of Edinburgh, but both, in their different ways, a means of saving herself.

Isabella returned to Scotland, but did not settle into a passive middle-class existence. She campaigned on behalf of slum-dwellers and Hebridean crofters and spent a lot of time in Mull. She worked on creating a book out of her letters to Henrietta, which became *A Lady's Life in the Rocky Mountains* (1879). But the familiar symptoms of neuralgia and depression returned, and again the remedy lay in travel. This time she sailed for Japan, a country in transition since it had opened its ports to foreign trade in the 1850s. Isabella was impatient to escape from the cities that were responding so rapidly to Western influences. Her subsequent account of her experiences, *Unbeaten Tracks in Japan* (1880), was frank in its description of the primitive squalor – dirt, disease, wretched food, rats, mosquitoes – she encountered in remoter areas. Her publisher, John Murray, tried to persuade her to tone down some of her descriptions. Some topics she addressed were deemed unsuitable topics for a lady to write about, or for ladies to read about. Her books – and she wrote about all her journeys – were popular.

At the age of fifty she married Dr John Bishop, who cared for her sister in her last illness, but had only a brief five years before he died. After his death she was on her travels again and on the move for most of the rest of her life, in Tibet, Persia (now Iran), Kurdistan, Korea and China. In none of these countries was she able to travel alone as she had done in the American West. At the very least, she needed an interpreter. In Persia she joined a larger expedition in the charge of Major Herbert Sawyer, who was carrying out a reconnaissance of territory where Britain, wary of Russian interests, was keen to have a presence. It was dangerous country. Isabella felt that travelling under escort entailed 'a certain abridgement of my liberty' and would have preferred to travel alone, but accepted the necessity of protection.

On the journey from Baghdad to Tehran they encountered blizzards as they crossed the mountains east of Kermanshah. The 'steady, blighting, searching, merciless blast . . . swept mountain-sides bare; enveloped us at times in glittering swirls of powdery snow which after biting and stinging careered over the slopes in twisted columns; screeched down gorges and whistled like the demon it was'. She was on mule-back, wrapped in several woollen layers, three pairs of gloves, sheepskin, a fur cloak and a mackintosh, but these 'were as nothing before that awful blast'. They passed the frozen corpses of some who did not make it. It was the worst of all her journeys. To her fellow countrymen, there was always the possibility that she was considered a burden, an impediment to the purpose of the expedition. 'Miss Bird's recklessness is a constant source of anxiety to the English officials who are naturally desirous that, as a British subject, no harm should befall her', commented one.

In 1892 Isabella Bird was among the first group of women to be elected fellows of the Royal Geographic Society, a move resisted by many of the Society's members. Lord Curzon, not yet Viceroy of India, made his views clear in a letter to *The Times* on 30 May 1893.

We contest in to the general capability of women to contribute to scientific geographical knowledge. Their sex and training render them equally unfitted for exploration, and the general professional female globe-trotters with which America has lately familiarised us is one of the horrors of the latter end of the 19th century.

It was considered a horror and a threat to established institutions and to the very fabric of society. The idea of a vicar's daughter roughing it in the wilderness in the company of a one-eyed ruffian, or riding a yak and nearly drowning while crossing a river in Ladakh, or in her sixties making her way up the Yangtze River with only some basic rations and her photographic equipment (she had taken lessons in photography), jeopardised fundamental assumptions about the role of women. If they could do these things, how did such activities reflect on the aspirations and expectations of men? And Isabella Bird, small in stature and quietly conventional in appearance, not only did these things, but wrote about them as well. She publicised her challenge to prevailing expectations.

The consequence of the controversy was that although the initial fifteen women members were not expelled, it was agreed that no more would be elected. Isabella herself did not join the debate. 'The fellowship as it stands at present is not worth making any trouble about', she wrote. 'At the same time, the proposed act is a dastardly injustice to women.' In other words, it was a gesture mired in prejudice and compromised by fear. The fellowship made no difference to her life. Soon she would be back in the Far East.

'It is pleasant', Isabella wrote to her sister, 'to be among people whose faces are not soured by the east wind, or wrinkled by the worrying effort to "keep up appearances"; who have no formal visiting, but real sociability; who regard the light manual labour of domestic life as a pleasure, not a thing to be ashamed of.' Travel was a kind of safe haven, the return from travel a re-entry into a world of limiting and dangerous convention: 'Every step now seemed not a step homewards but a step out of my healthful life back among wretched dragging feelings and aches and nervousness.' By choosing to avoid a smooth path through life, Isabella saved herself from a wretchedness that in her view was at least partially self-imposed.

In 1897, she was in Korea. 'I have freedom', she wrote to an Edinburgh friend, 'and you know how I love that! . . . I am so thankful for my capacity for being interested. What would my lonely life be without it?'

In 1904, she died in Edinburgh. She is buried in the Dean Cemetery.

More reading

Isabella Bird published many articles and books on her travels. Most have not been reprinted. One is included below.

Barr, P., 1970. *A Curious Life for a Lady. The Story of Isabella Bird.* Secker and Warburg.

Bird, I., [1879] 1960. *A Lady's Life in the Rocky Mountains.* Comstock Press.

Calder, J., 2013. *Lost in the Backwoods: Scots and the North American Wilderness.* Edinburgh University Press.

Hill-Murphy, J., 2021. *The Life and Travels of Isabella Bird.* Pen & Sword Books.

Woolf, J., n.d. *Isabella Bird Bishop. A Life of Adventures.* Royal Scottish Geographical Society. Available at: www.rsgs.org/blog/isabella-bird-bishop

SOPHIA JEX-BLAKE:
'A FAIR FIELD AND NO FAVOUR'

Jo Spiller

Jo Spiller has worked at the University of Edinburgh for sixteen years,
mainly in the field of digital education. In 2019, she put forward the case
for commemorating the Edinburgh Seven with posthumous degrees, 150
years after they became the first women to matriculate onto a full degree
programme at a British university. She has remained closely connected to
the ongoing recognition and profile-raising of the Edinburgh Seven that
the university has undertaken since then.

What did it mean to be a 'dangerous woman' in the nineteenth century,
at a time when on the one hand, the most powerful seat in Britain was
occupied by a woman, but on the other hand, the status of the average
woman, regardless of class, was practically that of a serf?

Sophia Jex-Blake and six other women who became collectively
known as the Edinburgh Seven discovered how dangerous the medical
establishment felt them to be when, in 1869, they set out to pursue the
study of medicine at the University of Edinburgh.

In Victorian Britain, there were limited opportunities for women
seeking employment. Working-class women and children did the most
dangerous jobs in the mines and factories, earning low wages.

Amongst the more affluent in society, the only profession open to
women had been that of governess until Florence Nightingale began
transforming nursing into a respectable profession. Attitudes to education were changing in late Victorian Britain, which meant that women
with skills, ability and character could pursue a nursing career. With
women demonstrating that they made good nurses, the question of why
they wouldn't equally make good doctors inevitably arose.

The Medical Act of 1858 stipulated that only those with recognised
medical degrees from British universities were eligible to register as
doctors. This meant that if women wished to qualify as doctors, institutions previously closed to them would need to be opened up.

In 1869, the University of Edinburgh was the first to open its degree
programmes to women when Sophia Jex-Blake successfully petitioned
the university for permission to apply to the medical faculty.

Despite there being support within the university and medical faculty, as well as from the wider public, there was also influential opposition to the idea of women as doctors. Sophia Jex-Blake wrote of one member of the faculty:

> [he] informed me women 'didn't understand their position', that they did their own work in the world badly, that they had not sufficient strength for medical practice.

Women's motives in seeking to practise as doctors were also considered suspect and potentially dangerous.

The same member of faculty who had articulated that women didn't understand their position stated, at a meeting of the University Council in 1870, that women seeking medical training could be 'basely inclined' and unless careful enquiries were made into their character, the institution could be harbouring 'Magdalenes'.

The debate was reported in many of the national papers, with most coming out in support of the women students and critical of the professors who opposed them, naming them publicly in articles published on the topic.

Throughout the first year of their medical degree, the women proved themselves to be both personally and intellectually equal to the demands of the discipline. They conducted themselves diligently and professionally in their day-to-day studies and demonstrated that they could match and even outperform their male counterparts in open examinations.

In the 'fair field and no favour' that Sophia Jex-Blake was requesting, some of the faculty staff acknowledged the women to be exemplary students. This led to growing tension with the wider student body, in part encouraged by hostile members of faculty, which led to the women being subjected to a mounting campaign of intimidation. They were regularly followed home, and had a series of obscene letters put through their letterboxes. Crowds would gather outside their Edinburgh homes to rattle their windows and door and remove their nameplate. They had peas and other objects thrown at them as they walked to and from their lectures.

The women stopped going out on campus alone and would not leave the house after dark. One significant event in the campaign took place at 4 p.m. on 18 November 1870, when the women arrived at Surgeon's Hall on Nicolson Street to sit an anatomy examination. They found their route blocked by a loud and unruly crowd of over 200 students and locals, throwing mud, rubbish and insults at them.

Many male students were shocked at the way their women co-students were treated that afternoon, and began to organise themselves into teams of bodyguards to escort them around campus.

The riot made national headlines and won the women many new supporters. The Committee for Securing a Medical Education to the Women in Edinburgh was set up with over 300 influential members including Charles Darwin.

The campaign was hard-fought throughout the following three years but ended in the courts, with the Lord Ordinary's verdict that the university had acted 'illegally' in matriculating the women in the first place.

Professor Masson, who was Professor of Rhetoric at the university and had been a steadfast supporter of the women students throughout, reflected that 'this is not the first time, and I suppose it will not be the last, when grave and wise men will be found defending a dying tyranny'.

Sophia Jex-Blake herself did not consider the Edinburgh campaign a failure, believing that 'it was the seed sown in tears in Edinburgh that was reaped in joy elsewhere'.

The women had successfully challenged the widely held assumptions regarding women's intelligence and shown that they were more than capable of meeting the demands of the medical profession. The events in Edinburgh began a national debate that would ultimately lead to the passing of legislation enabling women to access university education in 1877. James Stansfeld, MP for Halifax, who had been closely associated with the campaign, wrote:

> It is one of the lessons of the history of progress that when the time for a reform has come you cannot resist it . . . [Opponents] are not merely dragged at the chariot wheels of progress – they help to turn them. The strongest force, whichever way it seems to work, does most to aid. Dr Sophia Jex-Blake has made the greatest of all contributions to the end attained.

At its summer graduation ceremony in 2019, 150 years after first matriculating, the University of Edinburgh Medical School posthumously awarded the Edinburgh Seven full medical degrees. The degree awards were presented to seven current medical students representing Sophia Jex-Blake, Edith Pechey, Isabel Thorne, Helen de Lacy Evans, Matilda Chaplin, Mary Anderson and Emily Bovell. Since then, further initiatives to commemorate the women have included walkways around the BioQuarter in Edinburgh being named after them, and the creation of a tapestry commemorating the Edinburgh Seven, designed by the artist Christine Borland and woven by the Dovecot Studios, which now hangs in the newly opened Edinburgh Futures Institute.

More reading
Jex-Blake, S., 1886. *Medical Women: A Thesis and a History*. Macmillan.

LADY FLORENCE DIXIE: HONEYBALLERS AND THE DANGEROUS WOMEN OF SCOTTISH WOMEN'S FOOTBALL

Margot McCuaig

Margot McCuaig is the sole owner of purpleTV. She won Royal Television Society Scotland best sport film awards for documentaries she wrote and directed in 2015, 2016, 2019 and 2021. She also wrote and directed *Honeyballers*, a documentary film about the history of women's football in Scotland, and films about Rose Reilly, Sadie Smith, Julie Fleeting and *The Women Who Built Glasgow City*, all Scottish football icons. She is currently writing an autoethnography PhD at the University of Stirling, analysing gender, class and emotion in her documentary films, and in her own filmmaking journey. Margot is also a published novelist, with *The Birds That Never Flew* (ThunderPoint, 2015) and *Almost Then* (Linen Press, 2021).

In Mrs Matilda Pullan's *Maternal Counsel to Daughters* of 1855, it was argued that there is 'no better exercise for women in the world than rubbing a table or sideboard, or sweeping a room'.

This Victorian ideology was very much embedded in the notion that the legitimation of sport merely strengthened the legitimation of the dominant male preserve and the continuity of patriarchal assumptions. Women, it was argued, were neither emotionally nor physically able to participate in strenuous exercise. Femininity was therefore observed in the context of gentility and passivity and, crucially, in reproductive terms that ensured the nurture of the male, his children and the family home. While women were regarded as angels of the home, sport was the bastion of masculinity and defined the demarcation of the distinctive gender roles.

Fortunately, there were female transgressors, dangerous women who, in daring to play football, challenged stereotypical attitudes, and not only contested notions of the perceived norm but deconstructed concepts of femininity.

Women have been playing football for at least as long as men, from as far back as the 1700s. Records exist of women playing football in Scotland in 1628, but it was only in the late nineteenth century that the game began to grow in popularity. The first women's football inter-national in the world was played on 10 May 1881 in Edinburgh, when a Scottish side took on an English select. Albeit an unofficial interna-tional, Lily St Clair's goal for a victorious Scotland is recorded as the first goal scored in the history of women's football.

Whilst the women were revelling in developing ownership of a game that emancipated them from the restrictions of domestic responsibili-ties and passive exercise traditionally associated with femininity, the authorities were less favourable. In 1894, the *British Medical Journal* published a report in response to the increasing popularity of women's football. It was disapproving: 'Football should be damned out of hand as dangerous to the reproductive organs and breasts because of sudden jerks, twists and blows.'

Undeterred at attempts to discredit the women's game, another Scot, the aristocratic poet, writer, women's rights activist and adventurer, Lady Florence Dixie from Dumfries, was leading the way in the development of organised football in Britain. In October 1894, she published her inten-tion to create a 'British Ladies Football' team in a London newspaper.

The club founders engaged the services of an enthusiastic captain, Mary Hutson. Dubliner Mary played under the clever, attention-grab-bing pseudonym of *Nettie Honeyball*. 'Nettie' understood the importance of influential role models such as Lady Florence Dixie. Lady Florence was a well-known 'celebrity', and her brother was instrumental in bring-ing down Oscar Wilde. Together Dixie and Hutson strove to develop the women's game, in turn advocating equal rights for women.

Lady Florence Dixie was a curious and extraordinary Scot with a desire to make the world an equal place for women. The objective of her women's football team was to use the sport as a means to create oppor-tunities for women in a tense Victorian society constricted by entrenched gender bias and gross unfairness and inequality. With her captain, the aptly named Nettie Honeyball in tow, Lady Florence's team, comprised of middle-class 'ladies', began a campaign that continues, albeit on a different platform with a different agenda, to this day. The agenda is diverse, but the similarities are there. It is still about the empowerment of women and about dangerous women, who dare to challenge institu-tional norms and patriarchal systems.

Florence Dixie was resolute in her ambition to deliver equality for women. In an interview, a year after the formation of her club, she was clear about her objective:

I founded the association last year, with the fixed resolve of proving to the world that women are not the 'ornamental and useless' creatures men have pictured. I must confess, my conviction[s] on all matters, where the sexes are so widely divided, are all on the side of emancipation, and I look forward to the time when ladies may sit in Parliament and have a voice in the direction of affairs, especially those which concern them most.

With such unequivocal leadership in the form of Dixie, the early pioneers of the game remained resolute in their desire to develop the game further, and in 1896 a new team emerged led by the ambition of honorary Scot, Mrs Graham.

Mrs Graham played alongside Nettie Honeyball before forming the Mrs Graham's XI. Like Florence Dixie, she would also become a key figure in women's football. *Helen Graham* also played under a pseudonym. She was born Helen Matthews, and her determination to transgress led her to travel alone from Montrose in Scotland to play football in London, in a period when travel was expensive and arduous. This was a dangerous act in itself.

Women in football were regarded with distrust. They were considered dangerous. These transgressors were a threat to the cultural, historical and masculine value systems carved into the male football establishment. The critical foundation of a concerted campaign to exclude women from football was solidified in 1902 with a warning from the Football Association Council to its members not to play charitable matches against women's teams. This momentum grew, and support for women's football in the form of facilities was effectively banned in 1921. Whilst the 'ban' in Scotland was not formerly implemented until 1948, it was effectively in place from 1921.This restriction would remain in place in an official capacity until the 1970s. As a result, the game stalled dramatically, but the First World War provided a fresh impetus for women in society and the workplace, as women's football teams in munitions factories formed throughout the country.

New pioneers went on to pave the way for equality. Dick Kerrs Ladies, Rutherglen Ladies and munition factory teams in Scotland such as Beardmores Forge were pulling in large crowds, and respect grew for a game that was beginning to develop its own identity. This was not a game where women were trying to be men . . . This was women's football. It was not women attempting to imitate men and play the so-called 'man's game'.

Women like Sadie Smith, Nancy 'Cannonball' Thompson, Rose Reilly and Edna Neillis continued to pioneer and transgress, following in the footsteps of Lady Florence Dixie, Nettie Honeyball and Helen Graham. Their passion for equality altered history.

With passion comes determination and a will to push disappointment to the side and battle on. In today's context, the players and coaches in women's football have very little financial support and few resources. The players endure scathing attacks on the game as a craft, criticising their personal skill and capabilities as footballers, and they also have to listen to the boring and enduring notion that they are 'women trying to be men'.

That inaccurate picture clouds the real vision. In women's football, there is talent, passion and danger in abundance. This potent combination, which led to the banning of the women's game in 1921, has endured persistent attacks to discredit women and protect the male preserve. Excuses were unfurled, but the message was simple. With crowds of tens of thousands attending women's matches, men's position in society was being challenged. Instead of embracing something strong and admirable, the decision was taken to try and destroy it. Bizarrely, given women's football's popular success and persistent support since the nineteenth century, how the authorities hadn't envisaged the defiance that followed is a mystery.

Women continued to play and transgressed throughout the ban.

It was such determination that forced the official recognition of women's football in Scotland in 1974, despite the fact that, in some quarters, sexist ideologies were inherently fixed and unchanging; a reflection of the recurrent dominant ideas of gender that have been persistently associated with football, and indeed sport in general, since the nineteenth century. In 1956, Welsh International Trevor Ford had commented, 'football is not a women's game, it's not a pastime for milksops and sissies', and a women's charity match in London in 1971 was advertised as a clash between 'the world's most beautiful players'.

It's a cliché, an overused, boring anecdote that football is more than a game, but when it comes to the women's game, it is exactly that. It reflects a drive to succeed, a commitment to achieve and a will to challenge the world to wake up to itself and its outdated idiosyncrasies and inadequacies and make space for women on an equal footing.

Despite the unlevel playing field, women in Scotland are achieving great things in football. The Scotland national women's team qualified for the Women's World Cup for the first time in 2019. Glasgow City FC and Celtic Women have made great strides in recent years in the Champions League. While not all women footballers are brandishing banners depicting their call for equal rights, their determination to create equal opportunities is just as blatant and exciting. The understanding of what the women's game is, and what it is quite spectacularly trying to achieve, is becoming clearer thanks to their commitment.

Women aren't trying to be men; that notion has gone beyond laughable. It's just downright annoying. They are playing women's football, with women being the operative word. They are strong, independent individuals who collectively epitomise the fight for a new beginning and the recognition that they are equal. They utilise their skill, talent and knowledge to generate the passion and determination to allow us all, as women and men, to continue to grow.

Thanks to them, and the endeavours of Lady Florence Dixie, the struggle continues.

And my goodness, isn't it just fabulous to watch?

More reading

Dixie, F., 1880. *Across Patagonia*. Bentley.

Dixie, F., 1890. *Gloriana, or the Revolution of 1900*. Henry & Co.

Honeyballers, 2013. Directed by M. McCuaig [film]. Glasgow: purpleTV.

McCuaig, M., 1996. *Women in Scottish Football. Playing the Game 1880 to 1970*. Honours dissertation, University of Strathclyde.

McCuaig, M., 2002. *To What Extent can Bill Forsyth's* Gregory's Girl *Be Used to Reconstruct Football Culture in Glasgow in the Early 1980s?* MPhil dissertation, University of Glasgow.

McCuaig, M., forthcoming. In F. Skillen, G. James and H. Byrne, eds, *A History of The Growth and Development of Women's Football in Britain and Ireland between 1845 and 1890*.

MARY KINGSLEY:
BREAKING THE MOULD

Jo Woolf

Jo Woolf, as Writer in Residence at the Royal Scottish Geographical Society, delves into the archives in search of exciting tales of endeavour and exploration, many of which were told directly to audiences throughout the Society's 140-year history. Her book, *The Great Horizon – 50 Heroes of Geography*, was published in 2017, and she is currently working on another, to be published in 2025. Jo contributes to the RSGS's quarterly magazine, *The Geographer*. On her own blog, *The Hazel Tree* (www.thehazeltree. co.uk) she writes about history, landscape and the natural world. Jo is an Honorary Fellow of the RSGS.

What makes a woman dangerous, in any era? In the case of Mary Kingsley, it was the threat that she posed to the widely accepted principles of nineteenth-century society, and to the people whose status and reputation rested on the pillars of Victorian imperialism.

Not that Mary ever set out to topple the system. Self-deprecating to a fault, she claimed no sympathy with the women's suffrage movement, and she took great pains to dress and behave with the propriety expected of an unmarried woman with modest means and a negligible degree of formal education. But her deepest beliefs, the ideals that guided her life, became apparent from the very moment she stepped off a ship in Sierra Leone and strode purposefully into the rainforests of equatorial Africa.

Even by the standards of her day, Mary's early life was tightly restricted. She was born in Islington in 1862, the first child of George Kingsley, a physician and travel writer, and Mary Bailey, a London inn-keeper's daughter. From her father, she seems to have inherited her wanderlust and her fiery determination; from her mother, a resource-fulness and adaptability and perhaps also the spirit that allowed her to speak freely to people, regardless of their race and class. Mary's educa-tion was confined largely to what she could glean from her father's ample library. Not for her the dark romances of the Brontë sisters: she was a scientist by nature, and she mopped up books on anthropology and natural history while dreaming of voyages to distant lands.

Mary's ailing parents claimed all her time and attention until 1892, when they both died within weeks of each other. By that time, Mary was nearly thirty, an ageing spinster by the standards of her day. But she was suddenly and ecstatically free. Ignoring the horrified protests of her friends, she started to read about the requirements for travellers in the tropics and bought herself a one-way ticket to West Africa. Her purpose in going there was twofold: she would study the ecology of the rivers, in particular the fishes, and send specimens home to the Natural History Museum in London; and she would travel into the interior of the continent to find out more about the sacrificial rites and spiritual beliefs of the tribes who lived there.

In the light of the twenty-first century it is difficult to fully appreciate the enormity of what Mary was contemplating. Not only was she journeying alone to the place known as the 'white man's grave', where there were a thousand unpleasant ways to die, she was planning on staying with tribes known to be cannibalistic, who, it was safe to say, would never have seen anyone like Mary before. As for the European presence in Africa, most of the focus was on carving up the continent into portions that were ripe for exploitation and development by countries such as Britain, France, Germany, Portugal and Spain. Africa was still the domain of men, all of them ambitious colonialists and pioneers, stiff-upper-lipped statesmen and weather-beaten traders who had seen and heard it all and were willing to pour their worst horror stories into the ears of naive travellers on their passage south. A woman in such an environment was unprecedented, and, quite apart from the scandal, she was unlikely to come out alive.

But Mary was slightly more prepared than her friends might have thought. She read as much as she could about tropical diseases, and she bought herself a big waterproof bag in which to carry her possessions. She also realised that she would need an identity, a kind of passport to win the trust of strangers, and for this reason she set herself up as a trader. It would give validity to her journey, and it would help to explain her otherwise astonishing appearance. She was already wise, but she had yet to prove that she was capable.

Mary's insistence on feminine decency made no concessions in terms of clothing, and when she steered her canoe into the labyrinthine delta of the Ogowé River she was dressed in the same tight corset, voluminous skirts and high-collared blouses that she would have worn to a British tea party. By this time, she had gained the support of diplomats in the coastal towns – crucial for her purpose – and she had gathered a handful of African companions who were willing to accompany her on her mission. She knew that she might be depending on these men for her life: she never expected that they would be depending on her, for theirs.

The Fang tribe, whose reputation for capturing and eating their enemies was widely known, were more than willing to share their spiritual beliefs with Mary once they had overcome their initial surprise. Mary stayed with them as a guest, making a somewhat alarming find in her sleeping quarters that was obviously the remains of a recent feast, but at no time did she allow her fear to get the better of her. Her key, which was largely unrecognised in her own time, was that she met them with an open mind and treated them with respect. When her hosts found one of her assistants guilty of a crime and tied him up in readiness for a meal, it was Mary who found herself arguing for his release. The Fang trusted her judgement; her reward was their confidence and cooperation, and she was allowed to hear the stories of ritual and lore that underpinned their society, the unique blend of legend and history that defined them as a people.

As she marched through humid rainforests and paddled around the mangrove swamps, Mary faced extreme situations that tested her resourcefulness to the utmost. She had never wondered, for example, how she would deal with a crocodile that was attempting to board her canoe: a quick sharp rap on the nose with her paddle seemed to do the trick. A leopard, which had ventured into her camp and was now confronting her at close range, was discouraged by a number of random items thrown in his direction. On more than one occasion she fell into a game trap, a deep pit dug by hunters to catch unwary animals, and she found that her skirts saved her legs by snagging on the sharp spikes of ebony. She did carry a weapon – a Bowie knife – but she had left her revolver at the French outpost, reasoning that if she brandished it among the African people she would be asking for trouble.

Back in the drawing rooms of polite Victorian society, people didn't quite know what to make of Mary. After two visits to West Africa, she was gaining widespread recognition for her achievements, and she mingled with politicians and diplomats, writers and statesmen. The trouble was that they could not quite understand her message. She spoke out against the proposed hut tax in Sierra Leone, which she believed was an infringement of the people's inherent right to possess their own property. She expressed herself as a staunch imperialist, but she advocated a deeper sympathy with the African people. Wholesale subordination was not the answer. British civilisation, she argued, had taken centuries to develop and it was a mistake to imagine that these 'improvements' could be rolled out across Africa in the space of a few years.

Very soon, people were eyeing Mary with poorly concealed antagonism, and a public exchange of letters in *The Spectator* only fuelled the flames. Mary had been provoked into replying to a typically patronising view of the future of Africa, in which the perceived values of its people were dismissed with contempt. Africans were not brutal, nor degraded, nor cruel, she wrote. They had a sense of honour and justice, and in terms of good temper and patience they bore comparison with any other human beings.

That, of course, was the spark. The stiff-backed figures of state and Empire were incensed, and made no attempt to conceal their scorn. Mary had unwittingly found a chink in their armour, because if the equality of all humanity could be acknowledged across the globe, there would be no high ground from which to dominate. For that reason alone, she was seen as a dangerous woman.

Mary provided more proof of the capability of women, both mentally and physically, than she would ever actually admit. It was her actions, rather than her words, that spoke most clearly: she negotiated with honesty and fairness, and she received honesty and fairness in return. Her courage only seemed to falter when she was asked to speak to august institutions such as the Royal Scottish Geographical Society: rather than address the audience herself, she requested that her paper be read for her.

Mary's extraordinary spirit is still alive in her books. Her stories sparkle with the most delicious humour, and in many ways her voice is so timeless that she could have been writing yesterday. She regularly mocks the excruciating dilemmas that she found herself in, but her observations are acute. You feel yourself wanting to be her friend, and suddenly you can understand why she succeeded. And if a solitary and apparently defenceless woman could achieve so much in such unlikely circumstances, it is no wonder that her peers, raised on a diet of military glory, should have seen her as a threat.

There was no chance of Mary ever agreeing with this concept, simply because her low self-esteem would not allow it. And in any case, the potential never had a chance to develop. In 1900, moved by the plight of soldiers wounded in the Boer War, she travelled to South Africa where she became a nurse at a hospital in Simon's Town. Disease was rife, and within a few months she had died of typhoid. She was thirty-seven.

More reading

Bush, J., 2007. *Women Against the Vote: Female Anti-Suffragism in Britain.* Oxford University Press.

Frank, K., 1986. *A Voyager Out: The Life of Mary Kingsley.* Houghton Mifflin.

Kingsley, M. H., 1896. Travels on the western coast of equatorial Africa. *Scottish Geographical Magazine*, 12(3), pp. 113–124.

Kingsley, M. H., 1897. *Travels in West Africa, Congo Français, Corisco and Cameroons.* F. Cass.

Kingsley, M. H., 1899. *West African Studies.* Macmillan.

LOIS WEBER:
EARLY HOLLYWOOD'S
FORGOTTEN PIONEER

Shelley Stamp

Shelley Stamp is author of the award-winning books *Lois Weber in Early Hollywood* (University of California Press, 2015) and *Movie-Struck Girls: Women and Motion Picture Culture after the Nickelodeon* (Princeton University Press, 2000) and curator of the award-winning disc set *Pioneers: First Women Filmmakers*. She is founding editor of the journal *Feminist Media Histories* and currently edits the *Feminist Media Histories* book series published by University of California Press. She is Distinguished Professor of Film and Digital Media at the University of California, Santa Cruz, where she has twice won the Excellence in Teaching award.

The most profitable movie released by Universal Pictures in 1916 was a film on birth control and abortion, written and directed by a woman who was also the studio's most respected and highest-paid director. That filmmaker was Lois Weber, Hollywood's original dangerous woman, and the film was *Where Are My Children?* What Lois Weber accomplished over a century ago has become almost impossible to imagine in Hollywood today. As the film industry debates gender equity onscreen and off, Weber's legacy is vital to remember.

In her time, Weber was considered one of the three 'great minds' in early Hollywood, alongside D. W. Griffith and Cecil B. DeMille. While her male peers have long been celebrated as the fathers of American cinema, Weber has often been forgotten. Yet, of all the women active in the early movie industry, Weber produced the most sustained and substantial body of work. In a career that spanned three decades, Weber wrote and directed more than forty feature films and over 100 short films. She was the first woman to direct a feature-length film, in 1914 (*The Merchant of Venice*), and the first woman to be admitted to the Motion Picture Directors' Association in 1916. They had to make an exception to their men-only policy in order to do so. In 1917 Weber became the first woman to run a Hollywood studio – and one of the earliest directors of either gender to enjoy such independence. When the first Director's Committee was formed in the new Academy of Motion

Picture Arts and Sciences in 1927, Weber joined as its only female member. At the height of her renown, journalists dubbed Weber 'the wonder woman of the films', the 'super-woman of the silent drama' and a 'director deluxe of filmdom'. Yet, few recognise her name today.

Weber was best known for a series of popular films she made on controversial social issues while she was Universal's top director in the mid-1910s. If Griffith and DeMille sought to establish cinema's prestige by drawing on highbrow literary and historical material, Weber took an opposite tack. She seized upon the new medium's capacity to animate critical issues of her day. Cinema, she said, was a 'voiceless language', able to engage popular audiences in the era's most contentious debates. And that, she did. Weber tackled subjects like urban poverty and women's wage equity in *Shoes* (1916), drug addiction and narcotics trafficking in *Hop, or The Devil's Brew* (1916), capital punishment and police violence in *The People vs. John Doe* (1916), and the campaign to legalise birth control in two films – *Where Are My Children?* (1916) and *The Hand That Rocks the Cradle* (1917). Though she fought censorship battles on many of these titles, Weber developed a reputation as a thoughtful, socially engaged filmmaker. Critic Marjorie Howard noted at the time that Weber could 'deal successfully with subjects which other directors would not dare touch for fear of condemnation'.

Although she vowed to abandon such 'heavy dinners' when she left Universal to form her own studio in 1917, Weber remained a trenchant critic of social norms. Her films on marriage and domesticity, notably *Too Wise Wives* (1921), *What Do Men Want?* (1921) and *The Blot* (1921), provoke fundamental questions about changing sexual mores, traditional family structures and a rising culture of consumption in the Jazz Age. In later films like *The Marriage Clause* (1926), *Sensation Seekers* (1927) and *The Angel of Broadway* (1927), Weber produced highly reflexive critiques of stardom and Hollywood's glamour culture, particularly its commodification of women.

Towards the end of her career, Weber became increasingly outspoken about the limited roles available to women in Hollywood – both onscreen and behind the scenes. Complaining that female characters in too many Hollywood movies were treated as nothing more than 'cute little dolls' and 'over-dressed Christmas trees', Weber vowed to introduce a 'new feminine screen type', a 'womanly woman', who 'possessed both brains and character'. Critics began to notice that actresses who had formerly been given little to do onscreen aside from look pretty were, under Weber's direction, given fully formed parts and allowed to exercise the full range of their acting talent. Billie Dove, who became a star in Weber's films, remembered her as 'the best director I ever had'. Dove professed, 'I had a lot of men directors that I liked too, but she understood women.'

Throughout her career, Weber consciously mentored other women at all ranks of the industry – actresses, screenwriters and directors alike. She demanded a place at the table in early professional guilds, which had initially excluded women, and protested the growing climate of hostility towards female filmmakers in the 1920s. When a high-ranking studio executive proclaimed in 1928 that women did not make good motion picture directors, Weber penned a two-part syndicated newspaper article calling for *more* female filmmakers. Compared to when she got her start in Hollywood, Weber proclaimed, 'women entering the industry now find it practically closed'. Where she had once commanded tremendous respect on any set, by the late 1920s Weber found that male crew members were unaccustomed to working under a female director and sometimes even unwilling to do so.

For a filmmaker so renowned in her time, Lois Weber is remarkably unknown today, sidelined in most histories of American filmmaking. This is not for lack of trying. In the final decade of her life, Weber struggled against all odds to ensure her own historical legacy. Yet, even before she directed her last production in 1934, Weber was written out of Hollywood history, cast aside in the very first chronicles of American movie-making that focused exclusively on pioneering male figures and valued women only as stars. Scores of women like Weber, who had been essential to the early movie business as directors, screenwriters, producers, journalists and studio executives, were 'forgotten' in an initial rush to legitimise the newly powerful industry.

But this history is essential to remember. Even now, film industry executives and pundits continue to find themselves surprised that women make popular, profitable and interesting films, that female protagonists and female stars can carry a picture, even, astonishingly, that women watch movies at all. Female filmmakers still negotiate the awkward terrain of chick flicks; and being 'seen on the screen' is *still* considered women's primary role in cinema. These fictions have a long tail. Histories of Hollywood that forget pioneering women like Lois Weber produce a false narrative with profound consequences for subsequent generations of female filmmakers and filmgoers.

More reading

Mahar, K. W., 2006. *Women Filmmakers in Early Hollywood*. Johns Hopkins University Press.

Norden, M. F., ed., 2019. *Lois Weber: Interviews*. University Press of Mississippi.

Slide, A., 1996. *Lois Weber: The Director Who Lost Her Way in History.* Greenwood Press.

Stamp, S., 2013. Lois Weber. In J. Gaines, R. Vatsal and M. Dall'Asta, eds, *Women Film Pioneers Project.* Columbia University Libraries. https://doi.org/10.7916/d8-zsv8-nf69 (includes a complete filmography, with information about availability).

Stamp, S., 2015. *Lois Weber in Early Hollywood.* University of California Press.

ELSIE MACKAY: PIONEERING AVIATOR

Quentin Wilson and Fiona Wilson

Quentin Wilson was formerly an aeronautical engineer and worked on the Concorde and Hovercraft projects, as well as the Jetstream 41, built at Prestwick, by British Aerospace. Quentin grew up in Ayrshire, hearing tales of Elsie Mackay's bravery. Late in life, he extensively researched Mackay's final flight and co-authored this piece with his daughter Fiona. Quentin died in Prestwick in 2023.

Fiona Wilson is a poet, teacher and scholar and lives in New York City. She is the author of *A Clearance: Poems* (The Sheep Meadow Press, 2016), as well as essays on Scottish writing in the *Edinburgh Companion to Contemporary Scottish Literature* (Edinburgh University Press, 2007), the *Edinburgh Companion to Contemporary Scottish Poetry* (Edinburgh University Press, 2009) and the *Cambridge History of Scottish Literature* (forthcoming). Her poetry has appeared in *Poetry Review*, *New Writing Scotland*, *Literary Imagination*, *Edinburgh Review*, and on BBC Radio 3. She was an IASH Fellow in 2012.

Born in Simla, India in 1893, the Hon. Elsie Mackay was the third daughter of James Mackay, 1st Earl of Inchcape of Strathnaver, later the chairman of the Peninsular and Oriental Navigation Company. Money buys freedom, and more than most women of her era Elsie Mackay could afford to experiment with her life. Still, when she eloped with, and married, the actor Dennis Wyndham in 1917, her family cut her off.

Reborn as the doe-eyed silent-film actress Poppy Wyndham, she appeared in films with titles like *Snow in the Desert* (1919) and *Nothing But the Truth* (1920). In *Many a Slip* (1917), she played The Girl; in *The Tidal Wave* (1920), she was an artist rescued from the sea – and her own ambition? – by a ruggedly handsome fisherman. In 1922, she divorced her husband and was reconciled with her family. A more conventional life beckoned. Soon, she was doing interior design for P&O liners.

What she really liked to do, however, was to fly.

In 1923, a year after her divorce, she took up flying lessons at the famous De Havilland Flying School, becoming one of the very first British women – and certainly the first Scottish woman – to gain her pilot's licence. Flying was a new and dangerous activity in this period. Her father refused to even set foot in an airplane. In one famous episode, Mackay's safety belt broke in a plane performing a loop at 10,000 feet, and velocity almost dragged her from the machine. Back on the ground, her hands cut to the bone, she nonchalantly offered to repeat the move. Still, Mackay had a larger goal. Her dream was to become the first woman to fly across the Atlantic.

The 1920s were a period of intense public interest in aviation. Scarcely a day went by without a newspaper article related to airplanes, airships, flying men, and very occasionally, flying women. A weekly mail service to India was proposed and, also, the appointment of a Minister for Airship Development; solitary fliers attempted flights across Africa, or even to Australia. Each newspaper story was a saga that could be followed by readers as days, weeks and months went by, sometimes ending in triumph and sometimes in horrific disaster. One notable triumph that surely caught Elsie Mackay's attention was Charles Lindbergh's non-stop flight across the Atlantic in 1927. When the *Spirit of St. Louis* touched down in Le Bourget airport, near Paris, Lindbergh became an instant worldwide celebrity. Lindbergh had flown from America to France, west to east. Elsie Mackay's goal was not simply to be the first woman to cross the Atlantic, but also to be the first person to cross against the frequent headwinds of the much more difficult east-to-west direction.

Mackay had earned her pilot's licence, but to fly the Atlantic she needed the assistance of a flier with considerable experience, and so she approached Captain W. G. R. Hinchliffe with her plans. Once Hinchliffe's reluctance at the very idea of making an Atlantic flight with a woman was overcome, the two selected a machine called the Stinson Detroiter, with dual control and an enclosed and heated cockpit. The standard model had a top speed of about 130 miles per hour, but only a fraction of the range required for the Atlantic flight.

Mackay and Hinchliffe planned to compensate for this problem by carrying extra fuel in a large tank, with even more in cans. When required, the cans were to be poured into the cabin tank, and the fuel then transferred by hand pump to the main tanks in the high wing. Under normal flying conditions, this operation would have been cumbersome, but doable. Inside a tiny cramped fuselage, buffeted by strong winds, however, it must have been a very different matter.

By the end of February 1928, the airplane, now named *Endeavour*, was at Cranwell airfield, in the south of England, ready for take-off. Why were Mackay and Hinchliffe even contemplating a flight across the Atlantic at the end of winter? In the previous year there had been four such attempts, two of which had ended in disaster. Another attempt was in an advanced state of preparation. The time available at the airfield was limited and the press sensed that a new attempt on the North Atlantic was about to be made. If Mackay and Hinchliffe were to succeed in breaking records, their Atlantic attempt had to be made as soon as possible.

There was snow on the ground at Cranwell on the morning of Tuesday 13 March. Though the air was still, a brisk wind of 20 miles per hour was blowing 1,000 ft above the airfield. Nevertheless, the weather report available to the fliers looked promising. Around 8.30 a.m., the *Endeavour* took off. Three hours later, the plane was spotted at Kilmeaden in County Waterford, by Irish Civil Guards. Heavy snow was falling and visibility was low. Two hours later, it was sighted again, this time by the lighthouse keeper at Mizen Head, Co. Cork. Ahead lay the endless miles of the North Atlantic, with rough weather brewing.

Though Hinchliffe had left a note describing his plans, Mackay's involvement had remained secret. On 14 March, the *Glasgow Herald* broke the story with the headline: 'Big Flight Sensation – British Aviator Sets Out "to Fly the Atlantic" – Scottish Peer's daughter as passenger? – Aeroplane sighted by ships at sea.' By 15 March, it was indeed confirmed that Elsie Mackay was aboard the *Endeavour*. By now, however, liners on the Atlantic run were being asked to keep a look out for a plane 'distinguished by its dead black fuselage and brilliant gold wings, with the struts and supporting stays picked out in gold'. For the next few days, there were rumours of sightings, then nothing.

On 14 August 1928, the steamship *Seapool* reported the floating wreck of an airplane, but failed to salvage it because of darkness. Almost seven months later, the UK Air Ministry confirmed that part of an airplane undercarriage washed ashore in County Donegal had been identified as coming from the *Endeavour*. The finding was consistent with a sea landing in which water or ice floes had sheared off that part of the plane.

Had the *Endeavour* been brought down by severe buffeting, or by ice formation on the airframe or in the engine, always a danger? Or had it been driven far off course by strong winds? Was there a problem with the fuel transfer arrangements? The mystery remains to this day.

What is known is that in April 1928, three men (two German aviators and one Irish) became the first to complete the dangerous east-to-west crossing of the Atlantic. Two months later, the American Amelia Earhart became the first woman to complete the journey by airplane, travelling as a passenger in the west-to-east direction. In 1932, Earhart repeated the feat, this time as a solo pilot. It was not until July 1933 that Amy Johnson of England made the first east-to-west crossing by a woman, flying as a pilot with her husband Jim Mollison.

In her lifetime, Elsie Mackay was celebrated for her beauty and daring, as if those characteristics were somehow identical, and as if flying, for her, was little more than a kind of glamorous hobby. Pioneering women aviators were often diminished in that way. Yet, Mackay's most striking attributes were her raw physical courage and intense determination, the 'steel nerves' cited by a *New York Times* correspondent in 1928. Writing in that same newspaper, almost a century later, David W. Dunlap and Darcy Eveleigh suggested that, for women in the early twentieth century, flying had profound symbolic importance:

> Still hemmed in by all sorts of restrictions, still valued for looks and decorative skills, still steered toward passive accomplishments, [flying] was the ultimate escape: total freedom, total mastery – no interference. Total liberation. Women who became pilots won something additional along the way: respect.

Neither money nor good looks could achieve that. As Amelia Earhart put it to aspiring women pilots of the era: 'if and when you knock at the door, it might be well to bring an ax along; you may have to chop your way through'.

More reading

Baldwin, J., 2008. *West Over the Waves: The Final Flight of Elsie Mackay*. GC Books.

Butler, S., 1997. *East to the Dawn: The Life of Amelia Earhart*. Addison Wesley.

Jablonski, E., 1972. *Atlantic Fever*. Macmillan.

Jackson, J., 2012. *Atlantic Fever: Lindbergh, His Competitors, and the Race to Cross the Atlantic*. Farrar, Straus and Giroux.

Lebow, E. F., 2002. *Before Amelia: Women Pilots in the Early Days of Aviation*. Brassey's Inc.

Notaro, L., 2017. *Crossing the Horizon: A Novel*. Gallery Books.

BRENDA FASSIE: SOUTH AFRICA'S POP PRINCESS

Chisomo Kalinga

Dr Chisomo Kalinga is a Wellcome Trust Medical Humanities Fellow in the Department of Social Anthropology at the University of Edinburgh. Her Wellcome project is titled 'Ulimbaso "You will be strong again": How Literary Aesthetics and Storytelling Inform Concepts of Health and Wellbeing in Malawi'. It examines how indigenous literary practices (performance, form and aesthetics) are used to address community health. Her research interests are disease (specifically sexually transmitted infections), illness and well-being, biomedicine, traditional healing and witchcraft and their narrative representation in African oral and print literatures. She is working with colleagues at the College of Medicine and Malawi University of Science and Technology in Malawi to support the Malawi Medical Humanities Network (www.malawimedhumsnetwork. com). She is also an Africa section editor of the forthcoming *Palgrave Medical Humanities Reference Book on Race and Ethnicity*.

The South African pop singer Brenda Fassie (3 November 1964–9 May 2004) was affectionately titled 'MaBrrr' by her fans and proclaimed by *Time* magazine as the 'Madonna of the Townships'. Her outspoken, brazen and rebellious personality garnered unparalleled notoriety across Africa. She has long reigned supreme in my memory as the embodiment of the ultimate African diva (and you need only do a quick image search to see the variety of personas she inhabited).

On stage, she played the muse; her voice was melodic and her dancing, particularly when she wore traditional beaded Zulu-inspired mini-skirts, was playful and vivacious. In her personal life, her indulgence and bacchanalian exploits were well documented in the media. Her drug and alcohol abuse also drew comparisons to other fallen idols, as *Vice* magazine branded her the 'African Edith Piaf'. But these Eurocentric monikers never afforded full justice to the complex and unique figure that she was in Africa. She neither hid her addictions from the public nor did she retreat from inquisitions into her tumultuous relationships with both men and women lovers, which played out in the tabloids for most of her two-decade career.

By traditional and conservative African standards, she was by all means not a 'good girl'. The full force of her provocativeness only made her superstardom across the continent even more enigmatic. This is taking into account the double standard that embraces the same level of self-destructiveness from male artists as a nuance that complements their creative genius. And yet, despite her over-the-top and out-of-control diva personality, she was respected by her contemporaries throughout Africa and transcended the standard of success for black women set by her dignified elders such as singers Dixie Kwankwa, Dorothy Masuka and Miriam Makeba.

On the one hand, her popularity was justly gained through her presentation of powerful ballads about injustice such as 'Black President' (1990), a call to arms for the release of the then incarcerated Nelson Mandela, which became an international hit and a rallying cry against apartheid. In 'Sum' Bulala' ('Please Don't Kill Her/Him') (1997), she pleaded with South African taxi drivers to end escalating violence amongst rival operators in townships.

On the other hand, it was her carefree stage persona as evidenced in a 2001 performance of her bestselling, upbeat wedding song 'Vul'Indlela'('Open the Gates') (1997) that embodied everything that the public loved about Brenda.

She pranced barefoot in a short dress and jumped in the air, landing in the splits position with her pants exposed in the presence of Nobel Peace Prize Laureate and then President of the Republic of South Africa, Nelson Mandela. Every audacious move was met with cheers of support. Moments later, she leaped offstage and danced her way towards his table, first into the arms of his wife, Graça Machel, and then his. She pulled him away from his table and coquettishly pleaded with him to sing with her: 'Madiba . . . please, sing! Please, please!' He offered one abrupt syllable into her microphone before giving up. Her message was clear. At that moment, she, and only she, was in charge. And she had won over him and the entire audience.

Perhaps few outside the African continent are familiar with her legacy as a singer, a cultural icon and an outrageous success story to rise from the segregated townships of Cape Town. When IASH introduced the Dangerous Women Project and called for essays reflecting upon the question 'What does it mean to be a dangerous woman?', I felt compelled to share Brenda's story within the context of the black Jezebel narrative and stereotypes of black female sexuality that should have hindered her rise to fame.

Brenda was known as the 'bad girl' whose music even *gogos* (grandmothers) liked to dance to. Her success was in part defined by an unapologetic command of her sexuality both on- and offstage. She was a libertine and *enfant terrible*, yet she strategically confronted the Jezebel stereotype by challenging the racial binaries and heterosexist patriarchies that sustained this narrative within the South African apartheid social construct. Her celebration of South African traditions in her image and sound created an important space for deconstructing black female autonomy.

Despite the turbulence that affected her personal relationships, her fame and popularity were buoyed by her fans' acceptance of her narrative of empowerment against detrimental interpretations of black identity promoted by the apartheid regime. From the late 1990s onwards, her songs were less focused on English language, in favour of Sotho, Xhosa and Zulu. On stage and in her videos, she adorned herself in personalised traditional costumes reflecting the versatility of South Africa's indigenous textile cultures. Her music, which was first infused with Western pop sounds, soon adopted the local kwaito beats, a late twentieth-century African aesthetic that emanated from South African townships.

Watching Brenda in recordings of her performances, interviews and music videos, I often feel that she did not contrive to brand herself into an African feminist icon. Rather, there was an innate and raw disdain for injustice and oppression that informed her style, performance, imagination and sound. If her rebellion was ingrained, it perhaps was tested by a combination of her nature and a reaction against the apartheid state in which she grew up.

The black Jezebel narrative, within the context of feminist thought, is a trope that establishes a distorted and dehumanising framework to hypersexualise and objectify black women's sexuality; it historically demeans and overshadows the complexity and diversity of romantic experiences faced by women of colour. In its historical roots, particularly in the context of the European colonisation of Africa and the transatlantic slave trade to the Americas, it attributes shame and culpability for sexual interactions between white men and black women as a result of entrapment due to the manipulative and lascivious nature of African women, as Evie Shockley explains in her article 'Buried Alive'.

The stereotype traces its origins to hermeneutical interpretations of the New Testament in the Book of Kings; Jezebel was a Phoenician princess and idol worshipper who persuaded her husband, King Ahab, to abandon worship of Yahweh (God) in favour of pagan deities. In artistic representations, she is portrayed as a lascivious, dangerous woman who uses her sexuality to lure men into sin and other misdeeds. Hence, applications of the black Jezebel stereotype during colonialism, postcolonialism, slavery and the Jim Crow era justified the rape, sexual exploitation and degradation of black women by emphasising their feral sexual nature. Augustine Asaah, in 'Images of Rape in African Fiction', affirms that dominance over the African female body in creative representation continues to be framed by histories of postcolonial patriarchy, particularly in depictions of women's sexuality.

In African culture, the question 'Is she a good girl?' at face value is a polite enquiry; however, this question can also be a thinly veiled code to ascertain the level of promiscuous behaviour that a woman engages in. It reflects the conventional way that women are viewed within the troubling binary of either a 'respectable', 'honourable' African lady or a 'prostitute'. The anglophone African application of the word 'prostitute' classifies a spectrum of women who engage in sexual activities that involve premarital sex, particularly with multiple partners. This is contrasted with common applications of the word in a Western construct where it either identifies sex industry workers or is meant to insult a woman's sexual agency by associating her with sex workers.

The woman who has been labelled a prostitute in African discourse is devoid of humanity and is usually depicted as the source of demise, particularly through disease; she exists only to entrap the morally conflicted male to teach a lesson about promiscuity.

She is a Jezebel.

Paula Treichler examined the dialogue about female sexuality during the AIDS epidemic and revealed that although scientific discourse had a tendency to present women in general as 'incompetent transmitters of HIV, passive receptacles', this consideration did not apply to African women and sex workers. She argues in her 1999 article 'AIDS, Homophobia and Biomedical Discourse' that these two specific types of women in the public imagination were:

> seen as so contaminated that their bodies are virtual laboratory cultures for viral replication . . . [Their] exotic bodies, sexual practices, are seen to be so radically different from those of women in the [West] that anything can happen in them.

It demonstrates the severity to which the black Jezebel narrative had become entrenched in anthropological, communal and scientific understandings of black female sexuality.

Brenda used her music as a platform to confront both the African 'good girl' and 'Jezebel' narratives. In her song 'Good Black Woman' (1989), she woefully pleaded against her brother's imprisonment to apartheid police officers. Her frustration powered the melody, as she chastised the officers for having a bad attitude towards her and appealed to them to respect her value as a 'good black woman': one who fights against injustice.

While her music provided one avenue to discuss injustices against women, particularly during apartheid, she also used it as a platform to challenge perceptions that a measure of a woman's 'goodness' is conditional on her sexual demureness. In her aptly titled dance track 'I Am Not A Bad Girl' (1990), she responded to media criticism about her behaviour by declaring that she's not a bad girl seeking publicity, but just 'an ordinary girl' seeking acceptance to be 'the way I am'. In interviews, she matched these sentiments very candidly, particularly about her same-sex partnerships, and offered that her unrepentant stance of self-acceptance had a slight negative impact on her fame. In a 2003 interview with *Mamba Magazine*, she said:

> I am a lover. I've always been with women. When I was still married, I was also with women . . . People knew . . . Before people thought it was a bad thing in God's eyes . . . They don't bother me. It's nice to be the way I am.

In her last years, she came out as a lesbian. She was particularly adamant that who she loved should not prohibit her from also self-identifying as a good African woman.

The impact of the Jezebel narrative is most troubling in its tendency to both overtly and subconsciously undermine the sexual expression, identities and desires of black women. Many black women across varying cultures feel compelled to counter this stereotype by projecting an overemphasised demeanour of wholesomeness, piety and chastity. Asaah argues that this is reflected within African self-representations of female sexuality in particular: 'in spite of their thematic interest in the subject of sex, [African narratives], at the stylistic and technical levels, are muted and euphemistic portrayals of the sexual'.

Brenda, whose life and music were defined by racism, sexism and a counter narrative of empowerment, set forth an important dialogue that resonated across the continent through an interrogation of oppressive ideologies against Africans and women. Privately, she was a complicated and self-destructive character; but as an artist, she was a self-assured revolutionary. She offered herself and the South African music scene to the entire continent as a platform to converge and rebel against the legacy of ownership of black identity and sexuality. She seemed unfazed by the public exposure of her private life and allowed it to inform her activism and legacy.

Mireille Miller-Young argues in her 2008 article 'Hip-Hop Honeys and Da Hustlaz' that contemporary hip hop culture and its emphasis on pornographic, explicit and crude displays of black sexuality tend to cause anxiety within black communities and incite controversy around exactly what constitutes 'appropriate' representation of black sexuality. Though she acknowledges that misogyny and homophobia are rampant in hip hop culture, she advocates against withdrawing or toning down images of black sexuality as a protection and preservation mechanism against the historically rooted exploitation of the black Jezebel stereotype. Additionally, bell hooks, the prominent black feminist scholar, has advocated in the past for an 'oppositional gaze' or a new way of looking at and challenging the ways that society has accepted certain stereotypes about black women.

I found Brenda's life story intriguing because she used her celebrity to publicly denounce the principle that sustains the sexual expression of an African woman as an acceptable measure of her character. Instead, her articulation and embracing of her own sexuality encouraged us to theorise it as a practice of resistance against the black Jezebel narrative.

Black African female sexuality receives considerable analysis under heteronormative frameworks of postcolonial resistance and patriarchal subjectivity and fetishism. This engagement is vital to contextualise gender and feminist studies in Africa, but we need to engage more with the full range of experiences that the modern African woman faces. As a humanities scholar, I aspire to integrate more diverse narratives within the framework of African studies, particularly gender and LGBTQI+ experiences.

Brenda had an extraordinary ability to convert the discomfort that her sexuality elicited into an invitation to adore her. One of my favourite stories is how she handled a wardrobe malfunction at Zanzibar nightclub, a now closed venue in Washington, DC once popular with the African diaspora. Several of my relatives were in attendance that evening, and during a vibrant dance set, Brenda's breasts burst out of her corset in front of a stunned audience. Interpreting their silence as discomfort, Brenda paused her performance and cupped her hands under her bare breasts. She faced the audience and unapologetically declared, 'This . . . is Africa!' Once again, she was met with rapturous applause.

Brenda, at her best, epitomised black female empowerment and sexual liberation.

So what makes a woman dangerous?

The dangerous woman is an African woman who embraces her sexuality, who refuses to conceal it as an act of self-preservation against an antiquated narrative that vilifies her as a dark, voluptuous and indecent being. The dangerous woman is an African woman who is not afraid to challenge traditional perceptions of what it means to be a 'good girl'.

Brenda Fassie was a dangerous woman because she was a free spirit who wanted the world to love her unconditionally as a sexual black woman.

And we did.

Acknowledgement

A version of this chapter was published in *Dangerous Women: Fifty Reflections on Women, Power and Identity* (Unbound, 2022).

More reading

Asaah, A. H., 2006. To speak or not to speak with the whole mouth: Textualization of taboo subjects in Europhone African literature. *Journal of Black Studies*, 36, pp. 497–514.

Asaah, A. H., 2007. Images of rape in African fiction: Between the assumed fatality of violence and the cry for justice. *Annales Aequatoria*, 28, pp. 333–355.

BBC News, 2004. Brenda Fassie: A very human hero. 10 May. Available at: http://news.bbc.co.uk/1/hi/world/africa/3700309.stm

hooks, b., 1992. *Black Looks: Race and Representation*. South End Press.

McGregor, L., 2004. Obituary: Brenda Fassie. *The Guardian*, 11 May.

POLITICIANS

AND

PEACEMAKERS

In late 2024, Dr Harini Amarasuriya was appointed Prime Minister of Sri Lanka, the third woman to hold the role. Dr Amarasuriya is a graduate of the University of Edinburgh and conducted research at IASH in 2019, shortly before returning to Sri Lanka to become an MP. Her work while in Edinburgh focused on the women's movement and the influence of radical Christians on dissent in Sri Lanka, exploring ideas of intimacy in times of extraordinary violence and oppression – a starkly different kind of politician than often seen in the UK.

In this final section, we have gathered together profiles of political players both inside and outside traditional power structures. Harshana Rambukwella and Kanchana N. Ruwanpura provide a biography of Dr Amarasuriya's predecessor as Sri Lankan Prime Minister, Mrs Sirimivo Bandaranaike. As the world's first female PM, 'Mrs B' transformed herself from housewife to postcolonial leader. Similarly, Vijaya Lakshmi Pandit became the first woman President of the UN General Assembly in 1953, as outlined in Rosalind Parr's contribution. But individual firsts are not the whole story.

Activism as a route to change is also a focus here, from Mrs Barbour's Army fighting rent rises in Glasgow to Dagmar Wilson's campaigning for nuclear disarmament in the USA. Kathy Galloway quotes Helen Steven on her own fight against nuclear weapons, 'their power comes from our obedience'. This section celebrates the 'us' as well as the 'she'.

Daring to stand up to powerful groups, usually made up of men, defines the women showcased here. Some reached the pinnacle of politics while others preferred to lobby and organise, but whether local, national or international in reach, their actions helped form a more just social order.

MARY BARBOUR: BEWARE!

Catriona Burness

Catriona Burness is a historian who has published widely on the history of women and parliamentary representation in Scotland. She has worked with many local history groups and held university postdoctoral fellowships and lectureships. She carried out research on Mary Barbour on a voluntary basis as a member of the Remember Mary Barbour Association. The Association raised a statue as a lasting memorial to one of Glasgow's greatest heroes and the unveiling of the completed statue took place in spring 2017. The Remember Mary Barbour Association was formally wound up as a charity after the erection of the statue but some details on the campaign can still be seen at: http://remembermarybarbour.wordpress.com/

None of the definitions of 'dangerous' is reassuring. They include menacing, threatening, treacherous, hazardous, risky, dodgy, perilous and precarious. Asking about 'dangerous people' will produce a list of dictators, killers and/or criminals, mostly men. The immediate associations with 'dangerous women' seem to be with infamous convicted killers.

In the political context, the use of the term generally serves as a warning.

Born in Kilbarchan on 20 February 1875, Mary Barbour was the third of seven children, to her father James Rough, a carpet weaver. In 1887, the family moved to the village of Elderslie and Mary gained work as a thread twister, eventually becoming a carpet printer.

She married David Barbour in 1896, living first in Dumbarton. Their first child David, born a few months after their marriage, died of meningitis at the age of ten months, a loss likely to have shaped Mary's deep interest in health and housing issues.

By 1901, the Barbours had moved to Govan, and she was an active member of the Kinning Park Co-operative Guild. She also became involved in the Socialist Sunday School and the Independent Labour Party (ILP). The home focus of her activity was Govan and Glasgow. In 1914 housing was clearly Glasgow's greatest social problem and Mary Barbour had become the 'leading woman in Govan' within the newly formed Glasgow Women's Housing Association. As a political campaigner she was already challenging the status quo.

After the First World War started in 1914, thousands of workers flocked to Glasgow to jobs in the shipyards and munitions factories.

Property owners calculated they could raise rents for tenement flats. Instead, fury was aroused and the rent strike was the response. The historian James Smyth has noted that Govan was the initial storm centre and 'remained the major bulwark of the struggle'.

One of the key players in Glasgow's radical politics, Helen Crawfurd, gave a detailed description in her *Memoirs* of the tactics used during the rent strike:

> The Glasgow Women's Housing Association took up this issue, and in the working-class districts, committees were formed, to resist these increases in rents. Cards, oblong in shape, were printed with the words 'RENT STRIKE. WE ARE NOT REMOVING' and placed in the windows of the houses where rent increases were demanded. When the increased rents were refused, the property owners immediately took legal action for the eviction of the tenants.
>
> The women then organised resistance to these evictions in the following way. In the Govan and Partick districts the working-class houses were mainly tenements. One woman with a bell would sit in the close, or passage, watching while the other women living in the tenement went on with their household duties. Whenever the Bailiff's Officer appeared to evict a tenant, the woman in the passage immediately rang the bell, and the women came from all parts of the building. Some with flour, if baking, wet clothes, if washing, and other missiles. Usually the Bailiff made off for his life, chased by a mob of angry women.

Mary Barbour was involved in every aspect of the activities, from organising committees to the physical prevention of evictions and seeing off the Sheriff's Officers. Her contemporaries, Helen Crawfurd and Willie Gallacher, highlight her leadership role, with Willie Gallacher coining the phrase 'Mrs Barbour's Army'. In his *Memoirs*, William Gallacher later remarked that, 'In Govan, Mrs Barbour, a typical working-class housewife, became the leader of a movement such as had never been seen before, or since for that matter. Street meetings, back-court meetings, drums, bells, trumpets – every method was used to bring the women out.'

By November 1915, as many as 20,000 tenants were on rent strike and rent strike activity was spreading beyond Glasgow to other parts of the country.

The decision by a Partick factor to prosecute eighteen tenants for non-payment of a rent increase brought the crisis to a head in Glasgow's small debt court on 17 November 1915. Many of those in arrears were shipyard workers and there were strikes in support and deputations sent to the court. Thousands of women marched with thousands of shipyard and engineering workers in what the *Govan Press* described as 'remarkable scenes':

> Amid news of imminent ministerial intervention, the cases were dismissed. Within a month legislation was in place and the rent strike's place in history was assured. The Increase of Rent and Mortgage Interest (War Restrictions) Act 1915 introduced rent control whereby rents were restricted to their August 1914 level.

Joseph Melling, the author of the most detailed study of the rent strikes, underlines the importance of the way in which the industrial and housing protests combined to challenge the authority of landlords and the state. James Smyth considers that 'it may well have been the most successful example of direct action ever undertaken by the Scottish working class'.

Mary Barbour's involvement in this struggle made her a local hero in Govan and much further afield. In itself, this activity puts her firmly into the 'dangerous woman' category.

After the rent strike, Mary Barbour was involved in both protests against food shortages and anti-war movements.

Socialist groupings such the ILP and the Labour and Socialist Alliance campaigned for peace from the day the war started right up to the Armistice. The war split the suffrage movement, with some militant and constitutional suffrage societies suspending campaigning to support the war effort. The Women's International League (WIL) was formed in 1915 to offer a space to anti-war suffragists. The WIL was cross-party and according to Helen Crawfurd it carried out important propaganda work, 'Mrs Agnes Dollan, Mrs Barbour, Miss Walker, Mrs Ferguson and myself being the local propagandists.'

This same group of 'more active spirits' went on to found the Women's Peace Crusade (WPC) in June 1916. The aim was 'to hold a conference and take greater risks in our literature and propaganda methods'. The 'risks' involved taking an anti-war message out onto the streets and into working-class areas. Most of the neighbourhood meetings were held during the afternoon and often in back courts, making it easy for women to get involved.

Mary Barbour was a regular speaker at WPC rallies and spoke at the May Day rally in 1917. It must have taken courage. WPC meetings were frequently targeted by pro-war opponents and the police had to be brought in to restore order, as outside Glasgow City Chambers in 1917.

However, she seems to have been more restrained in her WPC and other activity than fellow activists, Helen Crawfurd and Agnes Dollan.

Alistair Hulett's song *Mrs Barbour's Army* refers to Mary Barbour having been arrested during the rent strike, but this seems to have been poetic licence on his part. I have not found any evidence of Mary Barbour being arrested for any of her wartime political activities, whilst it is evident from press reports that Crawfurd and Dollan were arrested several times. Agnes Dollan and Helen Crawfurd sought this out. Mary Barbour didn't. Churchill would certainly have called her 'dangerous', perhaps even more dangerous in her restraint.

Post-war, she was a natural choice in 1920 as one of the ILP council candidates for the Fairfield ward in Govan. This was one of the first elections after most women over thirty won the vote, and Lloyd George had made the memorable post-war promise of 'Homes fit for Heroes'.

Mary Barbour campaigned not only for better homes but for a higher standard of living generally, and fought for free school milk, children's playgrounds, municipal wash-houses and an end to slum housing. An article that she wrote for the *Govan Pioneer* concluded:

> The standard must be higher; better housing, and everything that makes life what it should be in the future must come first; the paying for it is the secondary consideration. Lloyd George has advised that you be daring in your demands. I hope the workers will be greatly daring in their demands, not only for better homes, but for a higher standard of living generally.

At the election she and four other women were elected to Glasgow Corporation, the first women elected in the city since the passing of the 1907 Act enabling women to be elected as councillors.

In 1924, Mary Barbour marked other milestones for women in public office when she became both a Bailie and 'the first fully fledged woman magistrate of the City of Glasgow'. Her support for Glasgow's first birth control clinic was more controversial. This went against the voting record of her Socialist MP colleagues, none of whom had supported the Birth Control Enabling Bill in 1922. The Glasgow Women's Welfare and Advisory Clinic opened in August 1926 at 51 Govan Road to give advice to married women on family planning.

In 1931, Mary Barbour opted to stand down from the council at the age of fifty-six, stating that she felt 'the difficulties ahead required young and strenuous fighters'. The *Govan Press* reported her farewell address as a councillor, which welcomed changes on health matters, but continued:

> Eleven years ago those who were returned as representing the working class went forward with certain ideals before them, ideals that they could revolutionise the life of the people of the city, both from a health point of

view and from a housing point of view. Those years had been to her a disappointment because of the fact that so little had been done.

When she died in 1958, her obituary in the *Govan Press* read:

> There are women in Govan today who think of Mrs Mary Barbour as one of the great leaders of the Labour Movement who truly represented its spirit and purpose, and I am inclined to agree with them . . . Mrs Barbour has been out of the limelight of public affairs in this city for many years now but there never was a more revered and loved local leader than she was in the heyday of her active life.

She undoubtedly challenged the status quo of her day, taking on landlords and the power of the state during wartime. She wanted not only to change but to revolutionise living conditions. In the positive sense of the term, Mary Barbour is a leading 'dangerous woman'. She is still relevant and 'dangerous' after her death.

Today, she is remembered, and inspires in Govan and beyond.

Acknowledgements

I gratefully acknowledge the research grant from the Lipman-Miliband Trust, which enabled archive research visits within Scotland and London and Manchester.

More reading

Burness, C., 2015. Remember Mary Barbour. *Scottish Labour History*, 50, pp. 81–96.

Canning, A., 2004. Barbour, Mary (1875–1958), *Oxford Dictionary of National Biography (DNB)*. Oxford University Press.

Llewelyn Davies, M., ed., 1977. *Life as We Have Known It by Co-operative Working Women*. Virago Press Ltd.

Note: Two of the pieces of further reading above – by Catriona Burness and by Audrey Canning – give Mary Barbour's date of birth as 22 February 1878. There was ambiguity in viewing her birth certificate and Audrey Canning, at the time of writing her article for the *Dictionary of National Biography*, was given this date by the Scottish Record Office (SRO). We have since had it confirmed by the SRO that the date of birth should be 20 February 1878 as cited in this entry for the Dangerous Women Project.

VIJAYA LAKSHMI PANDIT: 'EDUCATED, ATTRACTIVE, CHARMING WHEN SHE WISHES'

Rosalind Parr

Rosalind Parr is Lecturer in History at Glasgow Caledonian University where she specialises in South Asian and global histories of gender. She is the author of *Citizens of Everywhere: Indian Women, Nationalism and Cosmopolitanism* (Cambridge University Press, 2021) and has published research in *Journal of Global History* and *South Asia: Journal of South Asian Studies*. Her current research explores gendered histories of development in postcolonial India, Pakistan and Sri Lanka.

When the Indian independence activist Vijaya Lakshmi Pandit applied for a passport to visit America in July 1944, alarm bells rang across the British Empire. The purpose of the visit, as described in her passport application, was personal, enabling Pandit, who had been recently widowed, 'to have a quiet period' with her two daughters who were at college in America. Wartime imperial officials, though, were under no illusions. Pandit was a prominent anticolonial activist and, if permitted to go to America, she would undoubtedly use the opportunity to engage in damaging propaganda against British imperial rule. 'We must regard Mrs. Pandit', wrote one official in Delhi, 'as an enemy willing to traduce H.M.G. and the Government of India in every way possible in the USA'.

Pandit's application created a dilemma for the British authorities. If she were allowed to travel, she would be at liberty to publicise Indian nationalist grievances before an American audience. By drawing attention to the injustices of colonial rule, Pandit, it was feared, would undermine the unity of the Allied war effort, which was nominally built on a shared commitment to 'rights' and 'freedom'. Such a campaign might prompt unwelcome American pressure on Britain to withdraw from India, as well as stir up domestic tensions in India. On the other hand, British officials feared the propaganda value of any seemingly heavy-handed decision to refuse Pandit's application. The authorities were particularly wary because the premature death of her husband a year earlier was understood to have been precipitated by colonial prison conditions. Either way, officials agreed, Pandit was dangerous.

To the British, Pandit was dangerous because of who she was and what she represented. Born in Allahabad, North India in 1900, she was the eldest daughter of a wealthy nationalist family. Impeccably connected, her family had brought her into close association with M. K. Gandhi; and her brother, the eminent Indian National Congress leader Jawaharlal Nehru, was already a well-known figure in America. For her entire adult life, she had been a Congress activist and politician – a career that included three periods of imprisonment and two years as India's first woman Cabinet Minister in the United Provinces Provincial Government. A gilded upbringing, followed by years of activism and subsequent political office, had created a formidable communicator – a woman who was, as one official grudgingly described her, 'educated, attractive, charming when she wishes'. Quick-witted and confident, she spoke English with an authoritative 'Oxford accent' and conveyed a passionate sense of injustice. This made her, according to intelligence officials, 'the very person to interpret the Congress case to the American public'.

In the exclusively male space of the British bureaucracy, Pandit's femininity was perceived as a mysterious, somewhat slippery asset. Her 'undoubted feminine charm' and '"sob-stuff" appeal' marked her out from the rational, reasoned world of male politics and, it was implied, gave her something of an unfair advantage. Pandit herself was not above using the 'feminine charm' her enemies found so dangerous, remarking mirthfully many years later that as a younger woman she had 'used every weapon in my armoury unashamedly'.

As an anticolonial activist, what made Pandit's personal attributes so dangerous was the powerful symbolic value she possessed. If India could produce such a woman – educated, liberated, modern – the justification for colonial rule as a civilising mission was easily defeated. Her very existence refuted the image, so favoured in imperialist propaganda, of the subjugated Indian woman – a victim of Indian culture that could only be saved by European civilisation. Rather, she provided evidence of India's ability to self-govern. Yet after weeks of indecision, Pandit's passport application was approved. Fear of the political capital that might be made from the refusal to grant a recent widow access to her daughters ultimately overrode concerns about the effect of her propaganda in America.

When Pandit arrived in America in December 1944 she found sympathy, encouragement and ample opportunity for publicising her anticolonial message. Large receptions were held in her honour by prominent figures, including the novelist Pearl Buck, the *Time* magazine publisher Henry Luce, and the Chinese Consul General, at which Pandit spoke forcefully on 'The India Question'. Such high-profile connections exposed the contradictions at the heart of the American interventionist project, which at once purported to export American ideals of freedom while allying with the imperialist power Great Britain.

As a speaker, Pandit consciously tapped into the global ideological ambitions of the interventionist lobby. To an audience of over 900 dinner guests at an event in New York she made the claim for Indian independence in the name of 'liberty' for 'suppressed peoples everywhere'. Linking the Indian cause to anticolonial movements elsewhere, she argued that 'unless all people in all parts of the world are declared free and equal, there can be no peace and there can be no progress'.

Conditions in India provided much ammunition. In 1944–1945 almost the entire nationalist leadership and thousands of grassroots activists were imprisoned, enabling Pandit to make the damaging claim that India was 'one vast prison camp where 86,000 men and women have been detained in prison without trial'. Furthermore, the colossal tragedy of the Bengal famine (1943–1944) was still unfolding and Pandit, who had herself carried out relief and fundraising work at the height of the crisis, highlighted British failures in preventing mass starvation and the spread of disease. These colonial realities lent considerable weight to the nationalist argument that imperial rule was both ideologically unsound and disastrously ineffective.

Pandit's public utterances sent waves of concern across the Atlantic. At Churchill's request, Leo Amery, the Secretary of State for India, presented a secret report on Pandit's 'undesirable activities' to the War Cabinet. Her statements in America prompted a question in Parliament demanding to know what steps were being taken 'to counteract any harmful effect that such statements may have on public opinion amongst our allies'.

In reality, most Americans were content with the line put out by British propaganda that India was gradually moving towards self-government and the issue of Independence would be resolved after the war. Nevertheless, Pandit's activities in America rattled the British establishment. She was dangerous because she fundamentally questioned the right of Western powers to global dominance. In exposing the injustices of British imperialism and by asserting the ability of non-Western peoples to rule themselves, she countered the established racialised underpinnings of the international order. As Western powers jostled for position in the post-war world, her intervention represented a destabilising challenge to the future ambitions of those who sought to maintain European global influence.

It was in this spirit that Pandit travelled to the Allied-sponsored San Francisco Conference on International Organisation in April 1945 where she demanded a voice for the '600,000,000 . . . enslaved peoples of Asia [who] may not be officially heard at this Conference', adding the warning: 'there will be no real peace on this earth so long as they are denied justice'.

The following year she returned to New York for the First Session of the United Nations General Assembly (Second Part) as the leader of the Indian delegation. Here she heralded soon-to-be-independent India's arrival on the international stage with an attack on The Union of South Africa's discriminatory legislation against its resident Indian population. Through a resolution that framed racial discrimination as a global issue, Pandit led a historic defeat of the South African delegation and earned an international reputation as a champion of Asian and African rights.

Pandit's appointment as the only woman leader of a national delegation at the UN in 1946 was the beginning of a pioneering international career. She returned to represent India at the UN on several occasions and in 1953 became the first woman President of the UN General Assembly. She also served as Indian Ambassador to the Soviet Union (1947–1949) and the United States of America (1949–1951), and as High Commissioner to the United Kingdom (1954–1961). This exceptional career was subversive, countering universally dominant assumptions about women's place and abilities.

During her debut speech at the UN General Assembly in 1946, Pandit expressed the radical hope that

> women of all countries will have the occasion to participate more fully with men in all departments of life, including the work of this Assembly, thus helping to create a better and more balanced world.

Neither the role of such rhetoric in normalising the concept of gender equality, nor Pandit's significance as a pioneer and role model, should be ignored. However, her career as a dangerous woman is hardly a straightforward narrative.

Pandit was a product of the struggle between imperialism and nationalism, in which both sides sought legitimacy through their claim to emancipate Indian women. Working amid the competing claims of gender and nation, Pandit regularly traded on her own personal achievements in order to favourably contrast the status of Indian women with the sexism she observed in Western society. This was a riposte to the condescending attitude of Western feminists towards 'women of the East' and an anticolonial claim in itself. Yet, in her attempt to boost India's international prestige, she passed over the genuine gender, caste and class disparities of Indian society.

When it came to India, Pandit consciously nurtured her reputation as a trailblazer, remarking in her autobiography that

> as I see the new generation forging ahead, my heart is full of joy because it is my colleagues and I who built the road on which these girls can walk forward today.

This was a legacy she sought to cement in a book – planned but never published – entitled *Forgotten Women*, the aim of which was to honour

> the several women who have contributed to the national progress on many levels but who seem to have been completely forgotten.

Although gender equality was guaranteed in the Constitution of India (1950), advocates of women's rights faced strong conservative opposition in the decades after independence. The Hindu Code Bill, for example, which was designed to overhaul regressive social practices, made slow progress amid claims it signalled the destruction of the Hindu family. For social conservatives, Pandit's personification as a liberated, professional woman who operated outside traditional social constraints was indeed dangerous. At the same time, however, an unintended consequence of her international career may have been that it preserved the illusion of real gender equality in India while Pandit herself was 'forgotten' in domestic public life.

We can only speculate what impact Pandit might have had on Indian gender politics had she spent more time in India after independence. But if by working in the global public sphere she was marginalised in India, social conservatives might have concluded that a detached international space was the safest place for a dangerous woman to be.

More reading

Bhagavan, M. B., 2023. *Vijaya Lakshmi Pandit*. Allen Lane.

Brittain, V., 1965. *Envoy Extraordinary: A Study of Vijaya Lakshmi Pandit and Her Contribution to Modern India*. George Allen & Unwin.

Guthrie, A., 1963. *Madame Ambassador: The Life of Vijaya Lakshmi Pandit*. Macmillan & Co.

Nehru, J. and Sahgal, N., 2000. *Before Freedom: Nehru's Letters to his Sister*. HarperCollins Publishers.

Parr, R., 2021. *Citizens of Everywhere: Indian Women, Nationalism and Cosmopolitanism, 1920–1952*. Cambridge University Press.

MADGE SAUNDERS: PIONEER
IN INTERCULTURAL MINISTRY

Janet Lees

Janet Lees is a retired Minister of the United Reformed Church. She served at St James Sheffield from 1998–2004, where she first heard about the ministry of Madge Saunders. Janet led the group that visited her in Jamaica in 2002 and wrote about her life in the book *Daughters of Dissent* (United Reformed Church, 2004).

To be the first woman doing anything is often dangerous enough. Marjorie Prentice Saunders (1913–2009), a forgotten woman and Jamaican pioneer, had many firsts, making her a dangerous woman.

'You will find the vast majority of people in this country are friendly and willing to assist you', is a statement amongst the opening lines of the booklet *Living in Britain*, published by the British Council of Churches to help those arriving in Britain in the 1960s and 1970s to find themselves at home. The manuscript was by Marjorie Saunders, or Madge, as she was known. In the language of its day, the booklet narrates on employment, housing, health and children's services. There's the 'man who comes and empties the meter of all the coins you have put in', the male Landlord and Rent Officer and of course the male doctor, although I have no way of knowing whether all these men were directly from Madge's hand.

Certainly, her concern for children is there: 'Vitamin D is especially important for babies and young children' and furthermore 'Potatoes are better for your health than polished rice. Oatmeal and rolled oats are good for you', and also the address of the Vegetarian Society. There's also advice about how to encourage play and learning in young children. This is no surprise. Madge was one of the founders of the Basic School movement in Jamaica. Although Madge is thanked for her manuscript, the whole is credited to Douglas Tilbe, who was then Director of the Community and Race Relations Unit of the British Council of Churches (BCC). It was later reissued when Asian migrants from Uganda came to Britain.

Although the booklet affirms that a warm welcome awaits in Britain, Madge's own experiences were varied. She first came to Britain in 1946, when she studied Mission at Edinburgh's St Colm's House. She was the first Jamaican woman to be trained there. Then, a training house for women missionaries, her signature survives in the Birthday Book. It was a community of women from many nations and Madge mostly found this affirming, although she did encounter racism there. She returned to Jamaica and continued her work in education, both in Basic Schools, High Schools and in the church.

It wasn't until 1965 that she returned to Britain. In Jamaica, she had been involved in developing basic educational provision and in expanding work with girls and young women through the Girl's Guildry. This latter organisation had begun in Scotland, and later amalgamated with the Girl's Brigade. It was intended for the formation of young Christian women. 'Struggling' when Madge took on the work, she developed it into an international Caribbean organisation, and was always proud of the women who came through to leadership roles in Jamaica and other Caribbean islands.

By 1965, Britain saw many changes and challenges. Church leaders in Britain began to realise they needed help from Jamaican churches. The majority of Jamaican people coming to Britain were Christians, but the attitudes in British churches were a major part of the problem. In an interview about her life, Madge highlighted:

> When more than ten immigrants went into a church, the host people in the community left the church. This caused a financial crisis.

In response, Madge gave talks, led community discussions and study groups, spoke at conferences and on the radio and television. She wrote about 'being on call twenty-four hours a day, sleeping with a telephone by my bed ready to help anyone in distress'. She recalled racist graffiti being painted on the door of her flat after she was interviewed by a local paper about remarks made about immigrants by Enoch Powell. She recognised that the Church needed to be united in its efforts to combat racism:

> No one denomination can go it alone as we tackle the evils of racism, injustice and the moral and spiritual breakdown of our time.

Madge worked in an ecumenical project in Sheffield, serving a group of churches including St James Presbyterian Church, now United Reformed Church (URC), where she was ordained Deaconess on 26 January 1966. She also initiated a playgroup at the church, which still welcomes families from all sections of the community, offering support for the adults and opportunities for play and learning for the children. She led the St James community for ten years and also played a part in national ecumenical conversations.

Madge's ministry was a combination of these practical projects, and a recognition of the need to work in the community to further inter-cultural understanding. This meant serving in cultural organisations like the Sheffield and District West Indian Association as well as in local schools, play groups and youth projects. Her experience in the Basic Schools of Jamaica was an important foundation. There, she had encouraged the inclusion of breakfast and lunch to improve children's learning. This was no less necessary in Pitsmoor in the 1960s and 1970s as it had been in Jamaica when she opened a school kitchen at Galina Elementary School, earlier in her life.

Reflecting on her ten years as a missionary in Sheffield, the United Church of Jamaica (UCJ) described her as 'a bridge' between the white host and black immigrant communities. Madge was dangerous, because she supported a minority group, the black immigrants in Sheffield, and gave them a voice. She was persistent and did not stop, even when she herself was targeted by racists. She was dangerous as a pioneer, both in Britain and in Jamaica, tackling issues that many shied away from: nutrition for children, support for teachers, leadership for young people. She returned to Jamaica in 1976 to become the first woman ordained to pastoral ministry in the UCJ at the Salem United Church. She continued her work to develop leadership skills in young people, where the Madge Saunders Training Centre was named after her. She was dangerous because she continued undaunted all her long life, even giving up her house to provide bursaries for young people after she retired, and moving to a small bungalow, as she thought their education was more important than where she lived.

In her own words she summed up her philosophy, 'Sometimes you have to break certain traditions and laws to bring about positive change in life.'

In 2002, a group from St James Church Sheffield went to visit her in Jamaica. These were 'her Sheffield people', who remembered her pioneer-ing ministry in the city. Madge still had the scissors made of Sheffield steel that the Mayor had given her when she left to return to Jamaica. No doubt they had proved useful: she continued to encourage the UCJ right up until her death aged ninety-six in 2008. One participant in the visit from Sheffield to Jamaica recalled 'Everywhere we went people said, "Madge helped us do this."' It was this persistent effort on her part to sup-port and empower ordinary people that made her a dangerous woman.

More reading

Kaye, E., Lees J. and Thorpe, K., eds, 2004. *Daughters of Dissent*. United Reformed Church.

DAGMAR WILSON: 'HOUSEWIFE AND PEACE WORKER'

Jon Coburn

Jon Coburn is Senior Lecturer in American History at the University of Lincoln, UK. His research explores histories of protest and dissent in the United States with particular focus on the intersections of movements for peace, feminism and civil rights. His forthcoming book (to be published by University of Massachusetts Press, 2025) provides the first complete history of women's anti-nuclear group Women Strike for Peace, asserting the significance of maternal peace activism to histories of Cold War-era social movements.

Women have often been labelled as dangerous for expressing transgressive politics, but we must also recognise those who drew scorn while abiding by the rigid, gendered expectations of respectable behaviour that marked their lives. Peace and anti-nuclear activist Dagmar Wilson provides an exemplary case of someone who endured political criticism and even criminal accusation simply for calling for calm at a time of political hysteria.

Wilson modestly described herself as a 'mere housewife', a label that obscured her far-reaching impact on pacifism and politics. Born in New York in January 1916, Wilson grew up in the UK where she developed an 'upper-class British accent'. She later recalled her natural inclination to challenge 'traditional ways of doing things', and Wilson's childhood was steeped in the politics of dissent. Her parents were involved in the women's suffrage movement and were close friends with militant suffragist Betty Gram Swing. Wilson's father, CBS broadcaster Cesar Searchinger, exposed Dagmar to intellectual political discourse from an early age. Gandhi's visit to London left a lasting impression on the sixteen-year-old Dagmar, who remained proud about a school essay she had written on Gandhi's 'principles for peace'.

Wilson and her husband moved to Washington, DC just before the Second World War and raised three daughters. Her husband, Christopher Wilson, took up work in the British Embassy as a commercial attaché, while Dagmar balanced teaching, graphic design and illustrating children's books. Her political interests remained vibrant. Wilson joined the local Parent-Teacher Association (PTA), founded the Action

Committee for School Libraries and launched a school library pro-gramme. She also worked on the campaign for DC Statehood and applied her artistic skills to political purposes, converting statistics into graphics, charts and diagrams for use by the Committee for Inter-American Affairs.

Wilson's pacifist convictions drew her towards the anti-nuclear move-ment. She joined the Committee for a SANE Nuclear Policy (SANE) when it was founded in 1957, serving as secretary for the DC branch. However, Wilson quickly felt that existing peace groups lacked the urgency and inclusivity needed to halt the nuclear threat. When the US and USSR resumed atmospheric nuclear testing in 1961, Wilson urged SANE's leadership to take more direct action, only to be rebuffed. Failure to rouse the anti-nuclear movement's male leadership was, for Wilson, 'the last straw'. She recalled pondering, 'well, what about a women's action?'

Under Wilson's guidance, a new women-led anti-nuclear initiative came to life. Gathering her friends and colleagues in her Georgetown living room, Wilson planned a national 'strike for peace' and encour-aged women throughout the United States to join. Women Strike for Peace (WSP) was born, creating a powerful platform for women who felt they had a 'special responsibility' to protect the world's children from nuclear peril. Just six weeks after the initial meeting, on 1 November 1961, thousands of people mobilised in a massive display of peace advo-cacy. They declared that women should exert themselves in politics the same way mothers intervened in family disputes. In Washington, DC they picketed the White House and the Russian Embassy, presenting identical letters to Jackie Kennedy and Nina Khrushchev that urged them to influence their husbands to ban atmospheric testing.

Key to WSP's success was its deft negotiation of 1960s gender politics. In a period of heightened anti-communist fervour, women peace activ-ists' publicly transgressive politics risked particular backlash for lacking patriotism or defying the societal expectations of docile feminine behaviour. To counter this, WSP asserted its identity as middle-class mothers and housewives, avoiding critiques of masculinity and preserv-ing their domestic roles. Marchers assured the public that they were 'appalled at our own audacity, for we're just ordinary people, not experts'. WSPers explained that 'we are not striking against our hus-bands', with one member quipping that she 'will make the soup that they will ladle out to the children' while she campaigns.

This traditionalist stance sparked criticism from feminists. In her totemic 1963 work *The Feminine Mystique*, famed author Betty Friedan criticised Dagmar Wilson directly and declared that women in politics 'must make their contribution not as housewives but as citizens'. Yet this overlooked the significance of WSP's stance. The group asserted and embodied the view that 'traditional motherhood' was not a retreat from, but actually encouraged and facilitated, the 'radical politics' required for Cold War anti-militarism.

Through WSP, Wilson had an indispensable influence on the broader anti-nuclear movement, but she was a reluctant figurehead. Her colleagues thrust her to the forefront because she 'came closest to fulfilling the late fifties/early sixties ideal of nuclear family wife and mother' that WSP sought to reflect. Consummately modest and a little shy, Wilson disliked the spotlight and was 'scared to death of having to speak', not to mention the possibility of 'jail, loss of income, and ostracism' that could befall a leader of such activist initiatives.

Yet, she faced her anxieties with a quiet determination, leading WSP to become a formidable force on the social movement landscape. Having watched from the White House window as WSP women picketed in the rain, President John F. Kennedy praised the group and acknowledged that 'that their message was received'. Wilson led fifty representatives of the women's peace movement to confront negotiators at the Geneva Conference of the Seventeen-Nation Committee on Disarmament in March 1962 and received acclaim for lecturing national diplomats 'like a schoolmistress' for their failure to act cordially towards one another. UN Security General U Thant later met and thanked Wilson personally for her efforts.

Despite WSP's pacifying 'housewives and mothers' aesthetic, its public inclusion of women from any political background brought it under government suspicion. The feared House Un-American Activities Committee (HUAC) targeted WSP in December 1962, alleging communist infiltration and subpoenaing Dagmar Wilson along with thirteen other WSP activists. Merely an accusation from HUAC could tarnish reputations, cost jobs and ruin lives. However, instead of retreating, WSP women refused to be cowed. Nearly 100 activists rallied and offered to face the committee themselves. They petitioned HUAC to subpoena them too, declaring that 'if Dagmar Wilson is a communist, so am I'.

Across three days of hearings, WSP's activists used humour and maternal charm to belittle, ridicule and expose their accusers. When asked their occupation, each witness answered that they were 'a housewife'. The exception was Lyla Hoffman. She described herself as 'housewife and peace worker'. Blanche Posner laughed off an accusation that her wearing 'a coloured paper daisy' could imply communist affiliation. Apologising for her 'giggled' reply, she explained that 'it sounds like such a far cry from communism it is impossible not to be amused'. HUAC produced ominous evidence that Ruth Meyers had signed a Communist Party nominating position while living in Brooklyn. 'Are you the Ruth Meyers who executed that petition?' inquired lead investigator Counsel Alfred Nittle. Meyers duly informed the hearings that it was not her. She joked that her husband 'could never get me to move to Brooklyn'. The mistaken identity drew raucous laughter from the gallery.

Timed for perfect dramatic effect, HUAC scheduled WSP's leader Dagmar Wilson as the final witness on the last day of hearings. Throughout her entirely well-mannered and factual testimony she gently discredited the committee's paranoia, explaining that investigators had made WSP's prosaic activities 'sound terribly dramatic'. Wilson's well-mannered dismissal of the Committee's outlandish hysteria proved the perfect finale. In the hearing's closing exchanges, Nittle spied an opportunity to trap WSP's leader. The group's inclusion of 'women from *all* political backgrounds' prevented HUAC from depicting the group as a communist front. But Nittle believed that, if he could get Wilson to publicly denounce Nazism while accepting communist participation, he could use the hypocrisy to imply that the group did indeed harbour communist sympathies specifically.

Nittle set the stage by asking whether Wilson 'would knowingly permit or encourage a Communist Party member to occupy a leadership position in Women Strike for Peace'. Surveying the scene, journalist Mary McGrory wrote that such a question 'would bring a man to his knees with patriotic protest'. However, Wilson proved a more stoic opponent. She responded honestly that she had 'absolutely no way of controlling, do not desire to control, who wishes to join the demonstrations'. Nittle confidently levelled his loaded follow-up. 'Would you knowingly permit or welcome Nazis or Fascists to occupy leadership positions in Women Strike for Peace?' Wilson did not answer as Nittle had expected. To the committee's surprise, she calmly replied 'if only we could get them on our side'. Furthermore, she emphatically declared, 'unless everybody in the whole world joins us in this fight then God help us.' Her supporters in the viewing gallery rose to their feet with rapturous applause.

The HUAC affair demonstrated how maternal politics could dismantle the histrionics of Cold War anti-communism. Historian and WSP activist Amy Swerdlow affirmed that, by standing squarely upon traditional sex role assumptions, WSP had presented 'a radical critique of man's world' and raised 'women's sense of political power and self-esteem'. For Swerdlow, the hearing's importance lay in its demonstration of 'outraged moral motherhood', which allowed activists to challenge the government 'with more courage, candor, and wit than most men had done in a decade of inquisitions'. Journalists similarly celebrated the occasion. Political cartoonist Herb Lock mocked HUAC's investigators, suggesting that WSP's housewives had revealed the Committee's ignorance and depicting the absurdity of trying to determine if 'women or peace' were un-American. Wilson's noteworthy performance drew special praise. Russell Baker of *The New York Times* wrote that she had patiently tolerated her accuser 'as if he was a rather trying dinner partner'.

To its shame, HUAC continued to harass Wilson and subpoenaed her again in 1964 after WSP invited a Japanese pacifist to speak. Wilson and her co-defendants refused to testify without public hearings, and they were convicted of contempt of court, receiving suspended jail sentences. Though WSP rallied behind her, Wilson felt that that 'any satisfaction of martyrdom has been far outweighed by inconvenience, wasted time and personal outrage'. It brought renewed disruption to her life and stalled her attempts to revive a professional career.

Wilson's elevated stature in the peace movement thrust her unwillingly into the national spotlight. In a 1966 interview for her local newspaper, she described the challenges that leadership placed on her family by explaining how her home had become an unofficial mailing address for WSP. Public speaking took 'a tremendous lot out of' her, and she was never sure 'of being good that many times'. She continued anti-nuclear campaigning throughout her life, but gradually stepped away from public leadership after 1968. Even in later life, Wilson reflected that she had often felt 'unqualified' for the work she did, underscoring her humility and reluctance to view herself as a trailblazer.

Ironically, the very humility and restraint that made leadership difficult for Wilson also contributed to her historical importance. WSP demonstrated the formidable political power of 'traditional motherhood' that allowed women to counter Cold War extremism with a radical politics grounded in calm, maternal reason. But Wilson's personal experience also highlights how women have been targeted as subversive and 'dangerous' even while adhering to traditional roles. She modestly called herself a 'mere housewife'. But Wilson's use of conventional femininity changed the political landscape. It made her a powerful force, and a dangerous woman.

SIRIMAVO BANDARANAIKE: THE PARADOX OF SRI LANKA'S ELITE POLITICAL WOMEN

Harshana Rambukwella and Kanchana N. Ruwanpura

Harshana Rambukwella is a comparative literature and cultural studies scholar with an interest in the intersections between literature, history, aesthetics and nationalism. He is also a critical sociolinguist. Rambukwella is the author of *The Politics and Poetics of Authenticity* (UCL Press, 2018). He is an associate editor of the *Journal of Sociolinguistics* and serves on the editorial board of the *International Journal of the Sociology of Language*. Rambukwella is currently working on a project on the 'cultural life of democracy', looking at democracy in 'everyday life' as expressed in cultural and aesthetic artefacts. This work is partly funded by the Swiss National Science Foundation, and he also serves as a Project Fellow on the Reversing the Gaze team – an interdisciplinary multi-sited project attempting to interrogate how insights from the postcolonial world can be usefully employed in the analysis of populism and anti-democratic thinking in Europe.

Dr Kanchana N. Ruwanpura is a Professor of Development Geography at the University of Gothenburg Sweden and a Fellow at the Centre for South Asian Studies, University of Edinburgh. She holds a PhD from Newnham College, University of Cambridge and was previously a Humboldt Fellow at the University of Munich. The ERC, ESRC, British Academy and UNICEF have funded Kanchana's research, and currently she is working on a grant funded by the Adlerbertska Foundation in Sweden. She has published widely on themes related to feminist politics, ethnicity, labour and development; more recently, her research has moved to analysis around the political economy of debt.

In the UK, Sri Lanka is usually synonymous with cricket – particularly a brash and colourful South Asian version of the game. For those from an older generation, Sri Lanka, or Ceylon as it was known then, was an exotic tropical isle, which produced high-quality tea. However, rarely talked about nowadays, the world's first woman Prime Minister, Mrs Sirimavo Bandaranaike, was elected in Sri Lanka in the 1960s. Her election occurred during the heyday of the non-aligned movement

(NAM), a geopolitical bloc of 'neutral' nations from the Global South, in which she was also a key foundational player.

Sirimavo Dias Ratwatte Bandaranaike was a formidable woman. The scion of a powerful aristocratic family and the widow of one of Sri Lanka's most controversial and charismatic postcolonial leaders, S. W. R. D. Bandaranaike, Mrs B, or Sirimavo, as she was popularly known, was a housewife who transformed into a career politician following her husband's assassination in 1959. She held the premiership of the country on three separate occasions from 1960–1965, 1970–1977 and 1994–2000, in addition to being the leader of one of Sri Lanka's main political parties, the Sri Lanka Freedom Party (SLFP). No mean feat for a woman who was dubbed the 'weeping widow' by the press when she first ran for office.

Dynastic political succession in South Asia is nothing unusual. Yet, how did a woman, whom her cousin Paul Deraniyagala (quoted in a memoir of the Bandaranaike family by Yasmine Gooneratne) described as having 'presided over nothing fiercer than the kitchen fire', come to win the confidence of her almost exclusively male political peers? Moreover, how did she gain the confidence of the electorate on three separate occasions in a society in which, despite women's high educational attainment, men tend to call the shots?

In *The Nation and its Fragments*, Partha Chatterjee outlines the creation of a 'new woman' under anticolonial nationalism. In this period, the private or domestic sphere of life was cast as the repository of 'authentic' national identity, which is also seen as culturally, morally and spiritually superior to the West. Within this private-public split, the woman is conceived of as the bearer of nationalist authenticity. This is not, however, the traditional stay-at-home woman. Instead, a new bourgeois woman, educated and 'cultured', but with an inner core of tradition, is constructed. She has the freedom to move in the public sphere of life. This may offer a partial explanation for why the men of the SLFP were comfortable with Mrs B. A quotation from Mrs B, published in the biography by Maureen Seneviratne, explains the point:

> The women of Sri Lanka have never been chattels, never been in enforced servitude to the male sex. Whatever 'servitude' we render, is voluntarily undertaken, because there is a deep-rooted respect for the dual and different roles of father and mother in our society. According to Buddhist tradition, the family is a sacred unit and due all honour, and neither man nor woman are considered superior one to the other.

By the 1960s, when Mrs B first entered politics, Ceylon was a model of transition from colonial to democratic rule. Health and education indicators for both men and women were high, Ceylon had enjoyed universal adult franchise since 1931 – many years before its neighbours and many countries worldwide – and there was active voter participation at regular democratically held elections.

Though on the surface things looked well, a closer look reveals a different story. At the time Mrs B came to power, ethnic tensions, stoked by her seemingly liberal and cosmopolitan husband, had set Sri Lanka on a tragic historical trajectory leading to a thirty-year civil war. Women's position in society was equally tenuous. As feminist scholar Kumari Jayawardena notes in *Feminism and Nationalism in the Third World*, while Sri Lanka never registered the abhorrent practices of *sati* or child marriage of its near neighbours in South Asia and had impressive gender social indicators, it did not imply that the shackles of patriarchy were absent in Sri Lanka. They simply manifested in subtle and less insidious ways.

Sexist attacks and the caricaturing of the world's first female prime minister were quite common. Ranasinghe Premadasa, a member of the opposition UNP at the time, said that the PM's seat in Parliament would have to be purified once a month – stigmatising menstruation. Her portrayal and lampooning in the media reflected how the world's first female prime minster was considered a danger to the establishment, as a cartoon of the time – one of many in the media – suggests. The cartoon shows Mrs B and her daughter Chandrika, who became Sri Lanka's fourth Executive President, at the helm and the man in the backseat is Anura, the prodigal son. It parodies men who 'hang on to women's skirts' (in this instance the 'sareepota' or fall of the saree) to gain power. At the same time, it questions women's ability to lead – the car is on a narrow, precipitous road leading to an inevitable fall.

Yet, despite daringly and boldly taking on the mantle of head of state, she was hardly the agent of change feminists would have wanted the world's first women prime minister to be. This would matter for decades to come in Sri Lanka and continues to reverberate. This remarkable record, and the possibilities it could have opened up, but never did, are reflected in Sri Lanka's contemporary politics. While a few women politicians entered Parliament, none went on to lead the country again until 1994, nearly three decades later. Yet this too by no quirk was Mrs B's daughter.

While on the one hand, Chandrika Bandaranaike Kumaratunge, often referred to as CBK, was an upshot of dynastic political families in South Asia, she was also a politician of her own making. Her husband, like her father, was assassinated in 1988. Unlike her mother though, Chandrika was not necessarily seen as a 'weeping widow'. When she swept into power as Executive President in 1994, at the relatively young age of forty-nine, she had taken control of an emasculated SLFP and led it to a historic victory campaigning on a platform of human rights and the restoration of democratic values. She also resisted muscular majoritarian Sinhala nationalism, which her mother was complicit in nurturing, and, at least in her first term, tried to make peace with the estranged Tamil minority.

While both these women were symbolically powerful avatars for the women's movement in Sri Lanka and feminist politics in general, the danger they posed to the establishment was always curtailed by their lack of feminist consciousness. Despite being a forerunner to producing potentially dangerous women when it comes to women's representation in Sri Lanka's parliamentary system, it lags behind our South Asian neighbours. At a woeful 5 per cent of women parliamentarians, it is bottom of the pile in South Asia, compared to 34 per cent in Nepal, and it is surpassed, sometimes by miles, by Afghanistan, Bangladesh and India.

Shirin Rai argues that women's representation in Parliament is key for representative democracy, and where India, Pakistan and Bangladesh have adopted a quota system, its women constituents have benefited, despite the challenges that women politicians face. Yet, to its shame, Sri Lankan politicians and the political class skirt around and evade the dire need for this. The upshot is that in the contemporary juncture, Sri Lankan parliamentarians continue to think it is acceptable to make sexist and sexual remarks about the limited number of woman peers in Parliament. When Mrs Rosy Senanayake, an MP, faced sexual harassment in Parliament, she appropriately tore apart her harasser, given her streak of strong feminist consciousness. It was an incident that garnered worldwide attention including in *The Guardian*.

In contrast to the two women leaders that Sri Lanka has produced, Rosy Senanyake, was at the forefront of agitating for numerous women's causes, including for a quota system and for greater women's representation in Parliament. In many ways Rosy was the dangerous woman who was needed to challenge the patriarchal status quo in the Sri Lankan Parliament, and she was someone whom Sri Lanka's women's movement and Sri Lankan feminists respected.

Unfortunately, and perhaps because she had the potential to be a dangerous woman and disrupt the patriarchal political system, she was ousted from Parliament at the elections in late 2015. The birthplace of the world's first symbolic dangerous woman is then yet to produce a dangerous woman of the kind that Nicola Sturgeon calls for: 'When we are "dangerous" we can change the world and our place in it.'

More reading

Ruwanpura, K. N., 2024. A feminist politician, political furore: Feminist analysis for a new age. *Groundviews*, 8 October. https://groundviews.org/2024/10/08/a-feminist-politician-political-furore-feminist-analysis-for-a-new-age/

ROZANNE COLCHESTER: AN UNLIKELY ASSET AS ONE OF 'THE BLETCHLEY GIRLS'

Tessa Dunlop

Dr Tessa Dunlop is a historian, broadcaster and author of several books including: *The Bletchley Girls* (Hodder & Stoughton, 2015), *The Century Girls* (Simon & Schuster, 2018), *The Army Girls* (Headline Press, 2021), *Elizabeth and Philip* (Headline Press, 2022) and *Lest We Forget* (Harper North, 2025).

> I had never been abroad before, we went on a train. It was a terrific adventure – the wonderful mountains at night and waking up in the morning having arrived in Rome!

Long gone was the Yorkshire vicarage with its abundant garden. Now Rozanne, at a peachy fifteen, was deemed old enough to accompany her father to his latest posting. Charles Medhurst was appointed the British Military Attaché in Rome with a mission to monitor Italian rearmament. But to hear Rozanne reminisce, it is easy to forget that the Fascist state was moving inexorably towards war. She loved her time in Italy: the weather, the language and the people. From her schoolgirl perspective, the adventure has a naïve, occasionally comical quality.

Rozanne soon became familiar with Mussolini, or Musso as she refers to him. On their way to classes, satchels swinging, all legs and smiles, she and her sister walked past his Villa Torlonia.

> Oh, he used to come out at a certain time, just when we were going to school and wave at us.

The *Duce* was very fond of girls.

> Ha! He was rather a figure of fun among our friends, he took himself very seriously. He would put on a face, throw out his jaw and march about which was ridiculous. It was ridiculous that the Italians tried to copy Hitler. Middle-aged fat men full of spaghetti trying to do the goosestep at the head of their troops. It was the funniest thing!

At ninety-two, Rozanne remains an adept storyteller. She leans in: 'I even met Hitler! I shook his hand.' As a family member of the British diplomatic mission, sixteen-year-old Rozanne was there, waiting on the platform when in May 1938 Hitler and his circus of 500 Nazis arrived to woo the *Duce*. 'He looked much more normal in the flesh than I imagined.' She shuts her eyes, briefly his man's hand is back in her slender young clasp. 'I had imagined a Charlie Chaplin-type figure with a black moustache. But he did have fanatical blue eyes, I remember them vividly.' Then, the moment passed. Mussolini had arrived, and the military parade began. It was all so surreal, something of a game, but then Rozanne was only a child; a helpless bystander, blissfully unaware of the ugly political undercurrent.

In 1940, Italy entered the war and Rozanne returned to Britain. The lights were out in Paris, and a solitary soldier stood guard in their Channel ferry. 'One wondered if one would see a battle', but Rozanne didn't. Ducking bombs under a dining room table in Kensington was deemed too risky, so soon she had been bundled off to Yorkshire where she killed time as a typist for Northern Command. A slip of a girl, told off for wearing slacks to work by a harridan, it all felt rather pointless. Her brother was training to be an airman, her sister worked in Baker Street ('very hush hush') and her young beau was already dead. The midshipman David Bevan had been torpedoed in the Mediterranean in the summer of 1940.

> After David and Blitz I was longing to be involved. From then on, one was longing to be old enough to get in the Services. The Air Force was in my blood; I was going to join the WAAFs.

Although conscription for women, introduced in December 1941, was poised to demand it of her, square-bashing in a military uniform would have been a waste. Rozanne had a vital skill, honed in view of the Tiber River, practised in the Borghese Gardens and chirped in response to Mussolini's cheeky acknowledgements. She spoke Italian. Her father had been promoted to Head of Intelligence at the Air Ministry and, aware that his daughter possessed a valuable national asset, duly intervened: 'He explained to me there was a place called Bletchley Park and they needed Italian speakers there.'

In 1942, equipped with schoolgirl Italian and a scarlet bicycle, Rozanne entered Britain's most secret organisation. On the flats of Buckinghamshire, teeming with girls just out of school amidst mushrooming huts and blocks, a conveyor belt of corridors, closed doors and classified information, Britain's giant code-breaking centre was like nowhere else. Rozanne still enjoys recalling the peculiarities of the place, in particular the friendships she made: an Oxford don twice her age, and a professional actress whose à la mode style caught her eye. But what she actually did at Bletchley Park, a mere cog in a giant wheel, is harder to grasp.

That was deliberate.

The less said, the better. Unnecessary information endangered lives and all recruits had to sign the Official Secrets Act. Rozanne furrows her brow. She was in the Italian Air Force Section, responding to a war played out in real time. Under orders from Hitler, in March 1941 General Rommel's Afrika Korps had arrived in Libya to bolster the fleeing Italians. The subsequent war in the desert was a protracted bloody affair and the interception and decoding of high-grade Italian Air Ciphers proved invaluable. Far removed from the action, Rozanne was hunched over 'reams of paper [that] girls would bring in great bundles in haversacks'. She shakes her head.

> I was a decodist; there was a technique you learnt to break the code. It was quite specialised. You tried out various numbers until bits of words started to make sense. A lot of it was humdrum stuff.

Rozanne waves her hand dismissively. She is keen to underline the more important men who surrounded her.

The days streamed past in a haze of shifts. 'When we began work there was silence and total concentration', she explains. A tea break of ten minutes after two hours was followed by 'work and a concentrated silence again'. A young girl, albeit one who spoke Italian, Rozanne might have slipped through the war unaware of any specific mark she had made against an enemy she knew personally. Much of Bletchley Park's intelligence was based on the forensic decrypting and ordering of thousands of enemy messages, and Rozanne was part of this vast process. Her elementary decoding skills helped uncover patterns of communications and confirm logistical information. Not quite the noble war she had longed to fight. But then, war is unpredictable.

It was 01.30 in the morning and Rozanne was working late and alone, with the exception of Joe Hooper (later Head of GCHQ). It is easy to imagine her, gamine and pretty in a modest jersey and skirt, pearls resting on the nape of her long neck, head poised and attentive. 'I was decoding a message freshly arrived on the teleprinter. After many trials and errors ... the "groups" of numbers began to make sense, yes, and I found myself faced with a message that made sense.' Staring back at Rozanne in the middle of the night was an important Italian message she had personally unpicked. In a small room in Buckinghamshire, she sat reading something no one else in the Allied Forces knew. In three and a half hours' time at 4 a.m., Italy's SM.79 Torpedo Bombers and SM.82 transport carriers were due to leave Tripoli and head across the Mediterranean.

'Imagine the thrill! I told Joe Hooper about the message and he *leapt* from his desk in wild excitement. He tore along the passage to Josh Cooper's room.' With the Desert War over in early 1943, the crippled Italians were heading for Sicily, but thanks to Rozanne they never reached their final destination.

> It was the only time I did something useful in all the years I was at war. The whole place was alive with excitement. I got a pat on the back!

A rare accolade for a humble Bletchley girl.

And then suddenly, towards the end of her euphoric story, Rozanne's face crumples; she looks anxious, almost scared.

> It was awful, terribly sad to think of all those Italians being shot down. I lived in Italy; they were my friends.

Sunshine and silly old Musso, Italian mamas, pasta and pavement cafés: it all comes flooding back. Rozanne had fired a lethal shot into the heart of Italy without leaving her desk in England. Decades later, sitting in her comfortable Oxfordshire home, the triumphant young girl long gone, Rozanne is fleetingly revisited by the confusion of war and her own part in it.

She shudders. 'I loved the Italians but I'm jolly glad we won the war.'

More reading

Briggs, A., 2011. *Secret Days: Code-Breaking in Bletchley Park*. Frontline Books.

Hinsley, F. H. and Stripps, A., eds, 1993. *Code Breakers: The Inside Story of Bletchley Park*. Oxford University Press.

McKay, S., 2011. *The Secret Life of Bletchley Park*. Aurum Press.

McKay, S., 2012. *The Secret Listeners: How the Y Service Intercepted German Codes for Bletchley Park*. Aurum Press.

Smith, M., 2011. *Station X: The Codebreakers of Bletchley Park*. Channel 4 Books.

DAGMAR ŠIMKOVÁ: BRANDED A THREAT TO COMMUNISM

Kelly Hignett

Dr Kelly Hignett is Senior Lecturer in History at Leeds Beckett University, UK. Kelly's research relates to communist Eastern Europe, with a particular focus on Czechoslovakia. Her primary research interests include incarceration, forced labour, social repression, criminality, social deviance and experiences of 'the everyday' under communism. Kelly is particularly interested in women's experiences of communist repression, and she has co-authored a book titled *Women's Experiences of Repression in the Soviet Union and Eastern Europe* (Routledge, 2018). Kelly's current research focuses on the history and heritage of communist-era forced labour camps in Czechoslovakia. She is also writing a book about experiences of incarceration and forced labour in communist Eastern Europe.

In the years after the Second World War, the communist consolidation of control across Eastern Europe was accompanied by mass repression. Following the communist coup of February 1948 in Czechoslovakia, as many as 100,000 people were prosecuted for 'political crimes'. Most were sentenced to lengthy periods in penal institutions and forced labour camps. The vast majority of Czechoslovak citizens who were interned for political crimes between 1948 and 1954 were men. Only between 5,000–9,000 (5–10 per cent) were women. These women, who came from a range of locations, social backgrounds and ages, were held in numerous prisons and forced labour camps across Czechoslovakia, often alongside women sentenced for criminal offences, and *retribuční* (individuals who had been convicted as Nazi collaborators under the post-war retribution decrees).

While some of these women were actively engaged in anti-communist resistance groups, others were targeted simply because of who they were, coming from a suspect 'bourgeois' background. However, the new regime perceived them all as 'dangerous women', who posed a potential threat to communist stability. On this basis, they were incarcerated and subjected to forced labour in a range of areas including agriculture, textiles and industrial production. During their internment, these women endured poor living conditions, hygiene and medical care, and often suffered violence, abuse and humiliation from the penal authorities.

One of these 'dangerous women' was Dagmar Šimková, who later produced a detailed autobiographical account of her experiences in prison, *Byly jsme tam taky* (*We Were There Too*). First published by Orbis in 1991, a revised edition translated by Monika Elšíková was issued in 2010.

In *Byly jsme tam taky*, Šimková explains how her family were targeted after the communist coup of 1948 due to their 'bourgeois origins', because her father had been a banker. Their house was confiscated by the communists and both Dagmar and her older sister Marta were prevented from completing their university studies. Marta fled Czechoslovakia in 1950, but Dagmar became involved in underground resistance activities, printing and distributing anti-communist leaflets and posters mocking the new Czechoslovakian leader, Klement Gottwald. In October 1952, following a failed attempt to help two male friends escape to the West to avoid compulsory military service, Dagmar was arrested at the age of twenty-three. As the arresting officer led Dagmar Šimková to his car he told her to 'take a good look around, you reactionary bitch!' and taunted her that this could be the last time she saw her home or her mother for a very long time. She was subsequently sentenced to fifteen years in prison.

During her incarceration, Šimková passed through various prisons and labour camps in Czechoslovakia, where she was persistently reminded by the prison guards that because she had been sentenced for political offences, she was considered 'more dangerous' than the hardened criminals she was interred with. Although some of her fellow prisoners were murderers who had killed 'one person, possibly even two or three', Šimková and her fellow political prisoners had 'wanted to exterminate an entire nation' with their anti-communist activities.

Šimková documented the cruelty and harsh reality of life for women in communist-era prisons and labour camps in striking detail, describing how they were subjected to strategic desexualisation and gendered humiliation by the prison authorities:

> According to them, we are swines, bitches, smelly discharge, whores, and beasts . . . A woman had to be shamed for her femininity, she had to be deprived of her gender.

For example, she described how during one lengthy interrogation, she was repeatedly forbidden to use the toilet, and her eventual inability to control her bladder was characterised as a female failure:

> I was turning red, the tears were running down my cheeks, I asked them [two male guards] over and over if I could go to the bathroom. After another

hour my body gave up. I soiled the carpet. The agent screamed 'throw her out – that wet bitch!'.

However, throughout her long internment, Dagmar Šimková retained her fighting spirit. Her prison records include official observations about her 'brazen behaviour' and her refusal to conceal her 'negative attitude' towards the Communist Party. In 1955, she even successfully escaped from Želiezovce, a notoriously harsh agricultural labour camp in Slovakia, describing how she 'ran and fell in a field, to roll in scented flowers . . . it was an intoxicating feeling of freedom'. However, her freedom was short-lived. She was found two days later, sleeping in a haystack at a nearby farm and was returned to camp, where an additional three years was added to her existing prison term as a punishment.

Šimková also described the strong bonds of mutual solidarity, gentility and friendship that developed amongst women political prisoners. This was another source of strength that enabled many women to cope with their incarceration and resist the dehumanisation of the prison experience. In *Byly jsme tam taky* she even suggested that

Most of us survived with a healthy mind, and it was determined by the fact that we are women. Not that women had easy conditions in prison . . . but women developed different survival instincts compared to men.

Some women deliberately adopted what Šimkova called *Hedvábí-šustění* ('Silkrustling'), which she described as follows:

We oppose them [the prison authorities] with mutual tenderness, kindness, attention and courtesy. We called ourselves by diminutives . . . We are noblewomen. We are ladies. We watch our every move, intonation and expression carefully. It is constant self-control, which gives us a sense of respect and helps us to keep our dignity.

Other women prisoners also described *Hedvábí-šustění* as engaging in mutual care and gentle tenderness, often through participation in the ritual cleansing and purification of their bodies and hair in weekly 'beautification sessions', which helped them to bond with one another as well as restoring their sense of dignity.

During the final years of her internment, Šimková was held in Pardubice Prison near Prague, in the women's department 'Hrad' (Castle), which was specially created to house sixty-four women who were perceived by the authorities as being the 'most dangerous' political prisoners, in order to segregate them from the main prison population. Here, Šimková participated in several organised hunger strikes to demand better prison conditions, access to sanitary products and improved food rations. She was also an active participant in the secret 'prison university' founded by her fellow prisoner Růžena Vacková, a former university professor who gave underground lectures on fine art, literature and languages to the women of the 'Castle' department. Šimková remembered how 'We devoured every word. We tried to remember, and understand, like the best students at universities.' Some of the women even managed to compile some lecture notes into a small book that was secretly hidden, before being smuggled out of Pardubice in 1965.

After a total of fourteen years' incarceration, Dagmar Šimková was finally released in April 1966, aged thirty-seven. Two years later, during the temporary liberalisation of the Prague Spring of 1968 she played a key role in establishing *K 231*, the first organisation to represent former political prisoners in Czechoslovakia. However, following the Soviet-led invasion to halt the Czechoslovak reforms in August 1968, Šimková fled Czechoslovakia, eventually moving to start a new life in Australia, where she completed two university degrees, worked as an artist and prison therapist and even trained as a movie stuntwoman. She also worked with Amnesty International, continuing to campaign for better prison conditions until her death in 1995.

Today, women's experiences of political repression in communist Czechoslovakia remain under-researched and under-represented in the historiography. Women who endured communist-era repression have often been reluctant to disclose the details of the traumatic and humiliating experiences they endured during their incarceration. Dagmar Šimková's story is important, as she acts as a voice for both herself and the thousands of other 'dangerous women' who were simultaneously both victims and survivors of communist repression. In recent years, *Byly jsme tam taky* has been serialised on Czech Radio and dramatised by theatre groups, and it is currently included on the Czech Ministry of Education's list of recommended school texts.

More reading

A number of accounts from women who were imprisoned for political reasons in communist Czechoslovakia are available online, in English translation, at *Politicalprisoners.eu*: https://www.politictivezni.cz/en/life-stories.html

Hignett, K., 2018. Women's experiences of repression in Czechoslovakia, 1948–1968. In K. Hignett, M. Ilic, D. Leinarte and C. Snitar, eds, *Women's Experiences of Repression in the Soviet Union and Eastern Europe*. Routledge.

Pinerova, K. and Bouska, T., 2016. *Czechoslovak Political Prisoners: Life Stories of 5 Male and 5 Female Victims of Stalinism*. 2nd amended edn. Knihovnicka.

HELEN STEVEN:
A RADICAL PEACE ACTIVIST

Kathy Galloway

Kathy Galloway is a practical theologian, campaigner and writer. The major
focus of her work has always been peacemaking and social justice issues,
especially relating to poverty and gender. She was Head of Christian Aid
Scotland from 2009–2016, a former Warden of Iona Abbey, and Leader of
the Iona Community from 2002–2009, the first woman to be elected to the
post. She is the author of a dozen books on justice issues, spirituality and
poetry and her writings have been widely anthologised.

A history teacher in an exclusive girls' school in Glasgow sounds an unlikely
candidate for civil disobedience and non-violent direct action. Helen
Steven did not fit the stereotype of the subversive radical. With her hair
up, her polite, well-modulated tones, her love of climbing and gardening
and her enjoyment of Scottish country dancing, she could have been any
well-read, middle-class Scotswoman living quietly in rural Scotland.

But she wasn't. Helen had a burning passion for peace that led her to
the gates of nuclear bases and into prison, to the offices of NATO com-
manders and round tables with army generals, into the white heat of the
Vietnam War and the freezing chill of vigils and demonstrations and
marches. She spoke at thousands of meetings, went on television and
into print, preached, prayed and kept silence. She inspired, infuriated
and challenged, and was a thorn in the flesh to many. Helen was, at
one and the same time, a peacemaker and dangerous woman.

As a young woman, Helen went as a volunteer to Vietnam to do relief
work with the Peace Corps. She ended up campaigning for the cessation
of all work that facilitated the smooth running of the war machine. Face
to face with the horrors of modern warfare, in a war in which civilians
suffered in a proportion never seen before, she came to question not
just the justice of that particular war, but of all war. She returned to
Scotland with the woman she had met in Vietnam and who became her
lifelong partner, Ellen Moxley, another dangerous woman. Together
they raised an adopted Vietnamese daughter. She became a member of
the Society of Friends, attracted by their commitment to peacemaking,
and commenced her life's work. Many years later, she wrote:

History has shown time and again that justice won by violent means already sows the deadly seeds of the next conflict. When I worked in Vietnam, my sympathies were almost entirely with the North Vietnamese revolutionary struggle, and it seemed that the quickest way to achieve justice for the suffering Vietnamese was for the North Vietnamese to win the war as quickly as possible. Which is what, ultimately, they did, but, although the immediate prospect of peace was welcome, already, a new powerful group was oppressing, killing, torturing, and the cycle of violence and injustice remained unbroken.

This is where, I believe, nonviolence can provide a way forward. I totally agree that nonviolence which allows violating to go on is a form of violence itself-in fact, it is not nonviolence. The very essence of nonviolence is that it resists and opposes all forms of injustice and oppression to the last drop of its blood. It can never consent to anything that degrades the human spirit.

Nonviolence is about revolution. It is about finding creative, imaginative ways to overthrow all forms of tyranny and oppression, without becoming the oppressor in the process. It widens the options and holds out a possibility of a way out of the cycle of violence where dignity can be maintained.

From 1979 to 1985, Helen was the Justice and Peace Worker for the ecumenical Iona Community, whose members make a binding commitment to work for justice and peace at every level. Under her leadership, the Community opened a justice and peace centre and Fairtrade shop in the middle of Glasgow (Centrepeace), which raised awareness of development issues and offered training in non-violent direct action. With and through the Iona Community, the Quakers, CND and Trident Ploughshares, Helen campaigned tirelessly for the removal and disarmament of nuclear weapons and the ending of the arms trade.

She attacked the injustices of poverty and oppression that breed wars, and acted as a mediator in conflict resolution. She embraced the base at Greenham Common and travelled thousands of miles to speak on a variety of platforms, from large church councils to small meetings in village halls. She spent each summer on Iona, organising conferences and seminars, enabling young people, volunteers, parish groups and people of every political opinion and faith to engage constructively with the issues of peace and justice. The most notable of these was probably a series of Options for Defence events, where military generals and experts gathered alongside peace campaigners for a week, living together in community.

In 1985, supported by the Iona Community and the Quakers, Helen and Ellen opened Peace House in Perthshire, both a residential centre and their warm and welcoming home. Over the following twelve years, more than 10,000 people visited, stayed and took part in a whole range of courses, training, mediation and reflection. It was in Peace House, in the winter of 1990–1991 that *GulfWatch* had its genesis. *GulfWatch* was a daily bulletin of news and information about the First Gulf War, much of it differing from or extending what was presented through mainstream media channels. Well before the almost universal and immediate internet access and social media available today, *GulfWatch* information was collected from GreenNet, an early example of such networks, from fax messages and one telephone contact inside Iraq. It was mailed out each day of the war to church and peace groups and photocopied and distributed to thousands of people internationally. It became an alternative news service of global value, linking activists concerned with building peace internationally.

In 1999, Helen was involved in setting up the Scottish Centre for Non-Violence in Dunblane, which developed and widened the work that Peace House had been doing. It placed strong emphasis on conflict resolution and peacebuilding. She made friends with NATO generals, and found common ground with them wherever possible. But nothing of this prevented Helen from her consistent and persistent campaigning against Trident. She spent hundreds of hours outside the naval base at Faslane on the Clyde, watching, waiting, speaking to military personnel. She supported the peace camp there, and on occasion, locked on to, climbed over or cut through the fence. She attempted to take the British government to court. She was arrested twice, and on being convicted she refused to pay her fine and elected to go to Cornton Vale Prison. Civil disobedience was a hard boundary for one with her background to cross. But one of the things that made Helen dangerous was that in her non-violence training, she opened hundreds of people's eyes to the idea that 'their power comes from our obedience'.

In fact, it was Ellen, one of the Trident Three, whose civil disobedience became better known. Helen's support, advocacy and public organising for Ellen during her months in prison was as faithful as Ellen's had always been for her. She later wrote of this time:

Friends (Quakers) speak of holding someone in the light, and I have always found this a particularly helpful way of expressing it. The idea of going beyond words to a different level of being, to enfold another in the Light and Love beyond our physical experience, is a very attractive image.

A powerful experience of holding someone in the light occurred during the trial of the Trident Three at Greenock Sheriff Court. Ellen Moxley, Ulla Roder and Angie Zelter were on trial for dismantling part of the acoustic testing facility for the Trident nuclear submarines by throwing the computers in the loch. The three maintained that their actions were to uphold international law, basing their defence on the ruling of the International Court of Justice at The Hague in July 1996 that nuclear weapons are in contravention of international humanitarian law.

Only a few days into the trial, Sheriff Margaret Gimblett was faced with a crucial decision of whether or not to allow this defence under international law, or to treat it as a straightforward case of criminal damage. Everything hinged on her decision. She adjourned the court while she considered the case. Immediately a small group gathered on the pavement outside the court and stood in silence holding Margaret Gimblett in the light. In many ways similar to upholding the Clerk at Yearly Meeting, this was one of the most powerful experiences of focused prayer that I have ever had. An hour later, the Court reconvened, and her decision to allow a defence under international law made legal and campaigning history, as the trial moved on to the acquittal of the Trident Three four and a half weeks later. Sheriff Margaret Gimblett's profoundly moving summing up reflected the moral courage of the decision she took, influenced, I am certain, by the power of prayer.

Later, after retirement from paid work, Helen and Ellen moved to Raffin Stoer, Lochinver, and became active parts of the vibrant local community. But Helen continued to lecture and write. In 2004, her work – alongside Ellen's – was recognised with the joint award of the Gandhi International Peace Award.

What people do and will remember about Helen, is not just *what* she did, but *how* she did it. Her life's passion was demonstrated in her seeking after the consistency of ends and means. She fully owned the principle that there is no way to peace, for peace is the way. Her inspiring leadership and strategic brilliance were not just motivated by anger at war and the death-dealing arms trade. She was passionate for peace because she was passionate for life. Her protests at gates and fences were not simply gestures of dissent, but efforts to reach across where borders were most agonised and threatening. She proceeded with respect and reason, and with reverence for that of truth in the other. She was a great listener, not just to the words of others but also to their silences. She responded with grace to people's stories. And she loved the land and wrote about it with passion:

> One of my main reasons for believing in some kind of divine purpose comes from the sheer wonder and beauty of creation. Where we live in the far northwest of Scotland, we are privileged to be able to enjoy the darkness, and

even occasionally the wonder of the Northern Lights. Seeing great curtains of light flickering like searchlights in a great canopy across the sky, or pausing to reflect on the time it has taken for the light of an individual star to reach our tiny planet, makes me so aware of how infinitesimally small we are in the whole cosmos.

It is this love of the environment we live in, and of the infinite variety of people around me, that inspires in me a deep reverence and gratitude for life, and so moves me to action.

That gaiety, humour and delight of the lover of life often made her a somewhat disconcerting presence. Judges sentenced her with regret and admiration. Police officers hailed her as an old friend, having built up a relationship with her on so many demonstrations. And nobody wanted to send her to prison, because they could not be sure she would not start a branch of CND there.

After her death, the inspiration she was to many is living on, not least in the continued work of Women in Black. At her funeral, these words by Norman McCaig were read and stand well as her memorial.

> There will be nothing deathly in your death
> For your love always was the laughing sort
> That quickened life and would not die with death.
> And when you'd gone, I would not want to weep –
> That loving gaiety would still be there
> Filling with its own peace the quickened air.

More reading

King, M. L., 1981. *Strength to Love.* Fortress Press.

Lakey, G., 2012. *Towards a Living Revolution: A Five-Stage Framework for Creating Radical Social Change.* Peace News Ltd.

McIntosh, A. and Carmichael, M., 2014. *Spiritual Activism: Leadership as Service.* Green Books (UK).

Macy, J. and Young Brown, M., 1998. *Coming Back to Life: Practices to Reconnect Our Lives, Our World.* New Society Publishers.

Zelter, A., 2021. *Activism for Life.* Luath Press.

AFTERWORD

Jemma Neville

Jemma Neville is an award-winning author and freelance journalist based in East Lothian. Her debut book, *Constitution Street: Finding Hope in an Age of Anxiety* (404 Ink, 2019), is part memoir, part exploration of human rights in practice through the lives of neighbours on one street. It was completed while Jemma was a Community Fellow at IASH. She is Policy Director for national arts charity Creative Lives.

To be *daring* suggests bold adventure, the pursuit of bravery over comfort, risk-taking over safety, individual triumph. Truth or dare, spin the bottle, take a chance. It is about facing our fears.

Yet there comes a time in life, I have found – especially in mid-life and especially for women, regardless of personal ambition and circumstantial privilege – when you accept that you likely won't run the marathon, or summit the peak in record time, or win the top academic prize, or get the promotion, or write the bestselling novel, or teach your children multiple languages. At least, not all at once and not on others' terms. Not while changing nappies, paying a mortgage, remembering friends' birthdays, sorting the recycling and keeping a full fridge.

Choosing truth over dare is to affirm that women can do anything, but not everything. Setting ourselves up to believe otherwise is a familiar lesson in exhaustion and failure. Today's cost of childcare, inflexible work patterns, the division of household labour, a beauty industry premised on denying ageing, gender pay gaps and a medical profession that under-invests in women's reproductive health are some of the facts of this truth. As it always was. The official narrative of what constitutes daring adventure is one written by men for men. Most history is his story alone.

What do I know of my own infamous relations from history? King Richard III was a Neville. My great-great-uncle Daniel was eaten by a crocodile. James Smith set sail from Timberbush, Leith, for the New World as a cabin boy and returned a wealthy sea merchant. All daring and true, apparently. Some famous men, some forgotten. I know these family tales to be true, apparently, because of written diaries, embellished anecdotes and archived official records. Except that accounts of ancestral history are incomplete and therefore open to misinterpretation because of the absence of female voices – the gradual but persistent erasure and forgetting of our she-lines.

James Smith wrote a whole tome entitled *The Book of Occurrences* about his seafaring world adventures but included little detail about the women who supported his rise to fame and fortune from humble beginnings. Who fed and clothed him, nursed him when sick and made a home for him to return to? Who did his laundry or taught him how to write a diary? Likewise, I know nothing about the women who might have mourned the unfortunate demise of Daniel after the incident with the croc. The wife of Richard III, Queen Anne Neville, gets a substantial bookmark in history but only in reference to her king-making role in the English War of the Roses and as a woman educated and wealthy enough to wield power and influence among men. In less regal branches of an extended family tree, women appear briefly on the pages, if at all, to denote births, marriages and deaths. And upon marriage, they lose their maiden name and thus genealogical clues to their own identity. Beyond two or three living generations, maternal lineage becomes hard to trace and female footsteps eventually fade into anonymity.

And what does it mean to be remembered? The Tibetan *Book of the Dead* offers the concept of a second death. This is the moment in time when there is no one left alive who says your name aloud. This might not take long. For example, how many of us know the full names or something of the character of our great-grandparents? The span of remembrance and familiarity might be as short as a century.

Day-to-day, we don't always remember what someone said or did. But we do remember how they made us feel. This is embodied memory. Rather than being infamous for daring feats and endeavours, meaningful impact can also show up in everyday acts of caring, of conversation, of keeping company. Like this, the potential for extending love and kindness can reverberate down through generations we might never meet. Such a legacy need not be biological. Every encounter, every conversation, no matter how brief, has the life-changing power to make a lasting impact. Conversation means to turn around on the spot. It is about looking forwards and backwards in time.

The slow, often grubby, and poorly celebrated work of being a daughter, mother, partner, friend, colleague or neighbour is the stuff of courage, of taking heart. It is the ordinary ambition of a good life. When it succeeds, it is a shared endeavour that puts collective well-being ahead of personal enrichment. There isn't a guidebook or a map for how to do this. Navigating the right choices at the right time can be frightening and lonely and dangerous. Little of that daring day-to-day gets written down.

Therefore, the words that do get printed perhaps say as much about absence as they do presence. Reading can also be a form of bearing witness, of protest and testimony. It demands our time and attention. It is a generous act. And so, if you have read about the women in this collection, you have probably thought something too about the women in your own life, those infamous and those forgotten. Reach out a hand to those who will come next. Hold on tight.

More reading

Keegan, C., 2022. *Small Things Like These*. Grove Press.

Lavery, H., 2022. *Blood Salt Spring*. Polygon.

Levy, D., 2018. *The Cost of Living: A Working Autobiography*. Bloomsbury.

Morrison, T., 1973. *Sula*. Knopf.

O'Farrell, M., 2017. *I Am, I Am, I Am: Seventeen Brushes with Death*. Tinder Press.

Notes

Flora Tristan

Moses, C. G., 1984. *French Feminism in the 19th Century*. SUNY Press.

Cross, M. and Gray, T., 1992. *The Feminism of Flora Tristan*. Berg Publishers Ltd.

Caroline Norton

Blackstone, W., 1765. *Commentaries on the Laws of England*. Volume 1. Clarendon Press.

Sheridan-Norton, C., 1854. *English Laws for Women in the Nineteenth Century*. Pamphlet.

Sheridan-Norton, C., 1837. *Observations on the Natural Claim of the Mother to the Custody of her Children as Affected by the Common Law Rights of the Father*. Pamphlet.

Sheridan-Norton, C., 1838. *The Separation of Mother and Child By the Law of "Custody of Infants" Considered*. Pamphlet.

Sheridan-Norton, C., 1855. *A Letter to Queen Victoria on Lord Chancellor Cranworth's Marriage and Divorce Bill*. Pamphlet.

Letitia Youmans

Youmans, L., 1893. *Campaign Echoes: The Autobiography of Mrs. Letitia Youmans, the Pioneer of the White Ribbon Movement in Canada*. William Briggs.

Lumina Sophie Dite Surprise

Chivallon, C. and Howard, D., 2017. Colonial Violence and Civilising Utopias in the French and British Empires: The Morant Bay Rebellion (1865) and the Insurrection of the South (1870). *Slavery & Abolition*, 38(3): pp. 534–58.

Lee, V., 2021. Revolutionary Heroines, Insurgent Storytellers: Staging French Caribbean History. *Four Caribbean Women Playwrights*. Palgrave Macmillan.

Richards, J., 2019. The Fury Archives: Afterlives of the Female Incendiary. *The Fury Archives: Female Citizenship, Human Rights, and the International Avant-Gardes*. Columbia University Press.

Flora Shaw

Bush, J., 2007. *Women Against the Vote: Female Anti-Suffragism in Britain*. Oxford University Press.

Shaw, F. L., 1894. Australia. *Scottish Geographical Magazine*, 10, pp. 169–184.

Chrystal Macmillan

Anon, 1909. Report of Women's suffrage meeting in Dumfries under the auspices of Scottish University Women's Suffrage Union on 29 March 1909. Reported in *Dumfries & Galloway Saturday Standard*, 27 March.

Edinburgh University Court, 1906. Minute, 12 February.

Edinburgh University Court, 1908. Minute, 20 January.

International Congress of Women Zurich, 1919. Report, 12–17 May. WILPF.

International Federation of University Women (IFUW), 1929. *Report of Fifth Conference*, Geneva. August.

J. S., 1937. Obituary. *The Scotsman*, 24 September.

Joint Select Committee of House of Commons and House of Lords, 1923. *Report on the Nationality of Married Women.* HMSO.

League of Nations and Women's Cooperation, 1932. *The Open Door*, 9 August, p. 30.

Leneman, L., 1991. When women were not 'persons': The Scottish women graduates case, 1906–08. *Juridical Review*, 1, pp. 109–118.

Letter: Chrystal Macmillan to Secretary, British Federation of University Women, 11 March 1931 (BFUW correspondence; Women's Library, LSE 5BFW/03/08).

Letter: Ivy Williams to Sybil Campbell, 11 January 1930 (London: Women's Library, LSE 5BFW/03/08).

Macmillan, C., 1931. *The Nationality of Married Women.* Nationality of Married Women Pass the Bill Committee; Women's Library, LSE.

NUWW, 1913. Minute, 30 May. City of Edinburgh Archive.

Sheepshanks, M., 1914. Belgian refugees in Holland. *Jus Suffragii*, 9(2), pp. 194–195.

Lilian Lenton

'Citizens, awake!', *Votes for Women*, 8 March 1912.

Daily Report On Suffragette Prisoners In Holloway Prison, 20 February 1913. https://www.nationalarchives.gov.uk/education/resources/outrage-at -kew/daily-report-lilian-lenton/ (accessed 21 October 2024).

Lenton, L., 2001. Militant memories: Arson and bombs 1913–14. In Joyce Marlow, ed., *Votes for Women: The Virago Book of Suffragettes.* Virago Press, pp. 204–206.

Pankhurst, E., 2012. At the Royal Albert Hall, *Votes for Women*, 25 October.

Sentence on Kew suffragette. *Evening News (London)*, 7 March 1913.

Suffragette's insolence: Kew prisoner's defiant attitude. *Yorkshire Evening Post*, 27 February 1913.

The Women's Library at LSE, London, 7MLB/F, Transcript of recording, Interviews conducted by Lady Jessie Street with Suffragettes who participated in Militant Action, March 1960, pp. 1–43.

Adrienne Gerhäuser and Corinna Kawaters

Die Rote Zora, 1993. *Mili's Tanz auf dem Eis. Von Pirouetten, Schleifen, Einbrüchen, doppelten Saltos und dem Versuch, Boden unter die Füße zu kriegen.* Retrieved from: http://www.freilassung.de/div/texte/rz/milis/milis1.htm

ID-Archiv im IISG, ed., 1993. *Die Früchte des Zorns: Texte und Materialien zur Geschichte der Revolutionären Zellen und der Roten Zora.* ID Verlag.

Karcher, K., 2017. *'Sisters in Arms?' Militant Feminisms in the Federal Republic of Germany since 1968.* Berghahn.

Kawaters, C., 1984. *Zora Zobel findet die Leiche: Roman.* Zweitausendeins.

Red Dawns, 2014. *Red Dawns Herstory.* Retrieved from: https://rdecezore.org/?page_id=151&lang=en&l=2014

Anna Komnene

Annals of Niketas Choniates, 1984. *O City of Byzantium.* Trans. Harry J. Magoulias. Wayne State University Press.

Frankopan, P., 2009. Introduction. In Anna Komnene, *The Alexiad.* Penguin Classics.

Gibbon, E., 1907. *History of the Decline and Fall of the Roman Empire.* Volume V. Oxford University Press.

Kristeva, J., 2006. *Murder in Byzantium.* Trans. C. Jon Delogu. Columbia University Press.

Scott, W., 2006. *Count Robert of Paris.* Ed. J. H. Alexander. Edinburgh University Press.

Treadgold, W., 2013. *The Middle Byzantine Historians.* Palgrave Macmillan.

Harriette Wilson

Blanch, L., ed., 1985. *Harriette Wilson's Memoirs, Selected and Edited with an Introduction.* Century Publishing.

[*The Memoirs of Harriette Wilson* were first published in 1825 in four volumes by John Joseph Stockdale.]

Marjorie Fleming and Emily Pepys

Fleming, M., 1810–1811. *Diary.* Papers of Marjory Fleming, National Library of Scotland. MSS.1096-1100.

Pepys, E., 1984. *The Journal of Emily Pepys*. Ed. Gillian Avery. Prospect.

Pullan, M. M., 1855. *Maternal Counsels to a Daughter*. Darton.

Ruskin, J., 1865. *Sesame and Lilies*. Smith, Elder & Co.

Steedman, C., 1982. *The Tidy House: Little Girls Writing*. Virago.

Louisa Lawson

'About ourselves', 1888, *The Dawn*, 15 May, p. 1.

'That nonsensical idea', 1890, *The Dawn*, 5 June, p. 1.

'Wanted – women', 1892, *The Dawn*, 1 February, p. 11.

'Marriage not a failure', 1892, *The Dawn*, 1 August, p. 7.

'The woman of tomorrow', 1893, *The Dawn*, 1 August, p. 6.

'Learning to ride the bicycle', 1896, *The Dawn*, 1 October, p. 13.

'The greatest day that ever dawned', 1904, *The Dawn*, 1 January, p. 5.

Lawson, L. and Lawson, O., 1990. *The First Voice of Australian Feminism: Excerpts from Louisa Lawson's* The Dawn *1888–1895*. Simon & Schuster in association with New Endeavour Press.

Pearce, S., 1992. *The Shameless Scribbler: Louisa Lawson*. Sir Robert Menzies Centre for Australian Studies.

The Dawn can be found here: https://trove.nla.gov.au/newspaper/title/252#

Nellie Bly

Bly, N., 2014. *Around the World in Seventy-Two Days and Other Writings*. Ed. J. M. Lutes. Penguin Books.

Bly, N., 2015. *Ten Days in a Mad-House*. Open Road Integrated Media.

'Gender wage gap', OECD Data Indicators, 2024. OECD. [Online] available at: https://www.oecd.org/en/data/indicators/gender-wage-gap.html (accessed 5 October 2024).

Gregory, A., 2014. Nellie Bly's lessons in writing what you want to. *The New Yorker*. [Online] available at: http://www.newyorker.com/books/page-turner/nellie-blys-lessons-in-writingwhat-you-want-to (accessed 10 February 2017).

King, J., 2005. *The Victorian Woman Question in Contemporary Feminist Fiction*. Palgrave Macmillan.

Lutes, J. M., 2002. Into the madhouse with Nellie Bly: Girl stunt reporting in late nineteenth-century America. *American Quarterly*, 54(2), pp. 217–253.

Marija Jurić Zagorka

Dremel, A., ed., 2014. *Što žena umije. Zagorka, rad, rod, kulturna proizvodnja i potrošnja i vizualne reprodukcije književnosti* (*What is Woman capable of? Zagorka, Labour, Gender, Cultural Production and*

Consumption and Visual Reproduction of Literature). Zagreb Centre for Women's Studies.

Dulibić-Paljar, D., 2023. Celibacy for female teachers: Cultural phenomenon of the 19th century. *Croatica et Slavica Iadertina,* 19(1), pp. 169–189.

Roberts, M. L., 2002. *Disruptive Acts: The New Women in Fin-de-Siècle France.* University of Chicago Press.

Vujnović, M., 2009. *Forging the Bubikopf Nation: Journalism, Gender and Modernity in Interwar Yugoslavia.* American University Studies, Peter Lang.

Zagorka, M. J., 2008. *Kamen na cesti (The Stone on the Road).* Školska knjiga.

Ismat Chughtai

Asaduddin, M., 1999. Short stories and sketches. In *Ismat Chughtai: Monograph in Makers of Indian Literature Series.* Sahitya Akademi, pp. 75–113.

Asaduddin, M., 2013. Introduction. In *A Life in Words: Memoirs.* By Ismat Chughtai. Trans. Mohammad Asaduddin. Penguin, pp. ix–xxv.

Chughtai, I., 2004. Lingering fragrance. Trans. Syeda S. Hameed. In *A Chughtai Collection.* Trans. Tahira Naqvi and Syeda S. Hameed. Women Unlimited, pp. 190–224. (Reprint of *The Quilt and Other Stories, The Heart Breaks Free & The Wild One.* 1990, 1993.)

Chughtai, I., 2013. Conflict. Trans. M. Asaduddin. In *A Life in Words: Memoirs.* Penguin, pp. 61–75.

Chughtai, I., 2013. Leaving Aligarh once again. Trans. M. Asaduddin. In *A Life in Words: Memoirs.* Penguin, pp. 95–112.

Gokhale, S., 1993. Ismat Chughtai. In S. Tharu and K. Lalita, eds, *Women Writing in India: 600 B.C. to the Present.* Feminist, pp. 126–129.

Kudchedkar, S., 1997. Feminist voices from India and Canada. In Malashri Lal, ed., *Feminist Spaces: Cultural Readings from India and Canada.* Allied, pp. 1–10.

Naqvi, Tahira, 2004. Introduction. *A Chughtai Collection.* By Ismat Chughtai. Trans. and ed. Tahira Naqvi and Syeda S. Hameed. Women Unlimited, pp. vii–xxii. (Reprint of *The Quilt and Other Stories, The Heart Breaks Free & The Wild One.* 1990, 1993.)

Doris Lessing

Lessing, D., 1950. *The Grass is Singing.* Michael Joseph.

Lessing, D., 1952. *Martha Quest: Children of Violence.* Michael Joseph.

Lessing, D., 1962. *The Golden Notebook.* Michael Joseph.

Lessing, D., 1974. *The Memoirs of a Survivor.* Octagon.

Lessing, D., 1979–1983. *Canopus in Argos: Archives.* 5 volumes. Jonathan Cape.
Lessing, D., 1985. *The Good Terrorist.* Jonathan Cape.
Lessing, D., 1988. *The Fifth Child.* Jonathan Cape.
Lessing, D., 1994. *Under My Skin.* HarperCollins.
Lessing, D., 1997. *Walking in the Shade.* HarperCollins.

Anna Politkovskaya
Popescu, L. and Seymour-Jones, C., eds, 2007. *Another Sky: Voices of Conscience from Around the World.* Profile Books.

Hatshepsut
Creasman, P. P., 2014. Hatshepsut and the politics of Punt. *African Archaeological Review,* 31, pp. 395–405.
Ćwiek, A., 2014. Old and Middle Kingdom tradition in the Temple of Hatshepsut at Deir el-Bahari. *Institut Des Cultures Méditerranéennes Et Orientales De L'académie Polonaise Des Sciences Études Et Travaux,* XXVII, pp. 62–93.
Davies, V., 2004. Hatshepsut's use of Tuthmosis III in her program of legitimation. *Journal of the American Research Center in Egypt,* 41, pp. 55–66.
Laboury, D., 2014. How and why did Hatshepsut invent the image of her Royal power? In José M. Galán, Betsy M. Bryan and Peter F. Dorman, eds, *Creativity and Innovation in the Reign of Hatshepsut.* The Oriental Institute of the University of Chicago, pp. 49–91.
Nims, C. F., 1966. The date of the dishonoring of Hatshepsut. *Zeitschrift für Ägyptische Sprache und Altertumskunde,* 93, pp. 100–197.
Riaud, X., 2016. The dental identification of the Egyptian Queen Hatshepsut. *Journal of Dentistry and Oral Care Medicine,* 2(1), p. 108. Doi:10.15744/2454-3276.2.108.
Robins, G., 1999. The names of Hatshepsut as King. *The Journal of Egyptian Archaeology,* 85, pp. 103–112.

The Oracle at Delphi
Aeschylus, 2008. *Oresteia: Agamemnon, Libation-Bearers, Eumenides.* Trans. Alan H. Sommerstein. LCL 146. Harvard University Press.
Herodotus, 1998. *The Histories.* Trans. Robin Waterfield. Oxford University Press.
Lucanus, Marcus Annaeus, 2008. *Civil War, A New Translation.* Trans. Susan H. Braund. Oxford University Press.
Plato, 1914. *Euthyphro, Apology, Crito, Phaedo* and *Phaedrus.* Trans. H. N. Fowler. LCL 36. Harvard University Press.
Plutarch, 1919. *Alexander.* Trans. Bernadotte Perrin. Volume 7 of *Lives.* LCL 99. Harvard University Press.

Plutarch, 1936. *De Pythiae Oraculis and De Defectu Oraculorum*. Trans. F. C. Babbit. Volume 5 of *Moralia*. LCL 306. Harvard University Press.

Strabo, 1927. *Geography*. Trans. H. L. Jones. LCL 196. Harvard University Press.

Virgil, 2006. *The Aeneid*. Trans. Robert Fagles. Penguin.

Wu Zetian

Du, Y., 1936. *Tong Dian*. Shanghai.

Kinney, A. B., trans., 2014. *Exemplary Women of Early China: The Lienü Zhuan of Liu Xiang*. Columbia University Press.

Lo, P. W., 1814. *Quan Tangwen*. Imperial edn. Reprinted in facsimile in 1961 by Huawen Shuju.

Si, M., 1956. *Zhizi Tongjian*. Volume 201. Guji Chubanshe.

Twitchett, D., ed., 1979. *The Cambridge History of China, Volume 3: Sui and T'ang China, 589–906, Part I*. Cambridge University Press.

Wang, P., 1957. *Tang Huiyao*. Chunghua Shuju.

Yang, L. S., 1960. Female rulers in imperial China. *Harvard Journal of Asiatic Studies*, 23, pp. 47–61.

The Oseberg Burials

Arwill-Nordbladh, E., 1998. *Genuskonstruktioner i nordisk vikingatid: förr och nu*. Göteborgs universitet.

Pedersen, U., 2017. Vikingtidskvinner i maktens innerste sirkel. In N. Løkka and K. Kjesrud, eds, *Dronningen i vikingtid og middelalder*. Spartacus, pp. 99–125.

St Margaret of Scotland

Harrill, C. L., 2017. *Politics and Sainthood: Literary Representations of St Margaret of Scotland in England and Scotland from the Eleventh to the Fifteenth Century*. University of Birmingham. PhD thesis, University of Birmingham. https://etheses.bham.ac.uk/id/eprint/7548/

The Empress Matilda

Bradbury, J., 1996. *Stephen and Matilda: The Civil War of 1139–53*. Sutton Publishing Ltd.

Chibnall, M., 1993. *The Empress Matilda: Queen Consort, Queen Mother and Lady of the English*. Wiley-Blackwell.

Marguerite Porete

Lichtmann, M., 1994. Marguerite Porete and Meister Eckhart: The Mirror of Simple Souls mirrored. In B. McGinn, ed., *Meister Eckhart and the Beguine Mystics: Hadewijch of Brabant, Mechthild of Magdeburg, and Marguerite Porete*. Continuum Press, pp. 65–86.

Meister Eckhart, 1981. Sermon 52. In E. Colledge and B. McGinn, eds, *Meister Eckhart: The Essential Sermons, Commentaries, Treatises, and Defense*. Paulist Press, pp. 199–203.

Porete, M., 2002. Extracts from *The Mirror of Simple Souls*. Trans. A. C. Spearing. In E. Spearing, ed., *Medieval Writings on Female Spirituality*. Penguin, pp. 120–144.

Trombley, J. L., 2010. The master and the mirror: The influence of Marguerite Porete on Meister Eckhart. *Magistra*, 16(1), pp. 60–102.

Anne Askew

Adams, G. B. and Stephens, H. M., eds, 1901. *Select Documents of English Constitutional History*. Macmillan, pp. 253–259.

Beilin, E. V., ed., 1996. Anne Askew, *The Examinations of Anne Askew*. *Volume 1350, Women Writers in English 1350–1850*. Oxford University Press.

Christmas, H., ed., 1849. *Select Works of John Bale, D.D., Bishop of Ossory, Containing the examinations of Lord Cobham, William Thorpe, and Anne Askewe, and the image of both churches*. Cambridge University Press.

Dasent, J. R., ed., 1890. *Acts of the Privy Council of England Volume 1, 1542–1547*. British History Online, available at: https://www.british-history.ac.uk/acts-privy-council/vol1/pp451-475 (accessed 10 October 2024).

The Digital Humanities Institute, 2011. *The Unabridged Acts and Monuments Online or TAMO*. Available at: http//www.dhi.ac.uk/foxe (accessed 10 October 2024).

Nichols, J. G., ed., 1859. *Narratives of the Days of the Reformation, Chiefly from the Manuscripts of John Foxe the Martyrologist*. Camden Society, pp. 39–45, 299–313.

The Women of the Pendle Witch Trials

Clayton, J. A., 2007. *The Lancashire Witch Conspiracy*. Barrowford Press, pp. 188–221.

Lumby, J., 1995. *The Lancashire Witch Craze: Jennet Preston and the Lancashire Witches, 1612*. Carnegie, pp. 70–81.

Potts, T., 1845. *Potts's Discovery of Witches in the County of Lancaster*. Chetham Society.

Mary Somerville

Somerville, M., 2010. *Queen of Science: Personal Recollections of Mary Somerville*. Ed. D. McMillan. Canongate.

Sophia Jex-Blake
Jex-Blake, S., 1886. *Medical Women*. Preface to the 2nd edn. Macmillan.
Roberts, S., 1993. *Sophia Jex-Blake*. Routledge, pp. 1–3.
Stansfeld, J., 1877. Medical women. *The Nineteenth Century: A Monthly Review*, March, 1(5), pp. 888–901. Available at: https://www.proquest.com/historical-periodicals/medical-women/docview/2675121/se-2
The Scotsman, 1820, 20 April, p. 2.
Todd, M., 1918. *The Life of Sophia Jex-Blake*. Macmillan, pp. 236–245.

Lady Florence Dixie
Fishwick, N., 1989. *English Football and Society 1910–1950*. Manchester University Press.
McCrone, K. E., 1988. *Sport and the Physical Emancipation of English Women 1870–1914*. Routledge.
Magoun Jr, F. P., 1931. Scottish popular football, 1424–1815. *The American Historical Review*, 37(1), October, pp. 1–13.
S. B. D., 1895. Feminine footballers. *Daily Sketch*, 6 February, p. 60.
Ward, A., n.d. *Some Notes on the History of Women's Soccer*. Unpublished paper, p. 6.
Williams, J. and Wagg, S., 1991. *British Football and Social Change: Getting into Europe*. Continuum International.

Lois Weber
Drew, W. M., 1999. *At the Center of the Frame: Leading Ladies of the Twenties and Thirties*. Vestal Press.
Elliot, W. F., 1922. Exit flapper, enter woman: Lois Weber describes next screen type. *Los Angeles Times*, 6 August, III, p. 25.
Howard, M., 1917. 'Even As You and I', a drama of souls at bay. *Moving Picture Weekly*, 14 April, p. 18.
Weber, L., 1928. Many women well fitted by film training to direct movies. *San Diego Evening Tribune*, 24 April, p. 3.
Weber, L., 1928. Hostility of men drawback to women making success in picture directing, claim. *San Diego Evening Tribune*, 25 April, p. 13.

Elsie Mackay
Dunlap, D. and Eveleigh, D., 2011. Those magnificent women in their flying machines. *The New York Times*, 10 November.
Wilson, Q., 2008. The flight. Appendix. In J. Baldwin, *West Over the Waves: The Final Flight of Elsie Mackay*. GC Books.

Mary Barbour
Barbour, M., 1919. Women and housing. *The Govan Pioneer*, 3(1), June.

Crawfurd, H., n.d. Memoirs of Helen Crawfurd. Unpublished memoir. Marx Memorial Library, pp. 144–146.

Gallacher, W., 1978. *Revolt on the Clyde: An Autobiography*. Lawrence and Wishart Ltd.

Govan Press, 19 November 1915. The Mitchell Library, Glasgow.

Melling, J., 1983. *Rent Strikes: People's Struggle for Housing in West Scotland, 1890–1916*. Polygon.

Smyth, J., 1992. Rents, peace, votes: Working-class women and political activity in the First World War. In E. Breitenbach and E. Gordon, eds, *Out of Bounds: Women and Society in Scottish Society, 1800–1945*. Edinburgh University Press.

Vijaya Lakshmi Pandit

File 61/44 Poll (9), National Archives of India.

IOR: L/I/1/M82, British Library.

Pandit, V. L., 1969. The time of my life. Radio Interview with Mark Tully, 11 July. British Library Sound Recordings.

Pandit, V. L., 1979. *Scope of Happiness*. Crown Publishers, Inc., p. 313.

Pandit, V. L., 2008. India's case for independence. In B. Prasad, ed., *Towards Freedom: Documents on the Movement for Independence in India 1945*. Indian Council of Historical Research. Oxford University Press, p. 241.

United Nations, 1946. *Official Records of the Second Part of the First Session of the General Assembly. Plenary Meetings of The General Assembly*. Verbatim Record. 23 October–16 December.

Vijaya Lakshmi Pandit Papers, Nehru Memorial Museum and Library.

Madge Saunders

Saunders, M. P., 1972. *Living in Britain*. The British Council of Churches Community and Race Relations Unit.

Saunders, M. P., 1975. *The Challenge of Service*. 10th Anniversary Brochure of the United Church of Jamaica and Grand Cayman, 1965–1975.

Saunders, M. P., Nelson, B., McKenzie, T., Spence A. and Anderson, J., 2005. *Born to Serve: The Pioneering Ministry of Marjorie Prentice Saunders*. Faith Works Press of Montrose Road.

Dagmar Wilson

Alonso, H. H., 1993. *Peace As a Women's Issue: A History of the U.S. Movement for World Peace and Women's Rights*. Syracuse University Press.

Anon, 1965. Court crowd cheers 3 held for contempt. *The Washington Post*, 9 January, B3.

Baker, R., 1965. Observer. *The New York Times*, 15 December, p. 6.

Coburn, J., 2016. *Making a Difference: The History and Memory of Women Strike for Peace, 1961–1990*. PhD dissertation, Northumbria University.

Dudman, R., 1966. Dagmar Wilson: Striking for peace. *Washington Post Potomac*, 13 April.

Elshtain, J. B. and Tobias, S., eds, 1990. *Women, Militarism, and War: Essays in History, Politics and Social Theory*. Rowman & Littlefield.

Estepa, A., 2008. Taking the white gloves off: Women Strike for Peace and 'the Movement,' 1967–73. In S. Gilmore, ed., *Feminist Coalitions: Historical Perspectives on Second-Wave Feminism in the United States*. University of Illinois Press, pp. 84–112.

McGrory, M., 1962. Nobody controls anybody. *Washington Evening Star*, 14 December, p. 1.

Porter Adams, J., 1991. Dagmar Wilson. In J. Porter Adams, ed., *Peacework: Oral Histories of Women Peace Activists*. Twayne, pp. 193–199.

SHSW WSP Records, n.d. Dagmar Wilson: Striking for peace, MSS 433, 2:11. Biographical data on Dagmar Wilson.

Swerdlow, A., 1982. Ladies' Day at the Capitol: Women Strike for Peace versus HUAC. *Feminist Studies*, 8(3), pp. 493–520.

Swerdlow, A., 1993. *Women Strike for Peace: Traditional Motherhood and Radical Politics in the 1960s*. University of Chicago Press.

Taylor, E. B., 1998. *We Made a Difference: My Personal Journey with Women Strike for Peace*. Camino Books.

United States Congress House Committee on Un-American Activities, 1963. *Communist Activities in the Peace Movement (Women Strike for Peace and Certain Other Groups): Hearings Before the Committee on Un-American Activities, House of Representatives, Eighty-Seventh Congress, Second Session. December 11-13 1962, Including Index.* Government Printing Office.

Wilson, D., 2001. Tainting the antinuclear movement: HUAC and the irrepressible Women Strike for Peace. In B. Schultz and D. Schultz, eds, *The Price of Dissent: Testimonies to Political Repression in America*. University of California Press.

Sirimavo Bandaranaike

Chatterjee, P., 1993. *The Nation and its Fragment: Colonial and Post-colonial Histories*. Princeton University Press.

Jayawardena, K., 1980. *Feminism and Nationalism in the Third World*. Zed Books.

Jeyraj, D. B. S., 2015. Sirima Bandaranaike: 'Weeping widow' who became world's first woman prime minister. *Daily Mirror*, 18 April. http://www.dailymirror.lk/69505/the-weeping-widow-who-became-world-s-first-woman-pm

Kaul, A., 2012. Women's voices from the underground. *Asian Voices from the Underground*. February. http://www.asianconversations.com/SriLankaWomen.php

Rai, S., 2014. Political performance: A framework for analysing democratic politics. *Political Studies*, 63(5), pp. 1179–1197.

Saner, E., 2013. Top sexist moments in politics: Julia Gillard, Hilary Clinton and more. *The Guardian*, 14 June. https://www.theguardian.com/politics/2013/jun/14/top-10-sexist-moments-politics

Seneviratne, M., 1975. *Sirimavo Bandaranaike: The World's First Prime Minister*. Hansa Publishers Ltd.

Sturgeon, N., 2016. Scottish First Minister Nicola Sturgeon explains what it means to be a Dangerous Woman. *Dangerous Women Project*, 22 March. https://dangerouswomenproject.org/2016/03/22/dangerous-women-change-world/

Dagmar Šimková

Bursík, T., 2006. *Ztratily jsme mnoho času . . . Ale ne sebe!* Urad Dokumentace a vysetrovani zlocinu komunismu.

Formankova, P. and Zaloudek, D., 2010. *The Screeching Seagulls Are Flying Around Me*. Exhibition about the life of Dagmar Šimková, produced by the Ministry of Foreign Affairs, Czech Republic. http://www.mzv.cz/file/730310/exhibition_dagmar_simkova.pdf

Kuklová-Jíšová, B., 2007. *Krásná němá paní*. Nakladatelstvi ARSCI.

McDermott, K., 2010. Stalinist terror in Czechoslovakia. In K. McDermott and M. Stibbe, eds, *Stalinist Terror in Eastern Europe: Elite Purges and Mass Repression*. Manchester University Press.

Rehak, J., 2013. *Czech Political Prisoners: Recovering Face*. Lexington Books.

Šimková, D., 2010. *Byly jsme tam taky*. Patrick and Michael Murphey.

Helen Steven

Hulbert, A. and McIntosh, A., 1992. The Gulfwatch Papers. *The Edinburgh Review*, 87, pp. 15–71.

McCaig, N., 2009. If. In E. McCaig, ed., *The Poems of Norman McCaig*. Polygon.

Steven, H., 2005. *No Extraordinary Power: Prayer, Stillness and Activism*. Swarthmore Lecture. Quaker Books.

Steven, H., n.d. An idea whose time has come. *Coracle: The Magazine of the Iona Community*, 3(8).